Judith Locke Ph.D. is a clinical psychologist and former teacher who specialises in parenting and child wellbeing. She is the director of her private practice, and her training company Confident and Capable®. As a clinician, she provides psychological counselling to children, adolescents, parents and families. As a trainer, she provides dynamic psychological training sessions in parenting, resilience, staff wellbeing and related fields to parents and staff in schools, childcare centres, and government and community organizations, as well as private companies. Judith is also a Visiting Research Fellow at the Queensland University of Technology where she researches modern parenting, child and parent wellbeing, and how children and parents interact with academic environments.

The Bonsai Child is Judith's first book. She is currently working on her second, *The Bonsai Student*.

The Bonsai Child

Why modern parenting limits children's potential and practical strategies to turn it around

Judith Y Locke, Ph.D.

First published by Judith Locke (Kelvin Grove, Queensland), 2015

Design by Nic Lehman
Cover design by Nic Lehman
Cover concept by Judith Locke
Cover image by Justin Nicholas
Author image by Justin Nicholas
Printed by IngramSpark

Disclaimer
The contents of this book are intended for information purposes only. The information contained in this book is not a substitute for, and is not intended to replace, independent professional, legal, or medical advice. Readers should consider the need to obtain any appropriate professional advice relevant to their own particular circumstances.
Every effort has been made to ensure the information is correct at the time of publication. As psychological advice can change with new research on best practice treatment, you may be best to consult with a professional to ensure you have the latest advice for your child's or your own psychological or other issues.
This book draws on a number of cases the author has treated or been informed about over the years; however, the cases mentioned here are composites of typical cases, rather than particular people or particular situations. Any information that may identify a particular person has been altered or omitted.

Cataloguing-in-Publication details are available from
the National Library of Australia:
www.trove.nla.gov.au

ISBN 978 0 9943692 0 8

Suggested citation: Locke, JY 2015, *The bonsai child: why modern parenting limits children's potential and practical strategies to turn it around*, Judith Locke, Kelvin Grove, Qld.

I dedicate this book to all the families I have seen clinically over more than a decade. Your heartfelt experiences prompted my desire to better understand your circumstances; your selfless love and devotion to your parenting continue to inspire my commitment to solving the issues you face.

Contents

Introduction

It didn't add up. The family sitting in front of me should have had everything going for them…

The parents loved their daughter very much and had done everything to give her the best life they possibly could. They had sent her to great schools – a suburban government school near to home in her primary years and a wonderful independent co-ed school in her early high school years. They encouraged her to enjoy a wide range of interests, and happily paid for horse-riding and dancing lessons. They appeared to have a loving relationship with each other as well. Her mother now had a part-time job but had not worked at all during the child's first few years because she wanted to focus on being there for her daughter. Her father devoted his weekends to watching her play sport and taking the family on bush walks and to the beach. She seemed to have everything she wanted. They appeared to be the perfect family creating an ideal childhood for a 14-year-old girl. And yet here she was – depressed and angry, hating her parents and a life she deemed to be terrible.

This was not the only perplexing situation I encountered that week in my private psychology practice. Only two days before, I had spoken to a husband and wife in their forties, both intelligent high achievers, who were well respected middle managers in industry and government. And yet they called me to seek help because their four-year-old was making their lives hell with his constant demands and out-of-control behaviour: 'Can you speak to him and explain that he should listen to us and do as we say?' These two people advised politicians and senior managers, yet they couldn't manage their young child.

As a clinical psychologist who travelled the world treating parenting issues, I was used to seeing problems arise from two main areas – when parents don't have a good relationship with their child, and when parents are not consistent with discipline. However, the problems I was beginning to regularly treat in my practice appeared to arise from different causes. It quickly became clear to me that the old positive parenting spiel to improve their relationship with their child and be more consistent with discipline was not helpful to parents experiencing these new problems. These parents were putting everything they had into raising their child, but their well-meant efforts appeared to be inadvertently causing harm to the child and the family.

Why?

Intrigued, I started investigating. I began reading everything I could get my hands on about modern parenting approaches, including articles and research on helicopter parenting and lawnmower parenting and all of the other new terms for parents who seemed to do too much for their children by overhelping them and hovering too close. I went back to university to complete a PhD doing research into overparenting. I was informed by my research, but also by the many families I was treating in my private practice, and the thousands of parents I was educating in my seminars for parents of preschool- and school-age children. I also learned of important findings from other researchers; some of these are listed at the end of this book.

This book is the result of that investigation and work. It presents the common parenting situations I see in my private practice and seminar sessions, and explains how some of the popular views about parenting today can affect children and families. Most importantly, it gives practical strategies for parents to improve their child's and family's wellbeing.

In Part A, I discuss modern parenting and the changes in parenting approach from past generations to today's generation of parents. I explain the beliefs which have encouraged these changes: convictions shared by many people, despite flimsy evidence of their value. I show the detrimental effects on children, parents, and families that can occur when these beliefs dictate parenting behaviour. From my clinical practice, I present typical situations resulting from an intensive parenting approach.

In Part B, I provide strategies for parents of children of all ages – from the toddler years to young adulthood. These strategies give you techniques to genuinely improve your child's confidence, social skills, resilience and self-regulation. I show you how how to encourage your child to slowly develop their independence and maturity, which will help them do well in life.

My strategies may confirm the value of the your current approach, or give you ideas on ways to fine-tune or completely alter your parenting style. Either way, you will find them very useful.

My purpose in writing this book is to assist the many parents I have treated or addressed in my parenting sessions over the years. Many have expressed a desire for a resource they can refer to when they need an occasional reminder about the techniques we have discussed, or a guide they can share with their partner or friends. While there are many good parenting books out there, when I tried to recommend a book that encompassed everything I discuss, nothing suited exactly. I knew I had to write it all down in a book to be read and re-read by parents.

It is my sincere wish that this book creates a generation of parents I never see clinically, but whose children I encounter as I go about my daily life in the future – a generation who have become more confident and capable people as a result of their parents reading this book. I hope to see these adult children make important contributions to their community while living satisfying and fulfilling lives. And I hope your child or children will be amongst them.

CHAPTER 1

Do you need this book?

There are many different types of parents and many diverse views on parenting. How do you know that this book is right for you? To help you decide, I include four short quizzes about your parenting and your child. Answer these and your responses will reveal whether this particular parenting book is the one for you.

Quiz A – Your parenting style

Consider the following statements about your parenting approach and decide whether you agree with them or not.

1. If my child is having a difficult time, I do everything in my power to make things better for them
2. I am constantly vigilant to possible dangers in my child's life
3. I try hard to make sure my child is always happy
4. I put a lot of effort into praising my child to help them feel good
5. I need to stand up for my child with others.

If you agreed with most of these statements, you are putting a lot of effort into making your child happy. That's an admirable goal, but the strategies you are using may be at the expense of your child learning how to make themself content or developing skills to cope with difficult situations, both of which are essential for them to build resilience.

If this is the case, then this book will be very helpful to you. It will assist you to understand why you may be doing this and how to alter your approach. I suggest you make careful note of Part A before you move on to Part B.

Quiz B – Your parenting situation

Now consider the following statements in regard to your current situation.

1. I sometimes have difficulty getting my child to do things they don't want to do
2. I sometimes dread my child's reaction when I ask them to do things they don't want to do
3. My partner and I occasionally disagree on our parenting approach and discipline techniques
4. To make life easier for me, there are times when I do things the way my child wants them done
5. My child can be disrespectful to me or say hurtful things to me
6. My child has hit me in anger at times.

If you agreed with any of these statements, it appears that your child may be starting to take charge of the household. While it's quite normal for children to want to get their own way and become upset when they don't, parents should be in charge of the majority of decisions made in the home and confident that their child will comply with their requests. If a child is not able to comply with adult instructions, it is going to make it very difficult for them at school and in the workforce.

If you agreed with most of these statements, the strategies contained in Part B are going to be very important for you. Since there is likely to be a good reason why this situation has occurred, Part A will help too.

If you indicated that you and your partner don't agree on discipline techniques and parenting approach, I suspect you are doing a good cop/bad cop scenario with your child. In police shows that routine typically works very well to get the criminal, but in parenting not so well. Indeed, clever children quickly work out how to set off a good cop/bad cop routine to their advantage. Reading this book will help to get you and your partner back on the same page and ensure your parenting strategies genuinely complement each other and continue to be in the best interests of your child.

If you indicated that your child hits you or is regularly disrespectful to you, I consider this a *very big deal*. It needs to be addressed quickly before it becomes a significant problem for your child and yourself. I recommend you read this book, and if you don't see change very soon after you start to implement my strategies I suggest you seek assistance from a clinical psychologist or paediatrician right away. I give details of how to find that assistance in chapter 16.

Quiz C – Your parenting confidence

Now consider the following statements in regard to how confident you feel as a parent.

1. I sometimes go over and over decisions I have made (e.g. the manner of my child's birth, how long I breastfed my child, when I went back to work) and worry whether I made the best choice for my child
2. I sometimes agonise over parenting decisions I need to make and worry whether I will make a mistake
3. I compare my actions as a parent with the actions of other parents and feel uncomfortable when I am not making similar choices
4. I know I have done a good job as a parent when my child likes me.

Agreement with any of these statements indicates that sometimes you lack confidence as a parent. For all we know, you are doing a fantastic job and you have nothing to worry about, but that lack of confidence is going to make things really difficult, particularly at times when you might be in conflict with your child, such as the oft-dreaded teenage years. It's also going to take a toll on your wellbeing because you will always be second-guessing yourself and hesitant in your choices.

Reading this book will confirm for you that your actions are appropriate and in the best interests of your child. It will give you confidence in your parenting decisions, even when your choices differ from the choices of other parents around you.

Quiz D – Your child

Now consider the following statements about your child.

1. My child spends a lot of time by my side and regularly needs my attention or reassurance
2. My child seems to lack confidence and worries about many things
3. I need to spend a lot of time organising my child because they lack

motivation
4. My child argues a lot with my decisions
5. My child is often the centre of attention at home and frequently demands this attention
6. Regardless of how many things I buy my child, they always want more.

Agreement with any of these statements suggests that your child is not travelling well. Alternatively, your family might not be travelling well because you are all trying to accommodate the very demanding and time-consuming needs and desires of your child. Your child might lack confidence and need regular reassurance (numbers 1 and 2); have some motivation issues (number 3); might be a little oppositional (number 4); need the reassurance of a lot of attention (number 5); or expect a very charmed life (number 6).

If a parent suspects these types of issues in their child, typically one of the first things they do is organise an appointment with a psychologist. But don't grab the phone yet. Often all that is needed to get things back to normal and enable the child to go back to being a great kid again, is for the parent to change their approach and do things a little differently.

I am not suggesting that you never call that psychologist. I am just suggesting you try some of the strategies in this book first. And if that doesn't produce a significant enough change, then pay special attention to chapter 16 and start dialling.

If you haven't agreed with any of the quiz statements

Congratulations – you seem to have it all going on as a parent. That's great!

But hang on . . . What are you doing even investigating a parenting book? Is there a nagging doubt in your mind, or an issue with your child you can't seem to resolve?

If that is the case, then I suggest you read on . . .

Part A

CHAPTER 2

Parenting today

Parenting has changed enormously in the past 10 or 20 years. I'd guess most of you would consider your parenting approach to be very different from that taken by your own parents. Why has this change occurred?

Parenting has always been strongly influenced by the era in which it is delivered and the beliefs associated with the times. The 21st century has seen major changes in technology, communication, patterns of work and socialising, which have vastly altered family lifestyles. Our approach to life and our goals for raising the next generation have also changed. Indeed, many parents deliberately adopt a different parenting approach from that of their own parents.

Changes influencing parenting

Let's look at a few of the changes I see as having the most significant influences on modern parenting.

More prosperity

Many of you will consider yourselves slightly or totally better off than your parents. Oh sure, you may be in debt up to your eyeballs – but often that debt is for a pretty nice home in a pretty nice suburb.

Your children are probably experiencing what appears to be a very pleasant life. They have a nice bedroom and quite a few toys, including some amazing technologies. They can watch outstanding television, play awesome games, or listen to music with remarkable sound quality. They are probably attending a school where the educational opportunities are good and the teachers care for them. After school, it's likely they are able to participate in activities that are varied and interesting. Indeed, I'm guessing your child is experiencing a childhood that is pretty sweet.

While you have no doubt worked incredibly hard to be in your present situation, for many of you life will be sometimes stressful, but broadly rather good.

Prosperity brings new priorities

I'm assuming many of you are not involved in a famine or a war. (Having a hungry and argumentative child or teen might seem like it, but doesn't technically count.) So I suspect you are not having difficulty putting a basic roof over your child's head, or food on the table.

Because of this, you are likely to be pretty high up on Maslow's hierarchy of needs. For those of you hazy on what you studied in Psych 101, or feeling too lazy to google it, Abraham Maslow's hierarchy of needs is a psychological theory

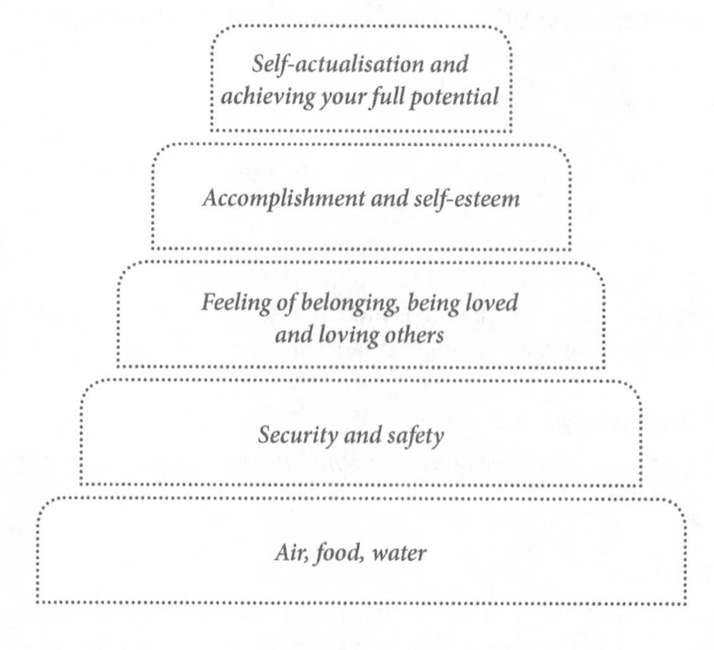

Maslow's needs hierarchy

which proposes that humans are motivated to achieve certain things. According to the theory, when you have the basic physiological needs taken care of, such as air, food and water, you seek higher levels of needs, such as security and safety. Once those are taken care of, you look to higher needs again, such as a feeling of belonging, being loved, and loving others. Then, once achieved, you look to be satisfied in the next level.

While there has been some controversy about the levels when they are applied across cultures, it makes sense that if you were stranded on a desert island, you would be more concerned about obtaining water and your next meal than you would be worried about enhancing your self-esteem.

In prosperous times, when basic needs such as food and shelter are taken care of, we tend to focus on higher levels of needs. I am guessing many of you reading this book are primarily focused on the esteem and confidence needs of your child. Even parents who are mainly worried about their child's issues with making friends are likely to be primarily concerned about the impact of friendship difficulties on their child's self-esteem and confidence. This is because most of these children are likely to have an already high level of care and love within their family.

This may partly explain why many parents place so much emphasis on self-esteem in children these days. It is not necessarily because of significant issues in children's confidence; it is because of a lack of issues in the lower levels of needs. When you can provide food, water and safety for your children, you become much more preoccupied with the things that may offer opportunities for improvement. Unfortunately we seem to be a little stuck on the self-esteem level . . .

More emphasis on self-esteem

We live in a time when the skills needed for future success are somewhat unclear. Years ago, if you had a basic trade or an education, you were assured you would always have a job. But things have changed recently. Now we are unsure of what is going to be the skill that will ensure a steady stream of employment. Without being certain of the expertise required in future job arenas, our fallback is the one trait that appears to be most important in mastering the necessary skills of everything. That trait is self-esteem.

The reason we have started to see self-esteem as the be-all and end-all is because some research findings have been incorrectly interpreted. As Martin Seligman so eloquently puts it, there are two important aspects to being satisfied in yourself and how you deal with the rest of the world – *doing well* and *feeling good*. As you can imagine, people who *do well* tend to *feel good* about themselves, and research has shown that the two traits tend to be correlated. But a misunderstanding of this research meant that *feeling good* started to be seen as an essential element of *doing well,* which is kind of putting the cart before the horse. So self-esteem, or feeling good, started to be seen as the precursor to doing well in life.

It is difficult to create good feelings in people without them actually doing something they feel good about. However, some people (read: parents) have developed shortcuts. These people use artificial means to produce good feelings in children or adolescents. They might praise the child so the child feels momentarily good about themself, or the parent might manipulate circumstances so the child does well (e.g. ensuring that they win, or making sure they get what they want). But producing good feelings in this 'express-post' way has problems. Firstly, these good feelings are only very temporary. They tend to dissipate quickly because they weren't really hard won and so they need to be topped up frequently. Secondly, the child becomes highly reliant on others putting in that type of effort for them on a regular basis.

There is another problem with this behind-the-scenes adult work when children face a potentially difficult experience. It makes the child miss an excellent opportunity to do well by actually facing the situation and learning that they can cope with something challenging.

Overcoming difficulty by learning how to either accept it, or undertake strategies to make it better for ourselves, is one of the true self-esteem building activities.

We eventually gain a sense of strength from coping with or overcoming problems. This allows us to become confident we can face any future tricky events. If other people in our lives deny us this chance, we will enjoy a temporary good feeling of winning or achieving. However, we will remain reliant on others and not become confident to step up to the next challenge without someone in very close proximity to defend us. Children are exactly the same.

Nonsense ideas out there suggest young people have to be constantly achieving and winning and receive regular praise to feel good about themselves. Consequently adults have taken on a lot of the responsibility for making children always feel good. Do children need to come from a loving home and feel they are important people in their parents' eyes? Absolutely – but love is not necessarily shown by ensuring your child is winning or successful *all of the time.*

Significantly, all this effort to make your child successful inadvertently sends a harmful message to them. If you do everything to ensure they always succeed and win, you are suggesting that their success is very important to you. It could also imply to your child how unacceptable they might be to you if they weren't successful. Even if you tell your child you love them regardless of their achievements and they should 'just do their best', the very fact that in the past you have manipulated things to ensure their victories might have given your child the message that they need to win to gain your approval, or even your love.

When your child is in difficulty, blame self-esteem . . .

This emphasis on self-esteem as the building block to doing good things means it is often blamed when a child isn't coping well or is not behaving appropriately. In fact, I don't think I have seen a parent in my clinic recently who doesn't believe their child's issues are in some way to do with low self-esteem, no matter what the problem.

Sidoney's parents telephone me. They are very upset. They say their 11-year-old daughter has low self-esteem and wonder if I can see her and help her. They state that for a number of years now, Sidoney has become increasingly argumentative, sometimes to the point of shouting and even screaming at them. She rarely agrees with anything they say or do; if they say 'black' she says 'white'. She appears to go from a very bad mood to one where she is easily upset and clingy with her parents. Her moods are extreme: she is often particularly awful, then particularly loving afterward. She called her mother 'fat' the other day, then later wrote a lovely note to her, apologising for making her cry. Every time something bad happens to Sidoney, she blames someone else. She also complains that nobody wants to be her friend. Sidoney's parents tell me they keep reassuring her that she is good at so many things and of course everyone likes her. They say the family stretched their budget to buy her horse-riding lessons last month to give her something special she can be really good at. But she still calls herself 'hopeless at everything'. She regularly accuses the family of not being nice enough to her, particularly when they ask her to do household chores or be nice to her brother. They say she is becoming 'really hard work', always arguing and refusing to do what they tell her to do. They believe if only she just had better self-esteem, she would be happier and have more friends.

Sidoney's case is not unusual. Clinically, I often find that when a child is particularly badly behaved, the parent believes the root cause is the child's low self-esteem or poor confidence. When I come across such cases, I am sure the child has feelings that aren't helping them. But we often overlook an important aspect of this poor behaviour. If children or teens are regularly disrespectful to their parents and receive no effective consequence to stop this behaviour, it has to have a negative effect on them. If the child or adolescent is in any way a reasonable person, there is no way, after these outbursts, that they are feeling good about themselves (just as we often feel really terrible about shouting at a slow barista or a co-worker).

Moreover, these children are being rude, argumentative, and perhaps even screaming at their own parents, i.e. the adults who are the major attachment figures in their lives. Attachment figures are very important to children because they show them how close relationships work. If a child is regularly disrespectful to a major attachment figure, such as their parent, they begin to establish bad patterns for how they will treat people who love them. This is a poor start to developing good relationships in their future.

I am concerned when I see children who do not care if they are disrespectful or even aggressive toward the people who regularly show them love and kindness. If parents do not give effective consequences to deter them from this behaviour, such children might be encouraged to feel a sense of entitlement. They may form an unreasonable expectation that they are at the centre of the universe and can do as they please in relationships and in their environment.

A sense of entitlement is almost the opposite of poor self-esteem, but it often looks like low self-esteem because the child's sense of wellbeing depends on constantly being the centre of attention or always having control of the household. Such children tend to become despondent when they don't have the power or the spotlight. This is a real clinical concern if the child is of an age when their need for constant attention should be starting to recede, typically after the age of seven or eight. Even at an earlier age, this attention-seeking behaviour is still of concern.

In many cases where the child has issues and is not travelling well, I am sure they aren't feeling good about themselves. But it is likely that low self-esteem isn't the sole cause. To ascribe it as such sets off a whole bunch of parenting actions, such as overcompensating for the child, providing high levels of adult assistance, and giving extreme praise. These actions inadvertently continue the problems. Because children become even more dependent on adult assistance, they begin to doubt their capacity to face life's challenges, and continue to not feel good about themselves.

It can get worse. Providing praise and attention when children aren't behaving appropriately confirms their impossibly high expectations of what the world should do for them. It affirms their assumed right to behave like a princess or an emperor – and this is a problem.

More information on child wellbeing and parenting

Parents' preoccupation with their child's self-esteem and constant success goes hand in hand with another modern change. There's more information out there on child wellbeing.

Since the sixties, many researchers and clinicians have focused on understanding ideal parenting approaches. Diana Baumrind initiated important research into parenting styles, which Eleanor Maccoby and John Martin further developed. They identified two key factors that determine parenting style:

> *Responsiveness*: a parent's tendency to be loving and responsive to their child's needs
> *Demandingness*: a parent's tendency to use rules and consequences to demand responsible and age-appropriate behaviour from their child.

Research has found that high or low levels of these two parenting factors result in different parenting styles, shown in the diagram below.

In this matrix, parents who are loving toward their children and also demand they behave appropriately are considered to be 'Authoritative parents'. Parents who demand that their children follow the rules (probably with a lot of shouting) and are not very loving or responsive to them are 'Authoritarian parents'. Parents who are very loving toward their children but who don't insist they follow certain rules of behaviour are 'Indulgent parents'. Parents who neither show love, nor insist on the child behaving responsibly, are termed 'Negligent parents'.

The authoritative parenting approach – high in both demandingness and responsiveness to children – has been shown by lots of research to be the ideal parenting method. It tends to be associated with improved wellbeing, resilience, sense of security, and popularity in children.

Responsiveness
A parent's responsive and loving actions toward their child

Demandingness
A parent's expectations of age-appropriate, responsible behaviour using rules and consequences

Demandingness \ Responsiveness	high	low
high	**Authoritative**	**Authoritarian**
low	**Indulgent**	**Negligent**

(Baumrind 1965, 1991; Maccoby & Martin, 1983)

So how has this influenced current parenting views? Typically, when research is done that has a finding of some sort, it is published first in journal articles for other researchers. This information then eventually trickles down to articles in newspapers and magazines for the rest of us, along with somewhat simplified details of the original research findings. For example, if researchers measure the health of people who don't exercise compared with people who do 30 minutes of exercise a day, and find the people who do 30 minutes more exercise have better wellbeing, you can imagine the simplified version of the findings featured in mainstream media might be 'do more exercise'. That is a really good headline for non-exercisers to pay attention to, but for people who are already doing one or two hours of exercise a day, following this advice might take a healthy amount of exercise into an unhealthy amount.

Likewise, when researchers found that children who are valued and loved by their parents do better than children who are not listened to or made to feel important by their parents, this finding was shared with the world. It resulted in headlines such as 'Make your child feel more important' accompanied by a lot of advice about listening more to your child and focusing on their needs. Now, that is a great message and does need to be shared with parents. But here comes the important caveat.

The only parents who need to listen to and act on the advice to respond more to their child, are the ones who are negligent or authoritarian.

The ones who are already highly responsive to their children need not listen to it, because they are already doing it.

Many parents, keen to listen to the experts, have acted on that type of headline in an effort to improve their parenting. The trouble is, following advice to make their child feel more important will sometimes take parents from ideal levels of responsiveness to extreme responsiveness. And this may not be helpful for the child.

In addition, most subsequent research has focused on the parenting approaches perceived to most need help: negligent and authoritarian parenting. This research has confirmed the negative impact of an unloving approach. As a result, there has been an avalanche of advice pointing out opportunities for parents to be responsive to children, but not a lot on the importance of demanding certain behaviours from children and how parents can do this.

If anything, the only debate on discipline in the media has typically been about whether or not to smack your child. Clearly, the act of physically hurting your child is inappropriate. Unfortunately, the media debate is rarely fine-tuned to include alternative ways to ensure a child behaves appropriately. Consequently, a parent who scans the media for parenting advice could easily start to think any discipline is harmful to a child. Combined with the plethora of suggestions that parents should make their child feel very important, this advice has resulted in the view that ideal parenting allows the child to dictate the terms in the family, rather than the parents.

Authoritative vs. authoritarian parenting

Another issue is semantic. The harmful strict and unloving parenting style, *authoritarian parenting*, sounds a lot like the very helpful, firm but loving parenting style, *authoritative parenting*. In the ideal parenting approach, authoritative parenting, the parents are authority figures who also demonstrate love and care for the child. This is in stark contrast to authoritarian parenting, which only uses authority and minimal or no loving actions.

Unfortunately these terms are often misunderstood and used interchangeably. As a result, the idea of a parent having or wanting any authority or higher status in the home has started to get a very bad rap.

A parent exercising no authority to guide a child is not in any way what researchers or psychologists suggest as good parenting practice. As the adult, a parent is in a very good position to decide the best things a child should do, such as whether the toddler should play with the electric saw or if the 14-year-old should go to the all-night rave. However, over time, research findings have been misinterpreted to promote a highly responsive and not very demanding parenting style. This has resulted in parents paying more attention to their child's wishes than their own common sense when making decisions about child rearing. This has been detrimental to parents and children.

More analysis of your own parents

With all of the effort you put into parenting, it is very likely you are thinking about your own experience of being parented. And I am guessing in the light of the current popular approach, which caters so much to children and gives them outstandingly lovely childhoods, your own parents' efforts might be starting to pale in comparison.

The parents I see clinically sometimes tend to view their parents negatively, often as 'very strict'. Many seem to remember things like their parents saying 'no' to a particular event, not being there for school presentations, or not buying something they really wanted as a child, like a pair of white roller-skates or a pony.

Often they also remember their parents as not being loving enough. They say their parents rarely told them they loved them and didn't hug them often. These memories seem to stir something in them during their early experience of being a parent. They can even bring on a Scarlett O'Hara moment. As the sun is setting behind them, they vow: 'If I have to lie, steal, cheat or kill, as God is my witness, ~~I'll never be hungry again~~ I'll never say no to my child.' Or 'I'll tell them I love them every hour of every day.' Or 'I'll give my child a pony.' And, great balls of fire! They make good on their promises to indulge their child more than they were indulged. Every. Single. Day.

While I am not suggesting these parents' memories are inaccurate, I do think it is unfair to compare your parents with parents of today. It was a different era and many parents were making the best of sometimes difficult financial situations. For many parents of past generations, putting food on the table in hard times was the most loving act they could manage. Remember, in tricky or financially challenging times, the focus is on the lower levels of Maslow's needs hierarchy. In those days, telling your child you loved them or hugging them regularly wasn't the norm. The workplace was not as understanding, and getting time off to see your child in a school performance was not prioritised by employers, or by parents themselves. In addition, schools actually weren't organising daily performances or communicating classroom activities to parents as they tend to now.

Am I suggesting your parents were not in any way flawed in their parenting choices? No, not at all. I am sure there are a few of you who had very tricky childhoods. But I am guessing many of you are still smarting over things that were, in the scheme of things, pretty minor. So why do parents do so much analysis of their own childhoods?

Thinking your parents failed you

The idea that adults are victims of their childhood is very prevalent. This belief has been amplified by popular but amateur psychology theory proposing that certain events in childhood make the adult, and that particular events or an omission of something in childhood ruins the child. This is true in serious cases, such as a child never being held or shown any sort of affection or love, but not in the majority of cases I see.

Why is this idea almost universally held? Well, it works for people. When you believe your parents somehow failed you, it does wonders for your self-esteem. It allows you to fantasise about the superstar you would have been had they just put in a little more effort and bought you Barbie's campervan, paid for your mime course in Paris, or told you that you were loved 24/7. And the thought of your parents holding you back from being a super success has the bonus of making you feel like you possessed unlimited potential, which was cruelly limited by them. These thoughts work wonders for your ego. They also put you in the victim's role, which is a very attractive thought for those times when we want to wallow gloriously in a deep, soapy bath of self-pity.

But wait – before you wax lyrically about how your parents done you wrong, strumming your twangy guitar – this way of thinking might have some ever so slight consequences. If you truly believe a few omissions in your parents' parenting choices have you suffering terribly today, then by the same token, every choice you now make as a parent is incredibly important. Get it wrong and you have completely ruined your child.

Doesn't feel so good now, does it? It's kind of biting you on the proverbial backside. Don't worry. It is completely untrue.

Children are actually pretty resilient to minor ups and downs, and even some events considered more serious. This idea that children are resilient is not very popular, but has been shown to be correct over and over in research.

If you are a loving parent with reasonable expectations of your child's behaviour, you will typically be getting it right.

Here's another important point I often make in parenting talks and in the clinic: even if your parents were the very worst parents, somehow you became a success. What is my definition of success? Well, you may have moved on from a problematic childhood to be educated, financially solvent, capable of love and desiring of loving relationships. That really does point to both your resilience and the fact that your parents' approach of not giving you everything gave you a hunger to succeed. Or it encouraged you to overcome barriers and develop a fighting spirit that gives you your ability to conquer future hurdles.

Who knows what would have happened to your drive if you had experienced a childhood of perfect abundance? Would you have ever left home? If you had been the absolute centre of your parents' attention, would you have been a superstar or could you have developed a sense of entitlement, which might have made you a little unemployable and slightly incapable of retaining friends or romantic attachments?

In most cases, forgiving your parents for doing the best job they knew how to do, will allow you to feel more loved as a child and give you a sense of greater good fortune. It will also give you a break from the pressure of being a parent now. You will be able to spend more time parenting the child you actually have, rather than parenting the childhood you believe you experienced when you view it through the untrustworthy but always self-serving *coulda, shoulda, woulda* binoculars.

More fear about what can go wrong

It is difficult to pick up a newspaper or scan a news site without seeing a story on something awful happening to a child. Whether it be assault, kidnapping or another terrible thing, these crimes get a lot of reporting, often because we feel devastated for the family and friends of these children and we become gripped by their sad story. The level of coverage of bad things happening to children can sometimes exaggerate the chance of this happening to our child. Parents become more fearful, so they become more protective and hug their children even tighter.

Despite the abundant reporting, the crime rate has not increased and statistics on child victims of crime have remained relatively static for the past ten or so years. And we aren't usually made aware of instances when children venture out into the community and remain safe, because the headline 'Child plays outside and nothing happens' wouldn't be considered publish-worthy news. So we think danger constantly lurks outside.

Research has shown that the community now tends to overestimate crime rates. The resulting increase in anxiety encourages parents to keep their children closer. They prefer them to play indoors rather than outdoors.

Unfortunately we forget that, in most cases, the offender of the crime is either a family member or known to the child. The emphasis on stranger danger doesn't reflect the truth and gives a false sense of where the potential danger in our child's life more likely lies.

Human nature contributes to this fear. In my time as a clinical psychologist, I have treated far more cases of fear of flying than fear of driving. This is strange because there are more motor vehicle accidents than plane crashes, and more people have an everyday experience of driving than flying. Why are planes considered more dangerous? People typically think things are more perilous when they aren't in control. When you don't know or are not sitting next to the pilot who is flying the plane you are in, you are likely to feel more scared than when you are in charge of a vehicle, regardless of their safety record vs. yours. This is because we feel more in control of a situation when we believe we are in control of the circumstances, including being or choosing the driver, or making the decisions. This is why we feel safer driving our child to school despite the high rate of traffic accidents and the fact that walking or using public transport, when they are old enough, is probably a safer option.

Believing greater protection will keep them safe

With more sophisticated technologies and better ability to control most things in your life – such as the temperature in the room, the curl or straightness of your hair, even the size of your nose – comes greater expectation of control over everything. This is especially true in parenting. Parents now believe it is possible for their actions to ensure their child's safety forever. So, strangely, parents believe that by keeping their child always close to them, they can protect them and make them perfectly safe.

There is a horrible irony in this increased protection. By keeping your child indoors all the time and driving them to school, they are more likely to be at risk of poor health and obesity due to insufficient energetic play and exercise. By constantly protecting them, they will also be less confident in the outside world because your shielding actions may suggest the world is a scary place.

It's only through experience that your child will develop the self-belief to deal with the real world.

Children eventually have to become independent. If you don't allow them to take gradually larger steps outside the home, they will fail to develop confidence and street smarts. Holding them back from this places them at risk of a compromised life.

More parental guilt

With this emphasis on the importance of parents' role comes another trend – parental guilt. Parents who see me in my private practice typically don't come to see me mentioning guilt as their primary concern, but I often see it as a complicating factor in their child's or teen's behavioural or emotional issues.

Parenting is the hardest job in the world and there is no one right way of raising children. Even when you feel you are handling one child relatively well, another comes along whose different personality seems to turn you back into a novice parent.

Because it is such an important job, many parents put their best efforts into making sure they do their greatest work as a mother or a father. Increasingly parents are told there is a right way and wrong way to parent. People fervently want to make the right decisions – choosing the best partner, choosing the best suburb they can afford (and sometimes one they can't really afford), choosing the right way to deliver their baby, choosing the best name for their child, even down to choosing the perfect pram.

Unfortunately, the best-intentioned and best-laid plans can go awry. Complications get in the way. Birthing plans go out the door to ensure the safety of mother and baby. What were once perfect suburbs become too expensive when circumstances change and both parents have to work or move to a less desirable location. Even once-wonderful relationships can become unworkable and a couple becomes two single parents. Usually all of these actions are chosen with the primary aim of doing the best thing for everyone involved. However, any changes to plans often add the complication of guilt to an already difficult job.

Guilt typically happens
when what you wanted to do
is different from what you did.

Guilty feelings are often backed up by two faulty beliefs that are becoming ingrained in our society. The first is that perfect parenting is possible and desirable; the other is that children will not recover from difficult events or tricky situations. The facts don't back up either of these beliefs.

Striving for perfect parenting is setting up an unrealistically high demand of yourself. It is likely to produce anxiety about your performance and guilt when you (inevitably) don't achieve the exact result you wanted. Even when you do exactly as you wanted, kids have a way of not responding to your efforts in the specific way you had planned.

Most things parents worry about are minor blips in a child's life that the child will forget quickly. Unfortunately, it is the parent's long, guilty memory of their past minor or unavoidable 'mistakes' that produces parental worry and distress. It can sometimes encourage an indulgent type of parenting that has the parent thinking they are making up for their perceived wrongdoings. This is not in the best interests of the child.

Children sometimes sense the guilty feelings of a parent and start to feel badly done by. A child may even feel like a victim, even though their life is good and their parents are doing a pretty darn fine job. This situation does nobody any favours.

So, the current era has seen many changes influence parenting, but that's not all. Our beliefs about ideal parenting have also changed. Let's look at these in the next chapter.

CHAPTER 3

Overparenting – too much of the good stuff

We are living in changed times for everyone. This is particularly true for parents. My research into modern parenting, together with my clinical experience with parents and families, indicate that the popular view of the best parenting approach for children is changing.

In the previous chapter, I introduced you to two major factors which determine parenting style. *Responsiveness* refers to a parent's nurturing, caring and loving actions toward their child. *Demandingness* refers to a parent's use of expectations, rules and consequences to ensure their child behaves appropriately for their age.

You will recall that differing levels of responsiveness and demandingness produce four broad parenting approaches: authoritative, authoritarian, indulgent and negligent. Researchers and clinicians consider the authoritative approach – where there are high levels of both responsiveness to children and demandingness of age-appropriate behaviour – to be the ideal parenting approach.

Today, however, changes in the degree of responsiveness and demandingness are affecting the popular view. I now see parents who are not just *highly* responsive to their children; they are *extremely* responsive to them –

to the point of being their friend or believing every single thing they say. Similarly, some parents are not simply demanding their child behave a certain way; they place *extreme* demands on their child to be successful – a talented athlete, one of the most popular children in their class, or always doing well at school. Other parents, in an effort to ensure their child is always successful and happy, overhelp the child to the point where they place *extremely* low demands on them because the parent does all of the work and the child does very little.

These shifts from high to extreme responsiveness, high to extreme demandingness, and from extreme to very low demandingness are linked. In my experience, they occur as a kind of chain reaction. Today's parents feel they are largely responsible for their children's sense of self-esteem and wellbeing, so they ramp up their responsiveness to their children in the belief this will ensure the children's current and future happiness and success. The predominant belief is that if a little love and attention gives a child some self-esteem, then a LOT of love and attention will produce a LOT of self-esteem.

This sharp increase in parental responsiveness appears to lead to a corresponding rise in the explicit or implicit demands and expectations parents place on children: because of the high level of attention they give to their children, these parents also inadvertently place pressure on them to do well because of the prevailing belief that a child must always do well to have good self-esteem.

Many parents hold such high expectations for their child's success and happiness that they consequently overhelp their child out of concern that they will fail to realise these expectations. The parent may do their child's homework, call the coach to get their child on the team, or bring their child's forgotten assignment to school for them. In this way, these parents actually reduce the demands they place on their children.

These actions are well intentioned but collectively they amount to an approach psychologists call *overparenting*. Just as overeating describes an important action (eating) done to excess, and overexercising describes a positive activity (exercising) done to excess, overparenting describes a parenting style in which important and positive parenting actions are done to an excessive degree. Being responsive to children, expecting good things from them and helping them are all good actions. However, too much responsiveness, too many expectations of success, and overhelping children to achieve will turn helpful actions into unhelpful actions.

Let me take some time to discuss the actions associated with each link in the chain reaction.

Extreme responsiveness

Today's focus on children's wellbeing and self-esteem (discussed in the previous chapter) has led some parents to take an approach Diana Baumrind calls *kind love.* She found that these parents do not require that their children become well behaved or well informed – only that they be happy. Because of this, they tend to go beyond what are considered normal levels of warmth and involvement with their children, to levels that are extreme and unhealthy.

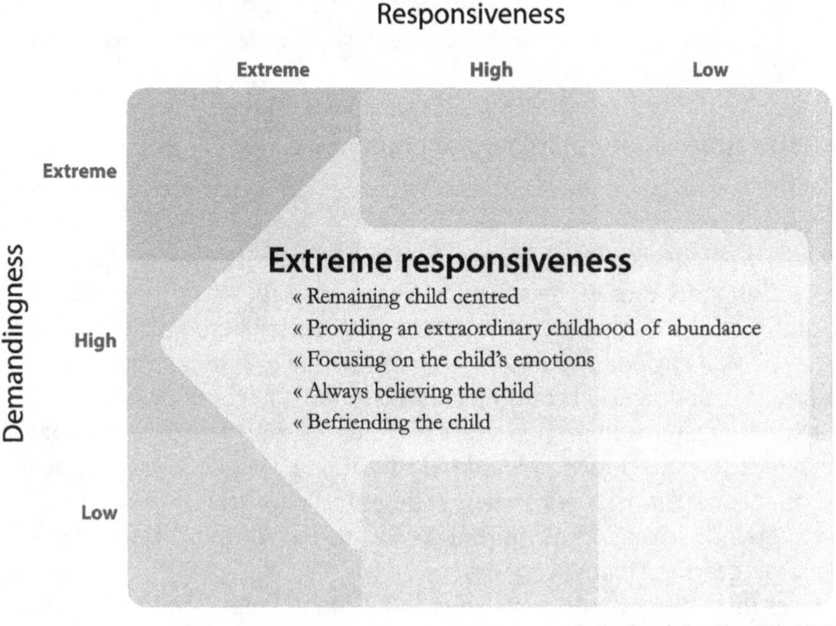

(Locke, Campbell, & Kavanagh, 2012)

Let me explain some of the parenting actions associated with extreme responsiveness.

Remaining child centred

Very early on, when you bring your baby home and in their first few months of life, the family is completely centred on the needs of the infant. This is essential parental care at this age. However, such extreme child-centredness is needed only in the very early stages of a child's life.

Unfortunately, these days, many families continue to completely centre their entire lives on their children.

For many households, the child's wishes are often the only ones taken into consideration in determining family actions, including which meal to purchase and what to do on the weekend. I have treated families where two working parents are exhausted by working in their jobs through the weekdays and then catering to every single desire of their six- or eight-year-old child on weekends. I know of many parents who put more effort into their child's or adolescent's social life than their own. The worst case I have heard of is a family where one parent had been offered a fantastic promotion to another city and they actually asked their child's opinion about the move. The upshot? Based on the decision of a four-year-old, the family stayed put.

Providing an extraordinary childhood of abundance

When a family is centred on the needs of a child, the family becomes focused on satisfying those needs.

Today, many parents consider abundant material possessions to be essential for a good childhood: beautiful rooms filled with wonderful toys; cute attention-grabbing outfits from designer stores; all the latest gadgetry in rooms where children can play all day. Many parents also consider the everyday experience of childhood must include special children's activities: out-of-school classes, such as gymnastics, ballet, or drama; trips to every children's show or Disney movie in town. Some parents have come to regard the education provided by government schools as 'inadequate' so they enrol their child in the 'best' school they can afford, even if their budget doesn't quite allow for the fees, or they have to drive a long distance to get them there every day.

Fear drives this – the parents' fear that without these things a child is deprived, their future set to be a little bleaker and their potential cruelly limited. To ensure this doesn't happen, every aspect of their offspring's childhood has to be extraordinary. Unfortunately, these parents tend to have a matching set of extraordinary credit card bills.

Focusing on the child's emotions

When you are always trying to make someone happy, you tend to really notice their emotions. You constantly examine their face and their verbal and non-verbal reactions to monitor their mood. This way you can quickly see when things are not going well for them, and you can step in and fix it for them.

This focused attention produces trouble. First of all, when you constantly look for potential issues in your child – such as every time they look hesitant, or every time they express some dissatisfaction with things or themself – you tend to build a somewhat one-sided profile of them, focused on their problems.

Once caught up in profiling, you become the amateur psychologist. You start to diagnose disorders in your child, such as anxiety, depression, low self-esteem, learning difficulties, etc. Once your diagnosis has been made, a momentum builds to continue to prove it, which encourages you to constantly decode your child's actions. You start to identify a psychological cause for any behaviour, including bad manners or inappropriate actions.

A child behaves badly and a modern parent scans their mind for reasons why. It is easy to see why a child's low self-esteem or depression are much more palatable causes to the parent than the possibility that sometimes their child is not so nice or not so well behaved. To add fuel to this, parents will often ask a child or adolescent why they did some sort of inappropriate action. Human nature starts working in the child's response.

Let's look at an example of how human nature creeps in. When your partner asks why you didn't take the garbage out, you wouldn't say, 'Because I'm lazy sometimes' or 'I knew you would do it, so why bother?' If you are crafty, you will give a reason that has them feeling sorry for you: 'I was exhausted after being at your mother's all day' or 'I am still so forgetful after the operation.' You might even mount a counterattack to make them feel guilty: 'Well at least I didn't record over the wedding with the football game.'

Children are just as clever. Rather than giving accurate responses, such as 'It felt good' or 'I'm feeling frustrated right now', they pull the *poor me* card: 'I miss Nanna' or 'I have no friends at school', or mount the counterattack 'Cause you won't let me go to the same school as my friends.'

It doesn't matter how tenuous the link is between the bad behaviour and the response: some parents will happily connect the two and accept the explanation or slink off guiltily after the counterattack. Over time children learn that these emotional responses let them off the hook and sometimes attract huge amounts of parental attention. Clever children will start using these types of responses as their get-out-of-jail-free card.

This attention towards issues and their diagnosis has another negative effect. If the parent simply diagnosed their child's issues and didn't do anything else, it wouldn't be so bad, but often the parent subsequently overassists the child, justified by a diagnosis that is not clinically proven. With mood issues like anxiety or low self-esteem, the parent's actions to help the child feel better can inadvertently make the issue worse.

Temporarily improving your child's immediate mood will not allow them to undertake actions to produce longer-term effective change.

When parents constantly interpret their children's emotions and seek to improve them, children often don't have to do too much to get their parents to jump to attention and make life rosy again. A slight frown on the face, a wail, a kick of the wall, and the parents are there making it better for the child. Sometimes children don't even need to express their feelings or make a request: they simply point to the teddy and it is handed to them; they frown and the parent offers ice-cream; they slam their books and parents help with homework.

No wonder these parents are worn out. Constantly interpreting and satisfying their child is an exhausting life for them. But I'll tell you what: it is a very, very charmed existence for their children.

Always believing the child

Extremely responsive parents pay attention to their child's or adolescent's every utterance. Their response to almost all statements: 'I believe you.'

Now, yes, I am sure many of the things that come out of a child's mouth are true. And I know you want to support your child as much as you can. And I hate to break the news, but, here goes . . . *not everything they say is correct.* When they are young their memory can be faulty and their imagination is often wild. That makes them great to play make-believe games with, but does not always make them 100 per cent reliable witnesses. Children are also egocentric when young and are not good at seeing other people's side of things. (Gosh, some adults haven't totally mastered this skill either!) They tend to see things only from their narrow, self-serving point of view.

Not only that, and I'll whisper this bit . . . they sometimes lie. They do. And it doesn't mean they are bad people; it means they are clever enough to see what effect the truth would have and adjust it slightly to make things go a little better for themselves. So saying they did nothing to deserve the detention and the teacher has got it in for them means they are thinking ahead, not that they are evil.

Many parents, slightly one-eyed about their progeny, and keen to demonstrate they are on their child's side, tend to always believe them. This results in a whole bunch of trouble for the person the child identifies as the true perpetrator of the crime, particularly if the parents are really keen to make the child happy again. So if you add a simple friendship fight at school (where both parties have some responsibility), to a parent who always believes their child and is keen to make them happy again, it equals a parent on the warpath to either the teacher, the friend or the parents of the friend, and a child who will never learn essential skills, such as the art of compromise, the ability to accept responsibility, and the capacity to sort out their own friendship issues.

Another issue arises when the parent's belief in everything their child says leads a parent to focus on every minor difficulty or injustice the child reports.

Believe your child is a victim all the time
and they start to believe it too.

Given the child's self-serving extensions of the truth often make them out to be the one suffering at the hands of others, you can easily see how a child or adolescent can start to believe they have terrible lives. This can foster a victim mentality that is very hard to shake off.

Befriending the child

I know that many of you might be thinking, 'But aren't you just describing the indulgent parenting approach?' And I agree that the parenting actions described above sound like these parents just need to have more rules, or make their child face the consequences of their actions and not allow their excuses to let them get away with it. But this parenting style is different because it provides extreme levels of warmth to a child, accompanied by an expectation that the child will reciprocate this warmth. These parents want more than a good relationship with their child: they want their child to be their friend.

These parents often want their child to be very close to them, confide in them, and see them as a buddy. They want their adolescent to come home and share intricate details about their day in the same way that close friends do. When not in their child's presence, these parents want to remain in constant contact with them on the phone, texting, or even on Facebook. These days, the adolescent texting under the desk is often replying to their dad; the university student on the phone in class is probably talking to their mother.

It's popular now to describe your child as a friend or a mate, and this is seen as evidence of good parenting. In some instances, the parent goes so far as to describe their child as their best friend. This particularly occurs with mothers and daughters, but can happen with sons and fathers, fathers and daughters, and sons and mothers.

This sort of relationship between parent and child is problematic. The very definition of a friend is someone you can confide in about everything and expect comfort and support when times are tough. To be a true best friend, it has to work both ways: the parent hugs the child when they are upset, and also expects the child to comfort them when they are distressed. This puts unnecessary pressure on the child.

When parents feel they need to be friends with their child, they put themselves in a difficult and compromised position. We look to good friends to provide support and approval for our choices. (Even better friends sometimes provide honest feedback, which can occasionally be uncomfortable for us to receive – but that is a different book I will write one day.) When a parent is friends with their child, they feel obliged to approve of everything their child says, and be cool with all of their actions and choices. So if the child shares information with the parent that is disturbing for the parent to hear, they may feel obliged to sanction or approve of it in order to remain their child's pal. In their effort to ensure their child considers them cool and treats them like a peer, they are likely to find they allow all kinds of things – swearing, purchasing bottles of alcohol for the child, allowing them to smoke, letting girlfriends or boyfriends stay over – sometimes at ages where it might be against the law.

If a parent wants to disagree with the child or adolescent about their choices, it becomes very difficult if their relationship is one of friendship.

Have you ever been promoted to a position where you are the manager of someone who used to be a peer and friend? It is a delicate task, particularly if you need to reprimand or redirect them. If a parent is their child's friend, they will have a very tough time disciplining the child. I find they often choose the easiest thing to do, which is to simply avoid discipline.

When parents and children are friends

Clinically, I find that when an adolescent or young adult describes their parent as their best friend, it indicates they may have many issues to resolve.

As a child develops and becomes older, there are some things I believe are best shared with a close friend of a similar age group, not with a parent. It is normal and healthy not to tell your parent every single thing about your life, particularly as you move into intimacy and romantic relationships. I find that those clients who describe themselves as best friends with their parents often feel guilty about things they aren't comfortable sharing with their parents because they feel these things must somehow be wrong.

Being very close friends with a parent can hold a child back from becoming an adult. For a child to successfully become independent, they need to move away from an extremely close relationship with their parent and become more autonomous in their decisions and actions. This is very difficult if they have allowed their parent to be their best friend.

Lydia is a 20-year-old who looks as if the weight of the whole world is on her shoulders. She comes to see me because she feels anxious about university. The more we talk, the more I realise she has another set of problems. Lydia describes herself as 'the only child of the best mother in the world'. She describes her mother as her best friend, who she tells everything to. (She does not see her father too often. This appears to be due to loyalty to her mother who still feels betrayed by the breakdown of the marriage ten years ago.) Lydia plans to spend a semester overseas next year, having been offered a prestigious internship. However, her mother regularly tells her how lonely she is going to be 'when my best friend leaves me'. Lydia tells me her mother doesn't like her to go out too often, so she is trying not to see her university pals on the weekend so much to allow her to spend more time with her mother. I try to discuss what her actual responsibilities are to her mother for the rest of her life, but Lydia only wants to talk about the sacrifices her mother has made for her and how she feels responsible for her. Lydia thinks she may not take the overseas opportunity after all, because she feels she would miss her mum too much.

When children or adolescents best-friend their parent, they don't have a vacancy for the best friend role and consequently don't need to put effort into finding a close friend of a similar age and circumstance. Friend-type relationships between parent and child also tend to be very one-sided, with the child getting the majority of comfort and attention. This can hinder the child or adolescent's development of reciprocity skills and reduce their capacity to be considerate of others' needs. In a cruel twist, the child has to continue to rely on the parent as their friend because they are not what their peers generally consider 'ideal friend material', often because of selfish, egocentric, or dominating behaviour in conversation. In addition, the parent may discourage the child from having close same-aged peer friendships or romantic relationships, because they fear their child will choose others to confide in or become close to – and the parent will lose their 'friend'.

Best-friending their child is also not good for a parent, who usually doesn't receive reciprocal support from their child/friend. They may also neglect their friendships with same-aged peers or socialise less often with long-standing friends.

By far the biggest issue when a parent wants their child to be reciprocally responsive toward them is that this parental need for affection from the child gives the child an opportunity for great power.

When a parent is dependent on the child for warm feelings, a clever child can easily start manipulating the parent's feelings and gain power over the parent.

As you would know, children as young as three can start this process of manipulation when you don't do what they want with statements like 'I not be your friend.' They often move on to something approximating 'I hate you' some time in adolescence. Confident parents can shrug off these statements: 'I'm the person in charge because I'm the sensible and loving adult. My child doesn't like the decision, and it makes sense that as a result, they currently don't like me.' But for the parent who wants the child to like them, this exchange becomes much more painful. Being a child's cool, approving friend removes the possibility of this problem ever happening, but, unfortunately, it makes a parent reliant on their child or adolescent being capable of and willing to make sensible decisions in day-to-day life.

And if the child is not making level-headed choices? Well, those two buddies are going to be in a whole world of trouble.

Extreme demandingness

Extreme responsiveness to children might sound wonderful: all of that parental attention, all of those wonderful activities, all of that effort to make children happy. These kids should be having a superb childhood, huh? Well, not always.

Unfortunately, when parents put such a lot of effort into making a child happy and successful, the result is a lot of pressure on the child to *be* happy and successful. When a parent gives up their weekend to ensure their child has a fantastic time, there is subtle pressure for the child to be cheerful all weekend.

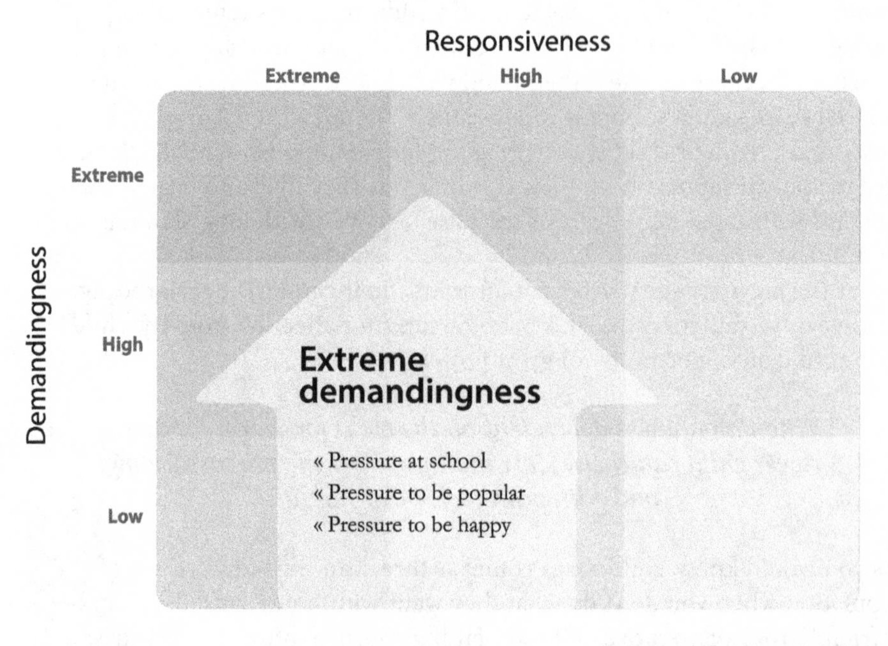

(Locke, Campbell, & Kavanagh, 2012)

When a parent goes into financial difficulty to give them ice-skating classes, they can place a burden on the child to show incredible dedication to the sport and provide hope for the dollars to transform into an Olympic career. So alongside extreme responsiveness to children, often come extreme demands placed on children to be always happy and continually successful.

Let me explain the types of extreme demands placed on children as a consequence of extreme responsiveness.

Pressure at school

Nowhere are these demands more obvious than in schools. As a former teacher in independent and government schools, I saw many parents expect their child to achieve good results in every subject, to be in the top team of the sport they played, to take the lead role in the play, and to be very popular with their classmates. Anything less was often not good enough.

These parents see their high expectations of their children as a loving act. To want their child to do well all of the time is seen as good parenting. To expect or accept anything less than great results from their child would indicate they don't believe in them enough. Subtle or obvious pressure on children to achieve success is seen as taking an interest in them and being caring. A parent's acceptance of their child's poor marks or failure to gain a place on the team or in the school play is seen as uncaring and negligent.

There are some interesting complexities in this pushiness and pressure. In some ways it is not completely the parents' fault they expect these things from their child. Savvy schools have determined that there are a lot of parents out there who want their child to do well in life. Because of this, schools have started to employ advertising techniques to appeal to these types of parents. Look at these phrases taken from advertisements for independent schools:

> 'X school: fostering self-confident, responsible, and successful students.'
>
> 'Our students are treated as individuals. Their unique talents and interests are recognised and nurtured; their goals and aspirations supported and encouraged.'

Understandably, these advertisements appeal to parents' desires for their child to be treated as a very special person, have their potential effectively nurtured, and become successful and confident. But the problematic element is that they are suggesting *all* children have the potential to be super successful if correctly nurtured: the parent has only to purchase an education at this school and their child will become a star. That's fine if the child is genetically blessed, but not necessarily truthful if the child lacks certain talents, or cognitive or physical prowess.

A fundamental element missing from discussions about children's achievements these days is the good old bell curve. The bell curve exists for pretty much every skill or ability – I swear to you! It basically shows that there is a normal distribution for everything and if you graded the whole population on A to E in any particular skill, say on mathematical ability, the majority would be in the middle and receive a C, with fewer receiving a B or D and even fewer receiving an A or E. Even if schools only gave A, B or C, the majority would still be in the middle receiving Bs and a smaller percentage would receive an A or C.

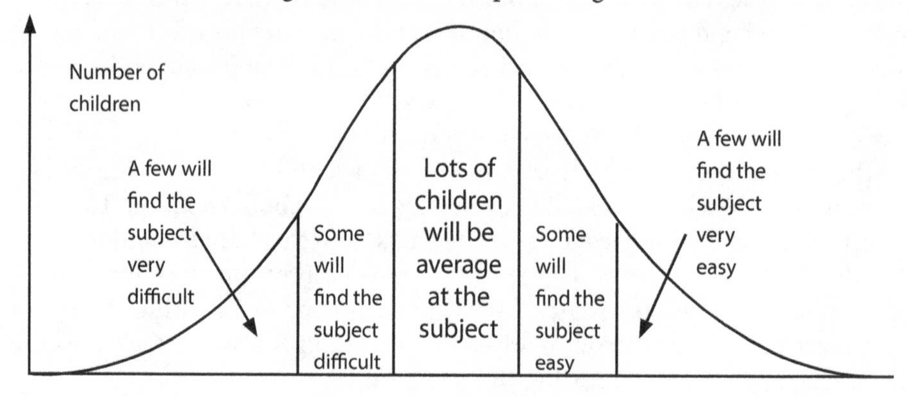

A good education can only take a child to the success their natural skill, basic intelligence and motivation will allow them to achieve, yet some parents think that by sending their child to a good school, they will reap rewards such as academic prizes and awards for sports performance. Somehow we now have an *effort equals achievement* mentality, where the more effort you put in, the greater the accomplishment you expect in return.

Schools inadvertently support this view when they are vocal about good grades their students have received. When parents hear of great results achieved in previous years at particular schools, they tend to equate attendance at those schools with academic triumph. So they scan the league tables and send their child to the top-performing schools to ensure their child's success. These parents become very cranky when their child does not achieve high results, and often blame the school for not giving their child what they appeared to promise.

I don't think that schools or parents are particularly at fault here. I understand schools want to show pride in their students' achievements in their advertising, and I understand most parents want to see these sorts of results from the school they choose for their child. Gosh, if schools told the truth – 'Locke College: We will do our best with whatever you hand us' – enrolments would dip significantly.

There is nothing wrong with wanting your child to have every opportunity you can provide for them. But there is a problem when you start to anticipate specific outcomes from these opportunities.

The main issue with these high expectations of success is that we have very high expectations of our children.

Many parents have very high hopes for their children. Lots of them expect their child to be very good, at least at something. They confirm their expectations by Facebooking their child's every achievement from a young age and making grand statements about them being 'a very good artist', 'a real little entertainer', and 'very good at reading', allegedly to improve their self-esteem. However, this behaviour starts to create a need for their child to achieve. Crowing about your child might be for their supposed benefit but it's a rare parent who doesn't get slightly ego-involved in their child's successes. This places even more pressure on the child.

Children quickly learn that when they are successful they get an awful lot of attention from their parents. And the pressure starts bearing down on them. The world tells them nonsense like 'believe in your dreams and believe in yourself and it will happen'. And that's fine if the belief is accompanied by a lot of hard work. However, we don't always acknowledge that there are some things that, no matter how hard they work, they won't achieve. No matter how much running, gym work, dieting and exercising I did, I was never going to be an Olympic athlete. To tell a child to *dream it and put effort into it and you'll be it* is often a cruel lie. Inspirational slogans like these can set them up to be crushed when their improbable dreams are not realised.

Are there lazy kids out there who could do a lot better than their average result? Absolutely. But not everyone can do better than average; some kids are average, and that is okay. Some can only achieve below the average mark in a class and that is also okay.

Truly loving parenting is about accepting their strengths and weaknesses, not always suggesting they should or could be better.

Pressure to be popular

We are familiar with the concept of the pushy parent who wants their child to be a sporting superstar or academic success. Unfortunately, pressure to perform doesn't end with schoolwork. Increasingly children face demands to be popular, to be invited to every party and have many friends.

I get numerous requests from parents of very young children who want me to speak to their seven-year-old who doesn't seem to have many friends. Schools report to me that all hell can break loose when there is a party and not every child in the class is invited. Even if the party is a small one, many parents take it personally if their child misses out.

Not all children develop friend-making skills uniformly. Some take a little longer to navigate social situations. Some just aren't as social. This doesn't necessarily mean they are on the autism spectrum; it just means they are a little more comfortable with their own company. There is a bell curve for social skills, and not every child is going to be class captain or be invited to every party. In the early years of school, many children won't be able to name a best friend or be clear on their social group. Indeed, the situation might change every day.

The trouble arises when many parents, in an effort to confirm to themselves that their child is socially successful, start to exert subtle pressure early on in the child's life. At the end of the first day at school a parent anxiously asks, 'Did you make any friends?' or 'Did you play with kids at lunch?' A negative response sees the parent earnestly asking the same thing the next day. They worriedly look up online forums on friendlessness or autism. They anxiously go through their child's school bags looking for invitations to parties. I can't tell you how many parents admit to me they spy on their child from the bushes at lunchtime to see if they are playing with other children. These parents start setting up play dates to get those firm friendships underway. You see how it starts to become a *thing* for the parent, which in turn suggests to the child that they may be lacking in the social skills department.

I have even had parents tell me their child has no friends *in front of their child*. If the child disagrees and stands up for themself, some parents make their point more strongly, 'No, you don't have any friends, no real friends.' Why on earth would they say this to a child?

Unfortunately, this pressure can cause a slightly sensitive child to become anxious, and can suggest friend-making problems where none exist. Or it can make children dependent on their parents to do all the work creating their friendship groups instead of developing their own social skills.

Imagine that at the end of every weekend, someone appeared at your door to ask you how many people called you or if you were invited to any parties. Imagine the pressure of a typical Monday if the question 'how was your weekend?' led to a judgement of your social success and popularity. Can you imagine how fraught your experience would be? What about the personal doubts if the other person looked terribly alarmed if you answered in a manner that didn't satisfy them? Now imagine that you are six years old and this is happening.

Pressure to be happy

Pressure doesn't end with academic, sporting or social success. Parents' desire to make children happy actually puts demands on children to be happy. Indeed, in the current parenting climate, I am not sure that some children have permission to be anything but happy. I think this is abnormal.

These days many children face not only the normal challenges of life and less-than-stellar days, they also deal with their parents' distress. When a child reports sadness to their parent, their parent despairs for them; when a child worries about a test, their parent can't sleep that night; when a child is annoyed with their friend for not inviting them to the party, their parent is furious.

> 11-year-old Liam and his mother come to see me. His mother explains that Liam has always had difficulty making friends. He seems to lack social confidence and has had a few headaches sorting out a group of boys to hang out with at school since a few of his former friends changed schools last year. Although he has a few acquaintances, he has no particular friendship group yet. Liam's mother cries during the interview, and tells me she also had difficulty making friends when she was young. When I interview Liam by himself, he tells me his mother questions him about socialising at school every day and, if his answer disappoints, his mother bursts into tears. Liam says he has decided not to tell his mother about friendships at school any more, because his mother becomes so distressed. Liam reports he is a little frustrated about the situation at school, but is more concerned about upsetting his mother.

I know of many children who hold back from telling their parent things because their parent becomes more upset than they are. Consequently, they present a happy face to their parent all of the time. I am convinced that many parents consider any form of worry, sadness or anger unnatural, when these are normal and often quite useful emotions to encourage us to alter things in our lives.

More importantly, being expected to be happy all of the time is really difficult and pressuring. Why do so many families fight at Christmas or after long days at theme parks? Because they have tried to appear loving, excited, and smiley for hours and hours. And ☺ It ☺ Is ☺ Sometimes ☺ Exhausting ☹.

Pain, depression, sadness, and frustration
are normal emotions and are part of the rich experience
of the full repertoire of emotions.

Children will be less resilient without some experience of these emotions. Learning how to face difficulties or occasional bad days gives children confidence that they can cope when they feel that way. Parents should allow their child to feel less than stellar every now and then to assist the development of this skill. Don't allow these sad or anxious emotions to go on for too long without seeking help, but don't feel you can or should erase them completely from your own or your child's life.

Why is this extreme demandingness?

These expectations are extreme demands because they are higher than many children's capabilities. If every parent expects their child to receive an A in a subject, the basic bell curve suggests that at least 80 per cent of them are expecting too much. If every parent wants their adolescent to be at Olympic level in their sport, the lead in the school play, or even invited to every party, it stands to reason that, for most children, this expectation is too high. If we expect a normal ratio of happiness to sadness to be 1:1 or even 3:1, then the parent's expectation of consistent happiness in their child is extreme, unrealistic and most likely doing some form of harm. This is not just 'do your best'; this is 'be superlative' and with this expectation someone is going to be terribly and regularly disappointed.

Low demandingness

What happens when the child or adolescent of extremely responsive and demanding parents does not achieve the success and happiness the parents want for them?

In my experience, many of these parents step in and help their child achieve success or make them happy. They do this in a myriad of ways. As soon as their child reports a difficult day, the parent thinks of ways to solve it for them. They will buy their crying child an ice-cream to make them feel better. They will sit down and help their adolescent write the assignment to get a good result. They will pack their child's school bag each night to ensure they don't forget their swimming gear or library book, or they will bring the forgotten item to school. They will continue to set up play dates when their child is 13 years old.

These parents have high expectations for their child or adolescent to achieve success. However, the person creating the achievement is the parent, not the child.

These parents actually place very low demands on the child, because it is the parent's effort that makes the child successful, not the child's.

This aspect of high-effort parenting is the hallmark of some of the more popular media terms for overparenting. 'Helicopter parenting' is so called because the parent hovers over their child with the intent to step in at the first sign of difficulty. 'Lawnmower parenting' gets its name from the way the parent mows away any obstacles that stand in the way of their child's success.

Parents do these things with the best of intentions, but at the expense of the child's opportunity to create their own success. They place low demands on the child to master essential skills, accept difficult things, or take on challenges that will improve their lives.

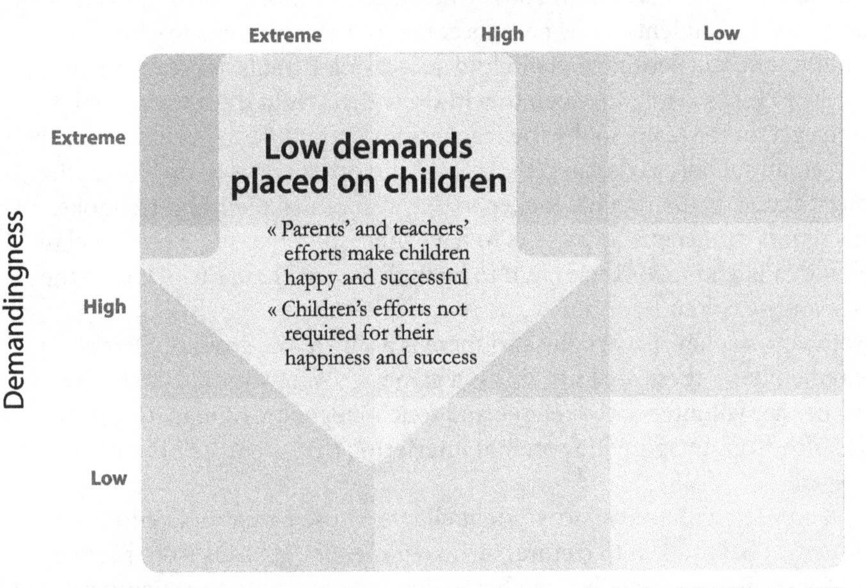

(Locke, Campbell, & Kavanagh, 2012)

My research shows that parents place low demands on children in many ways: carrying their toddler or putting them in their stroller when they are capable of walking; cutting up their ten-year-old's food; bringing a separate plate of food to the party for their 13-year-old picky eater; driving their 16-year-old everywhere because they won't let them catch public transport; not allowing a 17-year-old to take their driver's licence test because they believe driving is dangerous. Children who experience this type of parenting are often disadvantaged; some can't take care of themselves in normal school activities or real life. Some eight-year-olds are not able to attend school camps because they are unable to dry themselves, comb their hair or make their bed. I have treated university students who still rely on their parents to wake them every day with a phone call, even though they have moved out of home.

It is not only parents putting in this effort

Many parents agitate others to put in similar levels of effort to ensure their child is thriving and contented. These parents might contact the teacher to convince them to let their adolescent off the detention, demand the coach let their child play the whole game, request the kindergarten teacher to set up a friend for their child, or even insist that the parent of the birthday boy or girl ensures their child gets an invitation to the party.

I last taught in a classroom in 2001, when teachers were trusted to make the best decisions for students. Now parents come to their children's teachers and demand that the teacher make their child successful. Parents ask teachers to change their child's result, threaten to withdraw their child from the school if they don't get on the team, lobby the teachers for their child to get a lead role in the play, email schools to demand their child should not have to do a detention, or request access to their child's locker so they can return their library books. Schools report campaigns by parents to have their child put into a certain class and phone calls asking for their child to be in the school house which uses the child's favourite colour.

I watch my nephew play rugby and there is a sign at the ground: 'Parents please remember – these are kids; this is a game; we want your kids to have fun; the coaches are volunteers; the referee and touch judges are human; this is not the Bledisloe Cup'. Imagine the parental interfering that occurred before the sign was created!

I have worked with university student clients whose parents still edit their assignments. I have talked to lecturers who tell me they get calls from parents asking, 'Can you let my daughter do her assignment as a written assignment, she is not very good at oral presentations?' I have spoken to a university administrator who told me the mother of a first-year university student wanted to set up a camper bed and sleep by her 18-year-old son's side for the first two weeks in university accommodation to ensure he adjusted to college life. On the first day of semester, many universities develop activities to move the parent away from their child's side, because the parent wants to accompany them to their first university lecture to help them cope.

This help extends beyond their student years. I have spoken to managers who have received complaints from employees' parents when their young adult didn't get a promotion or received what they felt was an unnecessarily harsh performance review.

You think I'm kidding, right? But you can see how it happens. It is hard to drag some parents away from primary school classrooms when school starts. Keep that type of behaviour going as the child becomes an adult and you can see how behaviour that is abnormal can seem perfectly reasonable to parents who have always taken responsibility for ensuring their child's constant happiness and success.

When the child does not do well, the parent believes it is actually someone else's fault. I have lost count of the number of parents I have seen who blame their adolescent's educational issues on a 'bad teacher in grade four' or their child's behaviour problems on their current best friend. They believe that if you change the environment to be particularly supportive of the child then the child will become a super success. And yes, that might be temporarily true – but you will have to ensure the environment stays supportive for the rest of their life, and put it on wheels, because it needs to move around with the child as they go on to university or work, and if they move to other cities or countries.

Parents' actions to resolve their child's issues mean the child doesn't develop their own skills in facing the issues, accepting the situation, or resolving their difficulties.

Putting the onus on others to give the child a great life doesn't equip the child to make it happen for themself. They become used to a life where other people take responsibility for their happiness and success.

Today many parents subscribe to the idea they can give their children an ideal childhood through high parental effort and sacrifice. But don't believe the hype, this life ain't all roses. Let me explain further in the next chapter.

CHAPTER 4

The bonsai child

Some parents try so hard to ensure their child's success and happiness that they limit their child's potential to develop into confident, independent adults. This approach has resulted in a phenomenon I like to call *the bonsai child.*

Bonsai is the ancient Asian art of cultivating miniature trees. As a means of decorating a home or courtyard, trees of many varieties are deliberately made diminutive. Their owners plant them in small containers, and prune their branches regularly to make sure they fit into their environment.

The art of bonsai is quite intricate. Even though they are small, looking after these trees' needs is more time intensive than if they had been planted outside in the elements. To keep them small and attractively shaped requires much attention from their owner. New growth has to be trimmed back regularly and substantially to make sure the tree matures in an aesthetically pleasing manner, and to stop it from becoming too large to fit into its designated space. To ensure it maintains an attractive shape in its confined environment, the bonsai's branches need to be trimmed or realigned by wrapping them in wire. While bonsai are usually shaped and pruned to display the natural shape of the tree in its proper larger form, sometimes they are nipped and tucked to make the tree look a little more interesting, such as bringing about a windswept look.

Bonsai are highly dependent on their carers' protection. Trees must be checked regularly to see if they need water or fertiliser, and frequently re-potted. Because they are so delicate and small, they need protection from extreme conditions, and only thrive in environments that have constant temperature. Their position in the house has to be very well thought out due to their shallow root structure. Some varieties can only handle a small amount of direct sunlight.

Bonsai are beautiful but they are purely ornamental. They provide joy and value, but only for the occupants of the household in which they are housed. They fail to develop their full promise to enable the larger community to benefit from their capacity to provide oxygen, shade, beauty, and assistance for soil and fauna.

You can replant a bonsai outside – but you have to be very careful to put it in a sheltered spot because the plant is used to a customised environment. Even when planted outside, chances are the tree will never to get to the height of other similar varieties because of its earlier pruning and shaping. There is also a chance the tree will not cope in the elements because it is used to such a protected environment.

A bonsai child, like a bonsai tree, is stunted.

Overparenting produces children who are very much like bonsai. These bonsai children are similarly cared for with consistent parental attention to their every need, and any issues immediately solved. The bonsai child is deliberately placed in surroundings that suit them so they never need to adjust to a tough environment. As bonsai trees are not required to adapt to cope with variations in the weather, bonsai children never need to learn to adapt to differing conditions because their parent always puts them in a position that is specifically catered to them.

Bonsai children have childhoods trimmed of
difficult circumstances and the dead branches of failure.
Any flaws are quickly removed to keep them perfect.

Bonsai children's lives are mapped out by their parents, who bend and twist people and circumstances around them to keep everything about their offspring unblemished and lovely.

The bonsai child becomes used to their parent's constant attention and care. They are much less capable than others of facing the outside world. When bonsai children go beyond their home, they are surprised their needs aren't similarly catered to or that they are not figures of adoration. Accustomed to high levels of care, they start to believe they are unable to exist without this degree of consideration from others. If any winds of discomfort or difficulty blow on them, they are likely to break.

Bonsai children have reduced capacity to reach their potential because any new growth is limited.

Growing deeper roots or thicker branches may assist bonsai trees to become stronger, but strength is not the main aim for bonsai. Likewise, facing difficult circumstances may make the bonsai child sturdy, but the development of this sturdiness is a risk, because facing tricky things is not considered part of a perfect childhood. Any development of strength may make the child more capable than their environment allows, or their parent wants: they may experience events not part of their parent's plans for them, or risk not achieving the exact level of success desired by their parents.

Bonsai trees look like real trees but they are tiny replications. They haven't been nurtured in a manner that will easily enable them to fit in with other trees or in nature. Ironically, the effort to keep them looking exactly like miniature trees causes them to lose their potential to be real trees in a real forest contributing to the natural world. They are stuck inside – pretty, but reliant on others because of their small branches and shallow roots.

Likewise the bonsai children, whose childhoods have been trimmed and manipulated to be perfect, are reliant on the care and protection of others to continue their perfect shape.

Bonsai children are less likely to be able to contribute to the world because they have not been given or required to develop the skills required to fit in with real life.

A bonsai childhood is a pleasurable but ultimately empty start to life. It doesn't build a child's capacity to cope, and limits their potential.

CHAPTER 5

The effects of a bonsai upbringing

In my psychology practice, I have seen the effects of a bonsai upbringing on children for a long time now. Let me show you what happens when parents adopt this approach.

Clinically, bonsai children present a range of issues, including poor life skills, low resilience, anxiety, dependence on others, and poor behaviour.

Poor life skills

When parents constantly cater to their child's every need – packing their bag for school every day, driving them everywhere, solving their problems – the child doesn't learn life skills. When parents remember everything for them, the child doesn't progress the capacity of their own working memory. When parents take responsibility for solving the minor challenges of their lives, children and adolescents don't learn practical life skills or develop the capability to improve their own tricky situations.

Too much adult assistance makes children less inclined to learn skills to assist themselves. Research shows us that when parents do too much for their children, the children fail to develop autonomous motivation. My clinical experience confirms this. If a parent puts in all the effort for the child to achieve at school, the child has no motivation to try to do well at school. They may even blame their parents or the school when their results aren't up to scratch.

Many of my young adult clients expect others to step in and fix things for them. I am not sure I blame them; their expectations are somewhat logical if this has been the previous pattern. If your partner brought you a present every day and then one day turned up without a present, have they taught you what to expect? Would it be understandable if you were angry about the lack of a gift given the precedent your partner set up?

Likewise if bonsai children are used to their parents solving their issues for them, they won't feel the need to develop problem-solving skills. Unfortunately, it makes them passive, dependent on the support of others at all times, and unaccustomed and unable to effect change in their own lives.

Poor resilience

Children who don't face the normal ups and downs of life fail to learn the skills to face minor or major life challenges. They are fine as long as their lives proceed smoothly, but they are dependent on constant success and satisfaction.

I see many young adults who become melancholic when things don't work out perfectly for them. This is because they haven't had to develop any resilience in their childhood, as their parents have always smoothed things for them, no matter how minor the issue they faced. The bonsai child or adolescent has never learnt to cope with difficult things, nor have they learnt that they can endure things not quite going their way.

Bonsai children expect the world to always be a fair place where bad things don't happen, because their parent's actions have ensured they are always treated fairly and well. Accustomed to perfect conditions at all times, these children and adolescents receive a genuine shock when they encounter situations that aren't just or pleasant, and they can be very slow to recover.

The assistance given by parents to bonsai children also has a disturbing undertone.

High levels of help to children suggest to them that they need that level of support and imply that they lack skill to face issues on their own.

Help them a lot with their homework and they start to think they can't do their homework. Help them a lot with life and they start to think they can't really face life. Unfortunately, this level of assistance encourages bonsai children to have an external locus of control: they think their wellbeing rests on the actions of others and not on their own actions and choices. Ironically, over time, help makes them helpless.

Anxiety and perfectionism

Anxiety as a mental health issue appears to be on the rise. While I won't blame it all on bonsai childhoods, I'm going to portion a significant amount on the repercussions of modern parenting choices. The main issue is that too much parental attention has consequences: the level of interest in their achievements puts pressure on children to achieve; the degree of praising them as beautiful or handsome puts demands on them to be beautiful or handsome.

At some point in bonsai children's lives, the encouragement of their parents ceases to be enough. Genuine doubt will creep in about some particular qualities – attributes they now believe to be significant due to the parental attention lavished on them. The child whose beauty has always gained great attention from their loved ones will be more upset than others when they doubt their looks, because they think physical attractiveness is very important. On the other hand, the child who has not had a fuss made of their looks will not be as concerned when they are not feeling attractive or have a bad hair day. They will be able to shrug it off more easily because they haven't been led to believe that physical attractiveness is an essential quality for them to possess.

Praise isn't always a great gift. Imagine a colleague at work tells you how wonderful your clothing choices are, how you always pick out the perfect tie to go with a suit, or how you put together such stylish outfits every day. It is a nice thing for them to say, but imagine the pressure bearing down on you as you stand in front of your wardrobe the next day. And if you paraded in front of your wardrobe admirer in your day's sartorial choice, and they said nothing, would you imagine they think you are not up to scratch today? Would you be upset that you had let them down; would you double your efforts for the next day?

Praise easily becomes pressure over time,
particularly if it is laid on too thick.

Being the apple of others' eyes is also not always helpful for anxiety. When you imagine everyone noticing you, you focus much more on your performance. It makes you feel bad about even minor mistakes. Well-meant parental responses sometimes don't help. If bonsai children report failures, parents might deny a mistake was even made. A child does badly on the sporting field and some parents say, 'No sweetie, you were outstanding on the field, you were the best one there,' which is an inaccurate statement of the child's skills. While I understand that the parent wants to increase the child's confidence, children will reach an age when they know the parent's statement is nonsense. This makes them doubt themselves even more.

More importantly, the parent's denial of poor skills suggests to the child that not being good at the sport is unpalatable to the parent. If I said I had brunette hair to my parents and they disagreed, 'No, no you don't, you are a lovely blonde,' it suggests to me that being a brunette is unacceptable. If a parent denies the truth, it suggests the truth is unpalatable to them. You can understand that praise intended to build self-esteem actually doesn't build it at all. This is particularly so when praise is an extreme extension of the truth or an out-and-out lie: it causes a child to worry about their lack of skill (or blondness).

Too much assistance to enable the child to achieve also affects their confidence. Many bonsai children have been helped so much by their parents in the past that when their efforts start to be their own, their results pale in comparison, particularly when they have been praised for their great skills. They start to become fixated on their supposed failures. Often their parents are similarly obsessed.

Indeed, I would say perfectionism - the desire to be perfect, coupled with high anxiety and self-recrimination over minor mistakes – causes a significant majority of the issues I see in adolescents, young adults and adults. Often parents have inadvertently modelled this attitude through their extreme attention to their child's imagined or real success, and their complete denial of what appears to be unpalatable failure or average performance.

A sense of entitlement

If an entire household was centred around you, if your every utterance was doted on, and if others were always taking responsibility for improving your life and making you happy, understandably you would start to think you were pretty special. And that in itself is not a problem, but increasingly I find that parents are showing love to bonsai children at a level that inadvertently causes harm.

A sense of entitlement is a belief that everyone should always treat you in the exact way you want to be treated, and that your needs should be their primary concern. It can easily be encouraged in a child when they become used to the people around them being highly attentive and somewhat self-sacrificing toward them. This can easily become the reality to which bonsai children are accustomed.

Sure, those early months of infant care are all about parents forgoing sleep, not going out into the world, and a loss of adult fun. But there comes a time when parents should wrestle back some of the control and status in the family to be able to choose the meal, weekend activities, operation of the TV remote, the location of the annual holiday. If the child never learns to compromise then they start to feel entitled. I see egocentrism result in many clinical issues in children, teens and young adults, including difficulty keeping friends, temper issues, troubles with authority figures, and poor self-regulation.

Narcissism

Bonsai children are often narcissistic. This conceit is likely the result of being constantly praised for their talents, and having every failure explained as someone else's fault or unfair. A child is not always good at identifying that their achievements are primarily the result of their parent's efforts, and so they start to truly believe they are a talented artist or gifted student. A parent's extreme praise may lead them to believe they are a world-class singer or dancer. This belief may be slightly or very inaccurate (and the inaccuracy is sometimes humiliatingly proven on TV talent or idol-making shows).

When a child has developed narcissism, it is difficult to give them genuinely helpful feedback because their belief in their talent makes them deaf to suggestion. Narcissistic children will take any sort of constructive criticism very badly and either think of the judge as extremely cruel or become distraught because they are unused to anything but admiration. This makes progress toward improving themselves and actually achieving their dreams more difficult.

Too much reliance on others

Bonsai children and adolescents with inflated egos as a result of other people's efforts are often reliant on others in their lives to make them feel good through consistent nurturing and praise. This makes them needy of attention and needy in relationships, and this reliance reduces their independence and resilience.

People who are not overly reliant on others are better at being more objective in their judgement of relationships. They are more capable of assessing a person on the sum total of how they treat them, rather than becoming reliant on the person regardless of how they take care of them. Those who rely on constant attention and admiration from others tend to become besotted with people quickly and slow to withdraw from harmful relationships, which may come at a cost to them.

An unhealthy reliance on others comes at a cost to developing or insisting on healthy relationships.

I notice a worrying trend of adolescents being easily flattered and getting into relationships with manipulative and needy partners. These relationships are characterised by constant contact with each other, continual text messages, overt displays of affection and extreme romance. When the partner doesn't reply to the text message immediately or doesn't do exactly what the other wants, it quickly turns into possessiveness, emotional arguments and abuse.

I think it is no surprise that when you delve into their situation, you often find that people in these sorts of relationships have had a bonsai upbringing. They are accustomed to love being expressed through high praise, sacrifice and reliance on others. It takes an enormous amount of therapy to enable them to realise that true long-term love is not characterised by emotional manipulation, extreme personal sacrifice, and the constant drama of great displays of love followed by anger, abuse, or emotional tirades when the other person doesn't do exactly as you want.

Too much emphasis on emotions

Parents' focus on making their bonsai children happy puts much of the spotlight on the children's emotions. The children quickly learn that they get a lot of attention when even a little upset, and they start to think they should be happy all of the time.

> *Because of the focus on emotions, many children are erroneously convinced that anything but happiness is abnormal.*

A slightly difficult day is an aberration. A sense of melancholy is labelled depression; any trepidation is labelled anxiety. A friendship fight is bullying; a bit of sadness and the child is excused from school; or a smidgeon of self-consciousness and their parent writes a note for the child to be excused from the swimming carnival.

Unfortunately, everyone is an amateur psychologist these days and many are labelling any experience of difficulty as a mental health issue. This is not helped when low self-esteem is an easy cause for nearly every issue these days. This makes parents reluctant to give a consequence to poor choices because of their imagined diagnosis. Indeed, many parents (and sometimes even teachers too) suggest mental health problems, such as depression or anxiety, to children as potential causes of their poor choices. 'Did you kick me because you miss Daddy?' or 'Why didn't you hand in the assignment? Is your anxiety affecting you again?'

This adult concern is well intentioned and stems from a desire to make things easier for children affected by poor mental health. But it has unintended effects, particularly with children who don't have a diagnosable mental health issue and are simply looking for an easy way out. What child is going to disagree with the identification of an emotion or situation that is potentially going to absolve them from a misdemeanour? Sadly these easy excuses don't allow them to alter their behaviour for their benefit, and keep them victims of their alleged issues. So the child whose self-confidence would benefit greatly from completing an assignment successfully has an excuse never to do the work, and as a result never gains the achievement. Over time, if the child doesn't engage regularly in behaviours that will help them to feel better, a relatively brief mood can easily become a permanent mood.

Therapised children

Because of the emphasis on happiness, much attention is paid to brief negative moods. Psychologists and school counsellors are now regularly engaged to treat minor mood disorders.

Good therapy should help most issues and ideally teach children the skills to improve their lives relatively quickly through proven effective treatments. Bad therapy is just supportive counselling – talking about minor problems, sympathy from the professional, some inconsequential praise or life affirmations, and/or some ineffective suggestions for negligible improvements, such as 'try to be nice to your parents this week' – a process of patching up which is so fruitless it needs to be repeated on a weekly basis.

There are children with serious issues who need long-term therapy, but there are many regularly attending therapists who don't. Unfortunately a new breed of *therapised* children and young adults is emerging. They are so used to getting assistance for minor issues they begin to believe they need continual support. What should have been a short series of sessions to teach the patient effective psychological strategies to overcome unhelpful responses or deal with tricky situations sometimes goes on much longer than needed, often through client and parental pressure to have constant psychological support for minor challenges.

Therapised people start to believe they are somehow lacking in strength to face the world without regular therapy or special consideration from people around them. A long treatment time suggests an issue is serious, yet many clients are actually more capable than what is inadvertently implied. They undertake months of therapy for a short-term impact on their bank balance but no long-term impact on their mood or ability to independently cope with their circumstances.

Poor behaviour

Bonsai children are fine if they remain happily in their pots, basking in their parents' attention and care, needy but nice to be around. Unfortunately, bonsai children don't always remain like this. Some have a habit of taking over their surroundings and become more like house-sized evil triffids than tiny Japanese elms or miniature fig trees.

Parents are in an ideal position to help children make appropriate choices – they love their child, they want them to be able to fit into society, and they have an adult brain that can judge risk much better than their child. Indeed, the guiding part of parenting may be as important to children's development as hugging them.

It is the job of every parent to encourage and discourage certain behaviours.

Parents can manage behaviour using praise and rewards, or consequences such as Time Out or extra chores. Sometimes praise works best – say in situations where you are encouraging them to do something, such as weaning them off nappies and training them to use the toilet. But not everything can be improved with praise or encouragement. Sometimes the parent needs to give the child a brief and appropriate consequence for not following an important rule or for behaving inappropriately.

This consequence ensures the child understands they should not do a certain action. It may also give them an incentive not to do the action again. Over time this external policeman provided by the parent is internalised by the child or adolescent, and they begin to self-manage their behaviour to their benefit.

Bonsai parenting is great with praise and rewards but often hopeless with consequences. Many parents nowadays fear the results of consequences they give to their child. They tend not to assign them, or give ineffective ones.

Why? Parents who are fearful of their bonsai child not liking them are unlikely to enforce the sort of consequence that will make the child momentarily resent them. Parents who don't like their child being unhappy find it very difficult to endure the moments their children are placed in a short period of Time Out or briefly grounded, because they see their child's anger or slight anguish and believe it is causing their child harm. Either way, the consequences are too painful for parents to enforce.

Many parents of bonsai children become emotional when their child makes a poor choice or goes against their wishes. Often the only consequence chosen by the parent is a long lecture about their own disappointment and distress. In the course of the diatribe, the parent may become angry and emotionally manipulative. I have even seen loving parents get abusive in these tirades. I suspect this is because the act of bonsai parenting is so dominated by emotions that parents become too passionate when their children do the wrong thing. Many children's brains are not developed enough to feel real guilt. The parent, seeing that the child is not sufficiently remorseful, continues until they feel their child reacts appropriately.

Some parents who believe they show great love to their child appear to feel justified in showing great anger to them.

These deeply emotional interactions are horrible for all, but particularly for the child. Parents often feel guilty when they have calmed down, and then are super sweet to their child. And so the cycle of great love and sacrifice and then great anger continues . . .

Some parents of bonsai children give tangible consequences, such as taking an activity away from the child, but feel very guilty about doing this. These parents have the argument with their child and give them some sort of penalty; however, they spend a lot of time reassuring their child they love them during the disagreement or after giving the consequence. By doing this the parent suggests that their actions in reprimanding their child are unloving.

I would argue the absolute opposite.

If you are parenting your child only to make them like you all the time, you are too ego-involved and you will be ineffective in your ultimate task.

Somehow we are in a weird place now where people want to *feel good* more than *do good*. This sort of thinking does us *no good*. Good managers are occasionally not liked by their staff when they make important decisions; a considerate partner occasionally says some uncomfortable things to their other half to alter problematic behaviour. If you are in a relationship or workplace only to be liked then you are making it 'all about you' – often at the expense of those around you.

As a parent you take on many roles. While being the nice guy is important, being the tough guy with your child is at times even more important for their wellbeing.

These are the effects of a bonsai parenting approach on children. In my experience, these results aren't always seen at the same time in the same way. Sometimes things appear to go well in a bonsai household until the child is 10, 15 or even 18, when things start to go pear shaped. Sometimes I see families who aren't coping with their bonsai toddler's behaviour; sometimes I see parents with disrespectful adult children who are living at home and still causing their parents difficulty.

Over the last ten or so years, I have treated a broad range of issues – in children, adolescents, young adults, families and parents who aren't coping – which have been caused by bonsai parenting. I have characterised these issues as typical bonsai parenting scenarios. Let's look at these in the next chapter.

CHAPTER 6

Bonsai parenting – what I see in the clinic

A bonsai parenting approach is often responsible for many behavioural problems I see in my clinic. I will describe some typical scenarios to explain how bonsai parenting can affect children and parents.

When clients book an appointment with me, most briefly state their concern. As soon as I hear some particular concerns, I figure a bonsai parenting approach is involved. I've got to say my track record for accuracy is pretty much spot on. You may recognise some of these scenarios, perhaps even in your own situation.

Issues in children and adolescents

'Our four-year-old, Aaron, is ruling the house'

This is pretty much the gold standard case a clinical child psychologist sees. These predicaments can often be traced back to a child who was stubborn and strong willed when they were born. At first the parents placate the child and give in to them on issues that aren't a big deal, such as buying them the chocolate or letting them stay ten more minutes at the park. It makes a harried parent's life easier and avoids time-consuming and emotionally tough tantrums. However, the process of giving in to the child's wishes does not make a parent's life easier in the long run.

Always giving in to what your child wants does not allow them to learn self-control or how to fit in with others.

While giving in is relatively easy in their toddler years, doing only what their child wants becomes more and more difficult for a parent as the child becomes older. The process to get the child to comply with their wishes also becomes more and more challenging.

The parent has, in all probability, persuaded the child to do some things they didn't want to do, but often through a negotiated process where the adult seriously bargains with the child. So, the child might put on their shoes, but they do it because the parent has offered a reward, such as an ice-cream. The parent thinks they are in charge and are getting the child to comply with their wishes. However, if you asked the child why they put their shoes on, they would say that it was because they wanted the ice-cream, not because they wanted to do what their parent told them to do.

This parenting approach can only work for so long. Often it will come to a head, say when a child refuses to go to school, and the parent has absolutely no way of getting them to go. Another type of case I see is when the entire family, including siblings, are walking on eggshells with a miniature dictator. The family may always give in or try to appease the child because they have no available recourse should the child's mood turn unreasonable or angry. Sometimes the family goes along quite well, abiding by all of the child's wishes, until the day comes when they can't afford the private horse-riding lessons anymore, or won't let the adolescent go to the no-adult-present party. For once in the parent's life, they have to say no to the child without an alternative to make the child happy again.

Bonsai children or adolescents can become emotional and abusive when, finally, they face situations where they don't get their way.

My message for these parents is hopeful. Ideally I see this type of presentation early. If the child is still young, I am able to teach the parents new ways of being responsive to appropriate behaviour and more effective ways of dealing with inappropriate behaviour. Young children can adjust easily to changes in parenting approach.

Unfortunately, I don't only see this issue when the children are young. Some parents put up with this behaviour for a long time. They present to me when the child is an adolescent or young adult, sometimes when they are about to finish school. I can assist these parents, but it is a difficult task, and the changes aren't as simple. Like a bonsai tree, the child may continue to be slightly stunted and want to be treated as a princess or emperor for the rest of their life. These tendencies will make gaining and keeping employment and relationships challenging for them. They can turn it around – but it will take a lot of effort and motivation from the parents and, particularly, willingness from the child or adolescent to adjust their expectations.

'Our 14-year-old, Hannah, is always in a bad mood, saying horrible things to us'

This problem is often related to the issue above. Children anywhere between late primary and university years can start to behave this way. However, I've known of children as young as four years old telling their mother that she looks ugly or telling their father that they hate him. These children can be monsters at times: hitting siblings, yelling at everyone, and believing the family doesn't love them sufficiently.

Anger is not the only extreme emotion they display. Often, after an extreme bout of child anger and parental distress, these children begin a process of personal recrimination about how far they went in their tirade. They might start crying inconsolably; telling the parent that they're their best friend; talking about depression, loneliness, no friends, even self-harm. Perhaps they turn incredibly sweet, writing notes to their parent telling them how much they love them and how they are very sorry for being so awful. This begets a terrible cycle of anger and remorse, which plays out over and over again.

Some children are particularly susceptible to this scenario. The bonsai child is often used to getting their own way and quickly becomes impatient when adults give them instructions. They easily become angry and aggressive, then extremely upset after their outbursts. Their parent, concerned because the child is suddenly crying uncontrollably, is reluctant to give a consequence for the preceding bad behaviour in case it exacerbates the child's distress. However, if the bad behaviour is not curtailed by effective consequences, it will become worse, and the cycle will continue.

In situations like these, parents often become convinced the issue is depression or anxiety, and take the child or adolescent to see a psychologist. This often doesn't work out well in cases where the child has an aggression issue alongside a depression or anxiety issue because most children in the therapy room only talk about their internalised issues, such as their fears and sad moods. They rarely discuss the externalising issues, such as treating their parents appallingly and being aggressive or even violent towards family members. So the therapist often ends up treating them only for depression or anxiety. The child gains the idea they have a mental health issue, but does not receive assistance for their aggression. The parents become even more on eggshells with the child as they deal with the combination of a worrying diagnosis and ongoing angry tirades. It puts everyone in a difficult and unending situation.

When children display any form of aggression, the parents need to be involved in treatment.

Children under 12 years do not possess the willpower to learn self-control techniques and implement them in the heat of the moment. Their parents need to be given strategies to manage their child's emotional behaviour and assist them to develop self-control and willpower. These techniques can help the child feel good and behave in ways that don't impact on the rest of the family's happiness. This will have positive results for the child and the family, but many bonsai parents have to be convinced to regain their authority and build enough confidence to exercise it. This can take some time.

'Our 12-year-old, Eve, cries uncontrollably when she doesn't get A+s for her essays'

Many clients come to me with concerns about their child's fear of making mistakes and their desire to be perfect at everything. These children or adolescents are hesitant to try new things or things they may not be very good at. They are likely to have been born with traits of sensitivity or anxiety. But anxiety typically results from both nature and nurture, and you can assume that well-meant parenting choices have inadvertently contributed in some way to the child's tendency to be anxious.

The typical route to this issue is when a parent has determined, possibly accurately, that their bonsai child is a sensitive soul who seeks lots of reassurance to face life. The parent tries to help their child by praising them, reassuring them, and ensuring they are always successful (often through behind-the-scenes assistance). Unintentionally, these actions increase the child's anxiety for a number of reasons: the parent's emphasis on success places more pressure on the child to achieve success; the parent's help suggests the child needs help; the parent's assistance makes the child accustomed to constant triumph; and without facing tricky situations, the child doesn't learn to cope with occasionally not doing so well.

By seeing parents of children up to the age of 13 or 14 and altering their bonsai approach, I can turn this process around, even without seeing the child. When I treat an adolescent for anxiety or perfectionism, I also want to see their parents to ensure that their parenting choices are actually helping their adolescent learn how to face and successfully overcome their anxiety. I ensure, too, that the parent is receiving assistance in how to live alongside and help their child deal with a very difficult issue.

'Our 16-year-old son, Evan, is sitting alone in his room all of the time and won't do anything with us'

The cases of child or adolescent depression I see often stem from perfectionism or poor resilience, but they can also be exacerbated by well-meant parenting actions. Without opportunities to do good things – such as being part of the family, doing their chores, and participating in life – it becomes very difficult for children or teens to feel good.

There are definitely children born with melancholic tendencies but, like anxiety, depression can often be increased through parenting which inadvertently encourages the child's tendency to shut themselves off instead of firmly guiding them to re-enter the world and feel good about themselves again. Many parents of bonsai children allow their child to live their life exactly as they wish and don't insist they be present at family gatherings and involved in activities in the home. With this permission to be socially isolated, you can see how a child's minor mood issue can become a major mood disorder over time.

'Our son, Arjun, in year nine, has not been working at school and is starting to fail'

While this is a common scenario with adolescents in years eight, nine or ten, they can be in any year at high school, even year 12. Typically the parent calls me because the child or adolescent has started to not hand in assignments, is not completing their homework, and has to be coerced into doing their schoolwork with threats or rewards every afternoon. As a result, their marks are dropping significantly, or their parents are exhausted from doing the work to keep their child achieving.

When assessing this issue, I first ascertain the history of the child and their schoolwork. If the child has previously been keen and self-motivated in their schooling and this behaviour represents a real change, then I would be concerned about their mood. Sometimes a lack of interest in things that were previously pleasurable and engaging indicates a mood disorder and I would want to assess the child for depression.

While depression may be a factor, I typically find that the history in the family shows a more simple cause. Often the parents are heavily invested in their bonsai child doing well at school. The parents' eagerness for their child to do well sees them spend a lot of time assisting the child with their schoolwork by reminding them to do it every night, helping them with every piece of work, fixing mistakes prior to the child handing it in, and reminding the child to take the assignment to school or even dropping it off at school if the child forgets it. These parents are often more aware of their adolescent's or child's assignments schedule than the child is, and have sometimes created elaborate, colour-coded calendars of their school, sporting and extra-curricular commitments to ensure the child is organised and completes their school responsibilities.

Here's an interesting fact about motivation.

If someone else around you has motivation for you to do well, you don't need to develop your own motivation.

When parents willingly take responsibility for their child's achievements at school, the child can comfortably sit back and let their parent do all of the organising and reminding. This bonsai child doesn't have to put the effort in because their parent is so motivated for them to do well and is willing to do anything it takes for their child to achieve. Interestingly, the parent often reaches the stage where they tell their bonsai child to step up their effort and threatens that they won't help them. But the bonsai child isn't easily fooled. They are aware of their parent's extreme eagerness for their success and are happy to play chicken with them because they know the parent will always step in at the last minute and help them complete the task.

I usually see families at one of two points: either at the point where the parents want their child to be more responsible for their work, but still step in when the child fails to be organised; or at the point where the parents have completely stopped helping their child, and the child is starting to fail. In each situation, these parents are unable to get the child motivated to do their work. Because of the parents' excessive assistance, their bonsai children do not see schoolwork as their own responsibility. Scholastic success has been their parents' thing for a long time, and they don't see why things need or should change.

'Our 18-year-old, Daisy, dropped out of uni, and is now permanently on the couch'

Sometimes, the end result of a bonsai upbringing is this heartbreaking situation. Typically, the parent calls me, distressed and at their wits' end. Their child was a 'lovely kid' and they had a great relationship for many years. They put them through a good education. Things changed when the child started to be rude in high school or started to not do well at school or not be very well organised. The parents, and often the teachers, helped them get a reasonable final high school result, which got them into university.

The child, now technically a young adult, didn't like tertiary life when they got there and decided they needed a year off; or they wanted to do another course, which would start next year. Perhaps they have even started a few different courses or jobs, but they don't turn up to lectures or to the workplace, and they have a tendency to leave or be fired. They are always telling the parent that the lecturers or managers were 'idiots' or 'horrible' to them. It is never their fault – always the fault of others.

The adult child now sleeps until lunchtime. They don't do the simple chores the parent gives them. Amid bouts of volatility or extreme sadness, they mope around the house, primarily engaging with technology or with friends on social media. Their friends, who lead more interesting lives, may start to drop off their social radar. Sometimes they are awful to live with, screaming at the parent if they wake them up before ten in the morning, or angry if their brand of breakfast cereal isn't there when they want it. The parent is distraught for their adult child and suggests new courses or sets up work for them to do, but their young adult has excuses for everything or tells the parent they 'don't understand'.

These bonsai young adults are usually in this situation for a number of reasons. Their parents had all of the motivation for them to do well and the child has not developed ambition or the desire to achieve. The bonsai child has carved out a lovely space for themself in the house, with free internet, a private room, unlimited food, and a good range of technological devices. Their parent does their laundry and, despite threats to the contrary, also eventually does the chores they assigned to the adult child.

The bonsai young adult may have even got into a course they are not really capable of completing, because help from parents and teachers inflated their entry results. They may not have the aptitude to study or understand work tasks without large amounts of adult assistance. Because they are used to adults reminding them of everything, their memory and self-regulation skills may not be sufficiently developed. Perhaps they just didn't like the difficulty of the world outside. They may feel entitled and think the world doesn't understand or appreciate them. Perhaps they believe that unless the world continually caters to their needs and moods, they are best off inside the house where their quirks and special requirements are met.

Underneath it all, the bonsai young adult knows it is a tough world out there and that their parents' efforts have left them unprepared and feeling incapable of facing it.

More importantly, their life at home is pretty sweet. Why risk anything by heading out?

Effects on parents

Bonsai parenting is not great for kids in the short or long term, but it is also no picnic for parents. In my time treating parents who have adopted an overparenting approach, I have noticed many effects on mothers and fathers. I am concerned that these are rarely discussed amongst parents because it feels like a betrayal of their child or an embarrassment.

So let me be the one who spells these out.

'My son Kai is my entire world'

These days most parents feel pressure to experience being a mother or father as amazing, blissful and super meaningful. They feel obliged to be filled with constant love and admiration for the wondrous creation that is their child, to spend their days in endless delight with family life, and to enjoy every minute with their enchanting progeny. Gosh, what pressure!

As you will know, parenting can be an extraordinary experience and one that can produce intense joy. But the reality is that it is not always that way. There are days when it is tedious beyond belief or extraordinarily difficult. Sometimes it can feel like there is no reprieve from the weight of being a mother or a father. There are moments when, despite your great love for your child, you just don't like them much and fleetingly wish it was just you and your partner again. (Some days, even your partner's charms wear thin.)

When we revere the experience of being a parent to the point where it becomes an almost sacred experience, we place a great burden on parents to always experience it this way.

This expectation makes parents feel guilty when they aren't enjoying parenting or aren't feeling immense affection for their child. This guilt often prompts the parent to make it up to the child through grand gestures, which make the parent's busy schedule even busier, or a precarious financial situation even tighter. In most situations, parents are not responding to reality, but to the weight of impossibly high expectations and perfectionist *I should* feelings.

Parents aren't the only ones experiencing the weight of expectations. Children also are burdened by ideas that they should be consistently enchanting, wondrous creatures. In this scenario they have no permission to be ordinary and, occasionally, less than ordinary.

'My child wants to go to Gold Grammar, and it's a great school, but it's a financial stretch for me. What should I do?'

To give a child a perfect upbringing is a costly task. The pressure starts from the moment they are born to provide them with the perfect pram, essential organic food, ideal educational toys, and trend-setting clothes. The question of their schooling comes up immediately and parents feel pressure to buy the best education they can, or perhaps cannot, afford.

Twenty years ago, only parents who could genuinely afford the fees sent their children to non-government, fee-paying schools. Government schools were seen as adequate and capable of providing a good education for those whose budgets didn't stretch to paying more. These days, this is not the case and many see government schools as inadequate. These parents might stretch their bank account or incur credit-card debt to put their child through a fee-paying education they can't really afford, which may not actually be essential for their child.

The expenses don't end there. You could be sure 20 or 30 years ago that your child would move out when they became an adult. These days you are lucky to have them ever leave. A few years ago I met a 31-year-old man who was still sharing a room with his brother in their parents' house. Would it surprise you to learn this perfectly capable but totally unwilling man didn't have a full-time job?

When childhood stretches into adult years, it places a significant burden on parents who continue to support their adult children. With so many students going on to postgraduate courses or electing to work part time while continuing to live at home, you can understand why the Bank of Mum and Dad has become a major financial institution. Ongoing financial support of their young adult children has a big impact on parents' already stretched budgets. It also gives their children a huge sense of entitlement.

'I'm taking some of my holidays this year to help my eldest child get through their year 12 exams'

The financial expense of putting your child through the education and special activities that make up the 'perfect' childhood is not the only burden on parents. There is also an enormous emotional burden in keeping a bonsai child constantly happy, and this takes a toll on the wellbeing and happiness of many parents I see.

I have seen many parents completely lose themselves and their own happiness in the act of giving their child a superlative upbringing of constant joy. I have seen parents put more effort into their child having friends than into maintaining their own peer group and enjoying adult company. I have seen parents decline invitations to friends' and co-workers' important parties so they can drive their child to a children's party. This constant sacrifice of opportunities to be with like-minded peers comes at considerable cost to them. It also makes them reliant on their relationship with their child to fulfil all of their social needs. The situation remains manageable while the child is still a big part of the parent's life. However, the parent's happiness is completely ensconced in the life of the child and will be at risk when the child becomes an adult and leaves home.

A singular focus on their children also affects parents' other relationships, particularly their romantic relationships. It is ironic that the relationship which created the child is often the one that suffers most in making that child happy. You can see it in the smallest of interactions. Greetings to the bonsai child are ecstatic, 'Darling, how was your day? Give me a big hug!' but greetings to the partner are often curt, 'Did you take out the garbage?' Weekends are made up of extravagant visits to theme parks, and trips and presents for children; partners forget the last time they had a date with each other.

Relationships go through enormous stress when so much attention and sacrifice is directed toward the child. When you devote so much energy to one person, you rarely have much left for others. By putting all of your effort into your child's social life, you often lose your own. By summoning all of your energy to give your best self to your child, your partner gets whatever is left, which often isn't much. There is even less for yourself.

'My partner and I just separated and we're worried about the effect on our child'

Some parents stay together, unhappy but united for the sake of the children. I have also seen many parents split up as a result of intensively parenting bonsai children, leaving little energy for their relationship. This can set off a cycle that invariably makes things worse.

Typically when parents separate they are guilty about the impact of the event on their child and hypersensitive to any negative emotions expressed by the child about the separation. The guilt often leads a parent to increase their bonsai-type actions, because they are trying to make up for their supposed wronging of the child. So the child is given an enormous amount of affection, attention and many indulgences; this sometimes goes on for years after parents separate.

After separation, when sharing custody with the other parent, bonsai parenting can often become more intensive.

Many part-time parents become more intensive in their bonsai approach. Because they can do all of their chores when not with the children, they are able to give 100 per cent of their attention to the children when they do have them. If the other parent has the same approach, you get a child who becomes used to being the centre of the universe all the time, not even needing to compete with the washing machine or the lawnmower. I often see dangerous competitions between parents as to who can give the child the best life. Clever children will manipulate these situations to obtain even more advantages –'Daddy lets us play on his iPad' or 'Mummy buys me an ice-cream when we go to the shops'.

All hell breaks loose in these situations if one parent re-partners. This is because the bonsai child is used to having all of the parent's attention and does not react well to some being taken by another partner. Often the overparenting approach makes it impossible for parents to re-partner due to the child's extreme expectations and control over their parent's choices. This results in lonely parents starved of adult company, and children who feel even more entitled through being the only important people in their parents' lives.

'My teenager, Lee, does not appreciate the fact I have worked my fingers to the bone helping him'

When a parent has devoted their entire life to their child, when they have made financial sacrifices to give them a perfect childhood and education, when they have lost important friendships and relationships in the process of giving almost all their time to their child – well, that is one heck of an investment. And, as with all major investments, you can imagine that the parent is expecting some sort of return. I call this an *invoice.*

An invoice is the result of putting in effort so far above normal levels of exertion that you expect more out of the situation to make up for the extra you have given. By way of an analogy, let's imagine some situations where invoices are created.

Imagine it is your friend's birthday. You arrange for the two of you to go to a café, you enjoy a delicious lunch together, and you give them the latest CD by their favourite singer. All in all, it's a lovely day. I would imagine that level of effort and kindness for your friend's birthday doesn't create an invoice because you both enjoyed it, you haven't gone above and beyond in terms of your budget, and your personal coping resources haven't been strained through pretending to enjoy something you don't really like.

Now imagine that instead of that lovely lunch you organise an amazing lunch. You book a limousine to pick up your friend and take them to their favourite five-star Japanese restaurant (even thought you don't really like Japanese food) and you arrange for their favourite local singer to serenade them with their special song over the meal. You pick up the hefty tab knowing it's baked beans on toast for the rest of the month for you. And imagine at the end of the day you say to your friend, 'How was it?' and they say, 'It was pretty good, thanks'. How are you going to feel?

Well, I suspect you would feel somewhat hard done by. I suspect you would have expected a whole bunch of superlatives such as 'the best', and 'the most wonderful'. I suspect you may even have been rubbing your hands with glee at the thought of what your friend now 'owed you' for your birthday. Or maybe you were thinking that you had earned the title 'best friend forever'.

When you give more, you often expect more back.

Often the expectation is for gratitude from the other party. Sometimes appreciation is expected not only in effusive words, but also in consequent actions, such as agreeing with you all the time, calling you regularly, or acquiescing to do something for you.

The invoice of bonsai parenting is particularly large, and in many ways it's completely understandable. When parents have spent much of their money on their child's education, you can understand why they expect a good return in the form of good marks, outstanding reports, representation in sporting teams, maybe even prizes. When a parent has sacrificed a significant chunk of the family budget on ice-skating, gymnastics, or ballet lessons, you can understand why they expect sporting or artistic glory. When a parent has sacrificed their adult friendships for the sake of giving their child all of their attention, you can understand why they expect their child to provide them with friendship and a social life. But I am sure, as you read these words, you see the potential dangers in these expectations.

Unless the other person has agreed to the terms you have set up in your mind, you are potentially setting up a tab the other person has no expectation or desire to pay.

When a parent sets up a parenting effort tab, they do so without any permission from their child. I have never heard of a parent saying, 'I am going to sacrifice all of my personal relationships and a significant amount of my budget to always be there for you from your childhood to your adult years, but I make this sacrifice with the expectation that you will make up for it by being my best friend forever, remaining in constant phone contact, and staying very close to me for the rest of your life. Do you agree?'

As a clinician I have seen many adolescent and young adult clients suddenly realise they have amassed a huge account with their parent and that the payment terms are going to compromise their lives and their independence. As a school counsellor in high school, I often saw an almost haunted look come into the eyes of adolescent girls when they realised their accounts were accruing with their parents. (Boys are often pretty bad at caring about these bills and often even less concerned with paying them – bless them!) I have worked with clients who are unable to move more than a few blocks from their parents because of subtle or obvious pressure reminding them of all the parents have done for them over the years. Their debt is one of gratitude and proximity. I have seen many children who elect to spend as little of their time with their parent as possible because of constant reminders of this invoice and their failure to pay up on the parent's particular terms. I have also seen many parents remain angry about an unpaid invoice after their children have grown up and left home.

'My child has just gone to uni and I can't stop crying'

Some grief when children move out and don't need their parents anymore is normal. However, the sense of loss experienced by parents who have adopted a bonsai parenting approach can be extreme. When the bonsai child leaves home, the parent is bereft of any other interests to take up the space previously taken by caring for the child and catering to all of their needs.

Parents who have been completely focused on their child often have no other interests to fall back on when their child leaves home.

A parent whose main purpose has been to make their child happy, often has no sense of purpose outside that relationship and no idea how to make themselves happy in a manner that doesn't involve their child. Clinically I see these parents with issues of depression, anger about their child's lack of gratitude and 'abandonment' of them, and a real loss of life's purpose. At a time when these people should be free to live a life of new adventures, uncurtailed by the responsibilities of raising children, they are held back by regret, sadness and anger.

So, now you have read though this chapter and the previous one, something uncomfortably close to your situation may have made you wince. You can see that you might be a little too nurturing of your child, or possibly limiting them by not teaching them how to face the outside world. You can see what might happen in the future if you keep going the way you are.

You are starting to think you might be a something of a bonsai parent . . .

'But heck, Judith – it's a dangerous world out there. What are you asking me to do?'

I'm asking you to let your bonsai child experience a bit of blustery weather.

CHAPTER 7

Trees need wind

Now you know how an overparenting approach can reduce your child's potential, much like the art of bonsai limits the growth of a tree. How do you turn this situation around?

To successfully cultivate a bonsai tree, you need to decide when the seedling is very young that you will turn it into a bonsai. You place it in a carefully controlled environment. You protect and nurture it attentively.

You need to take great care to develop it into the sort of tree that will fit with your home and your ideal of what a tree should look like. You must ensure you cultivate it attentively, and provide it with the perfect conditions for it to stay healthy and aesthetically pleasing.

Similarly, a bonsai parent decides at an early stage exactly what the perfect conditions are for their child. They then mould the circumstances around their young person to ensure contentment and prosperity at all times. Once a bonsai child is used to the circumstances that make them happy and successful, they are very unused to any situation that is less than ideal. They need high levels of protection and care to continue to thrive.

A bonsai tree faces many threats if taken outside its protective environment. These threats include extremes of temperature, the sun, snow, and hail. However, the greatest threat to a bonsai plant is the wind. A sudden gust can be enough to break its branches, or blow it over and damage the pot or the tree itself. Because of this, bonsai owners have to be aware of the weather at all times and scurry out at the earliest indication of even slightly windy weather to bring their tree inside and keep it safe.

A bonsai parent is also very aware of the potential dangers lurking outside the family home. Indeed, many decide to take a bonsai approach deliberately, to ensure that those possible risks don't impact on their child. They intentionally keep their child away from environments and situations that might cause them a minor injury or make them unhappy or unsuccessful.

But in their quest to perfectly protect their child, bonsai parents forget one essential thing.

Trees need wind.

Wind helps trees grow. Swaying back and forth in the breeze assists plants by encouraging them to grow sturdier stems and roots so they can withstand squally weather. Strong breezes help trees to grow sturdy yet flexible trunks that accommodate occasional gales without breaking.

Sure, there are some powerful storms that can damage plants. However, trees that have been exposed to less than ideal conditions, such as winds and gusts, are better able to endure gales and storms because they have developed strength, flexibility, and a root structure that improve their chances of survival in tricky times.

Likewise, a child who has been given the perfect childhood can't cope with the less than perfect, but completely normal realities of adult life.

A child who has never faced anything but a supportive audience and successful outcomes is not used to life's normal complications and not sturdy enough to face the typical difficulties of living. They have not been put in situations which build their strength and flexibility. Sadly, many of these children and young adults know this and they lack confidence to go out into an unpredictable environment. They choose to sit inside their restrictive pot where their comfy environment keeps them safe and snug. Or they go out expecting others to protect them from any gusts of difficulty or challenge. It is an existence, but it is not a life, and they lack the core strength to cope.

Bonsai parents need to fling open the doors and windows, and let the wind in a little.

How, you ask?

Part B has all of your answers. It gives you strategies that will assist your child develop strength, resilience, flexibility and confidence while maintaining a reasonable relationship with all family members, even through the turbulent teenage years.

Sounds good? Well, what are we waiting for? Let's head into Part B!

Oh, wait on, hold up . . . Before we start, I need to find out what's happening with those people milling around at the back, quietly murmuring.

I'll just get closer so I can hear –

What's that? A little louder, please . . .

I think I can hear a chant coming from the people with their arms folded, their brows locked in concern or rolling their eyes.

I'll just tilt my ear toward them. What are they trying to tell me?

Oh. Now I hear it.

They are saying, 'But Judith, you don't understand . . .'

CHAPTER 8

But Judith, you don't understand

Almost all parents eagerly embrace strategies to support and encourage their child. But when it comes to strategies to overcome defiant or bad behaviour, many are held back by fears or doubts.

I used to take a different approach when treating parenting problems in my private psychology practice. In the old days, when a parent told me their four-year-old would not follow their directions, or their teen would not do their homework, I would go straight into the positive parenting spiel.

First I would describe techniques for improving their relationship with their child and encouraging their child to do the things they didn't want to do. Then in the second part of our treatment, I would give them the strategies a parent should undertake when their child refused to do things.

In my experience, parents lapped up the encouragement strategies, such as praising good behaviours and spending more time with their child. But when I started the second part I'd notice an odd thing happen to some of my clients. A slight frown would contract their brow. Some would fold their arms. There were a few pursed lips. When I explained strategies like having clear rules or being firm with their child, some clients would suddenly become teary or tell me the strategies were not going to suit their particular child.

And they often used the same phrase: 'But Judith, you don't understand'.

'But Judith, you don't understand' was always followed by a confession of a past misdemeanour on the part of the parent, or an explanation of the fragility of the child.

These parents were often reluctant to divulge details of the wrongdoing they believed they had inflicted on their child. But through some delicate questioning, their supposed felonies would come tumbling out, often accompanied by tears. Out they would pour: the birth was traumatic and they didn't have a natural delivery; they had difficulty breastfeeding and missed that special time with their child; their postnatal depression meant they weren't a good mother in the early weeks or months; they had to go back to work early because of financial difficulties and needed to put their child in childcare prematurely; they had to become a fly-in fly-out worker and missed their child's first birthday; they tried but couldn't have a sibling for their child who is now cursed with being an *only child*; they argued terribly in front of the child; they separated or divorced; their child lost one parent or a grandparent at an early age.

Some would report how difficult it was to have their child: they were on IVF for so long that when their child came along they felt so blessed and happy to be parents that the thought of being firm with their child would simply break their hearts. Some would report a difficult start to the child's life: their child was very sickly in their first few months and they feel they didn't bond well with them and need to make it up. Maybe they continue to think of their child as delicate. Perhaps their child went through some sort of extreme danger and the parent is reluctant to be tough with them because they feel so fortunate just to have them in their lives.

For many of you, the previous chapters will have clearly laid out why the approach you are taking may be harmful for your child. But some of you may still be caught up in thoughts psychologists call *cognitive distortions*: exaggerated thought patterns that cause people to perceive reality in a negative manner. As psychologists, our job is to help clients see that these negative amplifications of the truth are having a detrimental impact on their view of the world and themselves.

So here goes . . .

I do understand.

I do understand that you wanted to bring up your child perfectly and you believe you have let your child down in some way. I do understand that this makes you feel terribly upset or terribly guilty.

I do understand that by giving them a perfect childhood of abundance you believe you are making up for your supposed wrongdoing or the terrible world they encountered.

I do understand that you love your child very much and that you want to make them as happy as they deserve to be. I do understand that you believe your child to be so fragile that you always want to show them the love and kindness they ought to have and ensure that others do the same.

That is what I understand.

Now let's talk about what I know.

I know the mistake you believe you have made is not the end of the world for your child.

I know you or your child went through some sort of tricky time. I also know the experience was long ago, yet you act like it was yesterday.

I know that dwelling on your supposed offence or your situation makes you lack confidence in your ability to give your child a good upbringing. I know you have this ability, but you are refusing to see it.

I know this next bit is even more important.

You need to let that past stuff go.
It's doing you no good, and doing your child even more harm.

Your belief that you may be some sort of perpetrator of wrongdoing, or that your child requires special protection against the rigours of the world, is making your child become a victim. And your child has so much more potential than you allow them when you label them the *victim*, the *sickly one*, or the *poor kid*. You, too, are so much more accomplished than you allow yourself to be when you continue to focus on your one or two mistakes or past difficulties. You need to crank up that Ms Swift track and 'Shake It Off'.

I know you have tried to make your child's life perfect. And I know some of the strategies I speak of in the next section are going to be difficult for you, particularly if you lack confidence, or if your bonsai child is very delicate as a result of their personality and their upbringing. But you are doing them no favours keeping them in their pot, in their controlled environment, in their four walls. There is a whole wonderful world out there, which you are denying them.

So, come on, take my arm if you need to, we are heading into Part B.

Part B

CHAPTER 9

How to overcome bonsai parenting

Many of you will have bought this book with a particular issue in mind. You might want to go straight to the solution to your issue and read up on it right away. I recommend you don't. Instead, I urge you to read the following chapters in the order they are presented.

People read books in different ways – some read the information in the order it is presented, some buck the system. Going by my clinical experience, I assume at least a third to half of you are experiencing an issue with your child's behaviour at home, school or day care. If this is you, I bet you want to go straight to the section on dealing with defiance. I'm guessing about a third of you are concerned about your child's lack of confidence or their issues with friends, so you are keen to read the section on confidence. The other third or so of parents might have a combination of issues and are keen to dip in and out of different sections of the book; it might even depend on the behaviour their child displayed five minutes ago.

I have deliberately set up the chapters in Part B in the order in which I strongly recommend you read them. For those of you who want to read certain sections first, I'm going to give you a very good reason why you shouldn't pick and choose bits and pieces, but rather read this part from start to finish.

I have set up the book to assist the parent who has been influenced by popular parenting beliefs and is adopting the overparenting approach I call bonsai parenting. Statistically, I know that's going to be a lot of you.

Remember that bonsai parenting is about *extreme responsiveness* to children through intense nurturing, attention and protectiveness. This sometimes results in *extreme demandingness*, when excessive pressure is inadvertently placed on children to be successful and happy. Children's unhappiness when they occasionally fail to meet such high expectations can encourage bonsai parents to step in and overassist their children to make them satisfied again. This is called *low demandingness*, because other people are taking over the children's responsibility to achieve and overcome hurdles in their lives.

Because of these unintended adverse effects of the bonsai parenting approach, I will now take you on a well-considered journey. I encourage you to start the strategies in the order in which they are presented; I have deliberately designed the book so that you can begin to implement the strategies as soon as you read about them.

In the first section of Part B, I will give you strategies to be responsive to your child, but not extremely responsive – an essential element of authoritative parenting, the most effective parenting approach. In the second section I'll give you strategies on slowly increasing your demands on your child to enable them to step up and develop important life skills.

The first chapter is about helping your child to develop confidence. It will give you the means to assist them to build their own ability to achieve and make themselves feel good, rather than relying on you or others to do this for them.

The chapter on helping your child to be good company will assist you to model a relationship with them that encourages them to be a good companion to you and others. This will build their social skills and encourage them to take a positive view of the world.

Then, the chapter on developing resilience will show you strategies to help them learn how to cope with difficult days. This chapter will equip both you and your child to handle their occasional challenges without placing pressure on them to always be popular, happy and triumphant.

Once you have gone through these chapters, you will be prepared for the chapter on self-regulation, which will show you how to increase your demands of appropriate behaviour from your child and require them to step up and act appropriately. You'll be ready to do this because you will be confident that having certain behavioural standards and giving brief consequences for poor choices will not make you feel that you are being 'nasty'. You will guide your child to eventually manage their own behaviour rather than rely on others to prompt, tell or nag them. You will also learn how to assist your child to cope with authority – your own and others' – and what to do should they remain defiant.

The chapter on encouraging them to develop their maturity and responsibility will show you how to step back gradually and let them grow into adulthood.

Then I give you my answers to some questions I am always asked in the parenting sessions I deliver to schools and organisations.

I also explain how to get professional advice if your child's issues need professional intervention.

And finally, I give you something to implement when all else fails – the simplest but most effective parenting manoeuvre of all time. Seriously, of all time!

Righto, let's go.

CHAPTER 10

Help your child develop confidence

Confidence is an important cornerstone for building good life skills. Fleeting confidence doesn't help them much – but help your child develop *genuine* and *long-lasting* confidence and they will reap the benefits throughout their life.

Confidence is a belief in yourself: belief that you have good ability and personal strength to cope. Confident people are not necessarily exuberant or dominant. Indeed, some are quietly self-assured and do not need to be the centre of attention. People who are genuinely confident are not reliant on other people's responses to them and do not need to seek regular admiration or praise.

There are ways a parent can develop their child's confidence through their relationship with them, the time they spend with them, and the type of praise they give them.

A healthy and loving relationship with your child

At the beginning of this book, I warn about the danger of being too responsive to children by providing too much attention and putting too much effort into ensuring they are always happy. While too much responsiveness is a problem, when we look at strategies to give your child or adolescent the best start in life, we need to talk about the importance of parents building a good relationship with their offspring and spending quality time with them. The best person we can refer to is John Bowlby, known to psychologists as the father of *attachment theory*.

Bond with your child

Bowlby's work focused on the importance of attachment: the bond and trust established between parent and child. Bowlby concentrated on the important role parents play in ensuring a child feels confident and capable in future relationships based on the successful relationship they have with their parent. He emphasised the significance of a parent forming a close relationship with their child, through spending time with them, interacting with them, and responding to their needs. This essential contact gives the child their first positive experience of social exchange and assures them their parent loves them and will be there for them if needed.

The more confident a child feels about their relationship with their parent, the more secure they feel in life and in other relationships.

Many studies show that children who have what psychologists call *secure attachment* to their parent, are more confident and competent than children who don't have this bond. While ideally they would have this bond with both of their parents, having it with one is adequate. While single parents can be confident that their great relationship with their children can be sufficient, this is not to say they have an easy task. Bowlby points out that single parenthood puts enormous pressure on the sole parent, who needs support to do the demanding job of being everything for their child, particularly in the early years. (Like I had to tell you, huh?)

Spend time with your child

When a child is an infant, a parent needs to spend a lot of time with them, taking care of all of their physical needs (such as feeding, bathing, and changing their nappy) and also their emotional needs (such as playing with them, talking to them and showing them affection). As the child becomes more capable, they are able to spend periods away from their parent's attention, and become more able to amuse themselves and willing to be by themselves. Over weeks, months and years, the confident child is able to venture further away from the parent for longer periods of time, knowing they can return to their safe base. This starts when they are able to play by themselves, and develops into going to day care for a few hours, happily attending school for a full day, going away to school camp for a week, and finally being able to move to another city to attend university or work.

You should spend some pleasant time with your child or adolescent regularly. This is usually easy when they are young and seek your company: you can schedule walks around the block, time in the park, play on the rug with toys and games, and get them to 'help' you with grocery shopping and chores around the house. As they grow older there is still much you can do together: watch movies or TV shows, go for bike rides, eat a meal out, and share doing the gardening or cooking a meal.

Make sure this time together is also spent engaging with the world, seeing wonderful things around you. Reading books with your child is also a great thing to do: it provides special time together and encourages a love of reading. Even as they become older, reading in the same room together while absorbed in your own books is still a time of companionship that is pleasant for all.

Give affection to your child

Physical affection is a fantastic a way of showing love and improving your attachment to your child. Showing love to your infant child through touch, kisses and hugs is essential, and I imagine most of you do this regularly.

Let me remind you of a few important issues about giving and showing your child affection. Make sure your sons receive equal opportunities for physical contact as your daughters. Research has shown us that we tend to more readily hug our daughters than our sons, and it is important to ensure all children have the same opportunities for their parents' touch. While some might think of mothers as being the ones who do a lot of the kissing and hugging of their children, fathers can show this type of affection too.

Research shows us that another important role for fathers is rough and tumble play. This is physically energetic play, such as running around, pretend fighting or wrestling, or chasing games. It has been shown to be very important for child development and is associated with better wellbeing outcomes, particularly for boys. While I encourage this sort of play for all children who enjoy it, particularly in the primary school years, I would add one important caveat. There is some research that suggests the parent needs to be the more dominant playmate in this interaction, meaning parents should still be largely in charge of the action and not concede to their child's dominance all of the time. It appears that when parents broadly control the play and continue to set limits, it ensures children develop self-regulation rather than encouraging and increasing their aggression levels.

Am I saying that these roles and methods of showing affection are gender determined? Heck no! I don't see any problem with you bucking the trend and adopting a form of physical affection that is more often associated with the opposite-sex parent. It just needs to feel comfortable for you and comfortable for your child.

As your child becomes older, remember you still need to show them affection. This might be more subdued if that is now what they prefer, so while that first night they don't kiss you goodnight might be a big blow, make sure you keep touching them on the shoulder, high fiving them, and giving them hugs, even if you can only get them to accept a side hug in those often gnarly teenage years.

Finally, while it is important for you to show affection and occasionally receive reciprocal affection from your child, it is not a good idea to regularly request hugs or reassurances *from* them. You have to remain the adult in the relationship; it places too much responsibility on a child if they think they need to take constant care to make their parent feel better.

Talk to your child

It is essential, particularly in the early years, to talk to your child. Make sure you let them hear you talk from the moment of their birth, and use your voice to soothe them and communicate with them, as well as to show them affection. As your child begins to be able to understand words, it is crucial to converse and engage with them by asking them questions, particularly open questions which require them to give more elaborate answers than *yes* or *no*.

Maintain your relationship with your child

Spending time together in the early years is relatively easy. However, it can become tricky in their late childhood and adolescent years. Adolescents often tend not to seek time with you, but it is essential you maintain a good connection with them. There are some easy ways to do this that both of you will enjoy.

Some of the best conversations you can have with loved ones are in the car. When you are looking at the road (and not staring intently into each other's eyes), you tend to be more comfortable about deeper conversations. So make sure you use time driving your child around to reconnect with them. Make it a rule that you either talk to each other or listen companionably to music or the radio – maybe taking turns to choose the station or the music. Don't allow headphones or engagement with social media in the car, as these activities can be terribly anti-social. More importantly, driving them to and from activities while they are in their own world of technology puts you dangerously close to the role of (unpaid) taxi driver.

I know that some parents are happy for their children to watch DVDs in the back seat because of the peace and calm it brings – but I am not convinced it is good for family communication. I am concerned that children don't learn to sit with their thoughts or amuse themselves when they have screen entertainment always at their disposal. Staring at a big or little screen builds an unhealthy reliance on constant amusement; this is unhealthy for their posture, imagination and creativity. Try to use these amusements sparingly or for short periods, if at all.

As children grow older, it can be hard to find shared interests, but there is still much you can both do. It is a good idea to have a conversation with your adolescent and tell them that even though you know you are both busy, you would like to schedule some time together – possibly one or two hours a week or an evening such as every (or every second) Sunday night. Negotiate with them the sorts of things you could do and maybe agree to take it in turns to choose the activity. There are many things to choose from, such as video or board games, learning and playing sports like bowling or golf, watching reality TV programs like decorating or talent shows where you could each choose a team and make it a little competitive, or even going to the markets to get the weekly vegetables. Never forget that time together can also involve doing chores such as gardening or painting – like car rides, the shared focus on a task can make the conversations more relaxed. You also gain the added benefit of feeling proud of a shared achievement.

When your child becomes an adult and moves out of home, or even when they are an adult still living under your roof, it is still important to schedule time with them. It is essential to negotiate this with each individual child, as each child may have different views on the amount of time they would like to spend with you – and that's their choice. You can say to each child, when they are verging on their adult years, 'I would like to stay in contact with you but I want to make sure we are both comfortable with the arrangement. I was thinking maybe once a fortnight we go to a movie on Sunday afternoon and have a coffee after, or you could come for dinner every Tuesday night. What do you think and what would you prefer?' If they live in another city you may need to set up times for calls rather than rely on catching them at home and in the right mood for a chat. You could say, 'It is important to me that we stay in contact, how can we make sure this happens? Should we set up a time every week or fortnight when we call each other? Would such an arrangement suit you?'

Each child will want to spend different amounts of time meeting or talking with their parents. It's important you see this as a reflection of their personality and schedule – not their love for you.

Some kids are more social with their friends and not so social with their parents; others crave the attention of their parents. It's also better to go for quality rather than quantity.

Are you worried your child won't want to spend as much time with you as you want to spend with them? Don't be! By the end of this book you will have started to develop your own LAFP skills (Life Away From Parenting skills). Before they leave home, you'll have started to develop interests which don't involve your child, and this will help make the void not so great.

Quality time – not a quantity of time

Children need to be self-assured in their interactions with others. Their confidence in initiating a social interaction by engaging with someone is important for their ease in being with people. However, it's also their ability to let go of these interactions that improves their self-assurance about being alone. To ensure both, here are my recommendations about the time you spend together with your child.

Quality time with children is not necessarily endless time with them. While John Bowlby noted the importance of being responsive to infants and their needs, he also emphasised that social interactions between parent and child need to have a start and a finishing point. So, a good exchange between parent and child is initiated by one party, the other party responds, the exchange continues for some time and then one party ends it by looking away or walking away. It is a good sign when a child ends this interaction: it means the child is secure enough in the relationship to go on to do something else or explore the world independently, knowing their parent is a safe base they can return to.

Spend brief but frequent times together

Parents should not give their child a never-ending amount of time and they shouldn't feel guilty about concluding some interactions with their child. Ending time together is often caused by a parent's busy schedule of household chores and work responsibilities. Children actually benefit when their parent leaves them to do other things, and then returns. By terminating the interaction, the parent assists the child to learn to let go of an exchange, and encourages them to feel safe in the knowledge most separations are temporary and can be re-initiated easily. The child learns they can comfortably spend time amusing themselves and re-engage with their parent later. A child's comfort with ending interactions, and their confidence to be by themselves or go on to new interactions with others, ensure they will not be prone to issues such as separation anxiety, or want to cling to their parent's leg for long periods.

There is another important reason for quality time to take the form of brief but frequent periods: it is really difficult for both parties to stay happy and engaged for hours on end. Being super happy and pleasant with someone can take a toll on you. While we love spending time with our children, we tend to make an effort to be our best selves with them, particularly when they are toddlers or younger. This can sometimes become difficult to keep up and we may even lose our temper easily when we have continually smiled and cooed with them for long periods of time. Not making it an endless amount of time together will help the interactions remain positive and pleasant for all.

If you keep your times with them brief and come back to them regularly, you assist them to develop their independence, and the exchanges won't be too intense or lengthy for you.

Untie your child from your leg

There will be parents out there who feel like their child is permanently tied to their leg. Despite their best efforts to disengage with them occasionally and set up independent activities for them, their child might have a tendency to follow them around the house a lot, showing them everything they are doing or insisting they play or talk with them *all the time*. This is often more likely when children have no siblings or ready-made playmates.

For these parents, I suggest you start to tell your child what you are going to do and then remove yourself from the situation. Say something like, 'I'm going to put the clothes in the wash now. Then I'll come back and see what you've done by yourself.' When you re-enter the room, reward them with praise for what they have done by themselves. Play for a little while and then tell them again what you are going to do. Go away to return later and praise them for playing on their own. The period of time you spend away from them can start to get a little longer each time. The important thing is to assure them you always return and they should not be worried you will be gone forever (or their version of forever which might be about ten minutes). For some parents I recommend a reward chart used for a couple of weeks, such as giving them stickers for playing by themselves for ten minutes or more without coming to see you.

Make sure your praise is not so effusive it encourages them to seek your opinion on everything they do. Imagine if every time I wrote a sentence or a paragraph of this book, I grabbed my partner or friend and asked them to tell me what they thought. Imagine if they replied, 'A really amazing sentence, Judith. I can't believe your talent!' You can see I would be tempted to invite my cheer squad in on a regular basis. Likewise, don't be super enthusiastic about everything your child shows you, particularly if they are regularly seeking you out for an exhibition of their latest masterpiece. While you can praise genuinely good work, occasionally it is a good idea not to enthusiastically show your approval every time; this will ensure they are not manipulating you into shaking the pompoms for them all day. Try an approving hum (mouth closed, going from a very high to low tone). Try it and you will understand what I am saying.

Which brings us to the whole topic of praise. And that's a really important one when discussing your relationship with your child and building their confidence.

Praise

Many parents are in the habit of praising their child and it's not a bad habit to be in. Praise is well known to be beneficial to younger and older children: it draws attention to their appropriate behaviours and encourages them to do more of the same.

Because parents are major attachment figures for children, parents' opinions matter to them. That's why children are keen to get their parents' attention and feedback on the things they do. Clever parents use praise as a means of encouraging their children into prosocial behaviours, such as being kind and helpful, or doing activities which are going to assist them, such as playing with an educational toy, becoming toilet trained, or learning to ride a bike.

Praise can be very useful but, as I have already explained, modern parents sometimes praise too much. This can counter its effectiveness and result in a range of problems.

These days, praise is often overused.

I understand many parents have very good intentions with their praise. They aim to use praise as a means to develop confidence in their child and that's a great goal. But it is important to put in a huge caveat about the risks of praise and constant attention. There is a huge difference between confidence and narcissism. Confidence is when a person believes in themself; narcissism is self-admiration to the point where the person moves through life constantly looking for the appreciation and attention of others.

In their attempt to create confidence and self-esteem in their children, parents can sometimes inadvertently go a little too far in their praise and attention. This results in the creation of little narcissists who expect everyone to pay them a lot of attention and constantly treat their minor issues with great care and importance. Unfortunately, sometimes on the road to developing high self-esteem in our children, we mislay their cheerful selves and pick up some bloated egos in their place.

Egotistical people tend to rely on other people giving them a lot of attention and making a big deal of them at all times. If the other person does not admire them, an egotistical person is adversely affected because their wellbeing is so reliant on the responses of others. Confident people are more comfortable in their own skins and do not look to others for validation of themselves and their minor achievements all of the time.

Bonsai children, used to high levels of attention, can start to rely on an hourly shower of compliments to cope.

Praise can be beneficial but it must be used with some thought and consideration of its benefits and potential pitfalls. Let me take you through some broad strategies that will ensure your praise remains helpful to your child.

Respond like a poker machine

I will visit this again when I deal with defiance in chapter 13. Here I will give you a general strategy to keep in mind at all times, particularly with children under seven or eight. It is a really helpful one to think about when responding to your child's behaviour.

Kids want your attention. They really do. Of course, ideally, they will receive your positive attention, where you approve of what they are doing and give them encouraging feedback. But if that seems too difficult, then they are happy with the runner-up: negative attention. In homes where they don't fear extreme punishment, children would often prefer to be in trouble than to be ignored. Any attention is better than no attention.

John Gottman discusses this in his great book, *The Relationship Cure*. He points out that relationships are maintained through emotional bids, which are a request for emotional or social connection. Bids can be anything from questions, to gestures, looks, or a touch of the arm. They are ways of seeking evidence from another person that they care about us or understand us.

Typically there are three ways another person responds to an emotional bid. Imagine I say to you, 'Look at that puppy!' – that's a bid to share an experience with you. You could respond:

'Isn't it cute!' – a positive response.

'I don't have time to look at dogs!' – a negative response.

'. . . ' – an ignoring response.

Gottman's research found that couples who give positive responses to emotional bids tend to have good relationships and stay together. No bombshells there. But would it surprise you to know that the couples who make negative responses to each other's emotional bids tend to stay together longer than the ones who ignore each other? It's true. So what does that suggest? It suggests a negative response still represents some interest in the other person, even if it is just to criticise them. Being ignored, however, can mean the other person doesn't even care enough to argue.

The interesting thing about parental responses to children is that often the negative attention is more interesting to the child than positive attention. Let me explain. Say your toddler is playing in their room quietly and you pass by. If the toddler is simply stacking their red and yellow blocks, many parents would simply walk past or perhaps say a noncommittal 'good-o'. But what if a parent sees their toddler drawing on the wall with their favourite pricey lipstick? That response is going to be much more passionate: it is likely to involve yelling, vigorous arm movements and some wild action from the parent. In short, a lot of noise and colour will ensue. So good behaviour gets a small response from the parent and bad behaviour gets a whole lot of hullabaloo.

Now imagine that the parent is a poker machine (work with me here – it will soon make sense). Poker machines have been deliberately designed to keep punters gambling. They make winning exciting and memorable: they announce it with loud noises, flashing lights and catchy melodies. When you lose on a poker machine you lose without fanfare – no sound, no flashing lights – so a loss on a poker machine does not remain in the gambler's mind. The loss is a non-event. But gamblers keep putting money in, hoping for the win accompanied by its excitement, while barely noticing their silent losses.

So if you were a poker machine and your child was gambling on particular behaviours, which choice would stand out for them as more exciting? In the case I describe above, the behaviour they would remember would be the lipstick drawing rather than the block stacking, because the lipstick ensured the most colourful presentation, both on the walls and via their parent!

To ensure your child gambles on good behaviour (rather than naughty or inappropriate behaviour), you have to make your responses to their appropriate behaviour loud and exciting like a win on a poker machine. You also have to make your responses to their poor behaviour choices relatively boring and predictable.

Be loud and unpredictable with their good choices,
and calm and predictable with their poor choices.

You can ensure your child will be inclined to gamble on the appropriate or socially acceptable choices if they come accompanied by animated and unpredictable praise. (We will discuss appropriate ways to deliver boring and predictable consequences in chapter 13.)

Animate your praise

Early in your child's life, particularly in their toddler and early schooling years, you can use animated praise to great effect to encourage them to do things they might not necessarily want to do. Animated praise is praise with lots of liveliness and excitement in your voice, often accompanied by movements such as shaking imaginary pompoms in your raised hands, or punching the air as if your child has scored a goal. Your child will love these moments and will be encouraged to repeat the sorts of behaviours that promise this level of excitement from you. 'You cleaned up your room? Yaayyy!' 'You did a poo in the toilet? Woo hoo!'

Vary your praise

People are more likely to do things when they genuinely don't know the response their actions are going to invoke. This is the reason why children often gamble on bad behaviour because their parent might provide a very animated negative response (if they are in private at home and perhaps a little stressed) or a slight response accompanied by extreme facial expressions (if they are in public and reluctant to draw people's attention to their child's behaviour).

To keep your younger child purchasing tickets in the positive behaviour jackpot, it is important that your responses are unpredictable. One time when you see them putting their shoes back in their room when you asked them to, you might high five them, saying, 'You've put your shoes in your room!' or 'You did what I said!' Another time when they pick up their toys from the floor, shake your tail feather as you squeal, 'Woo hoo! You cleaned your room, I am going to do the clean-room dance!' and dance away with them. If they share with their sister, come in and say, 'Wow, you guys are playing so cooperatively, can I join in for five minutes?' When your child takes their plate into the kitchen for once without you asking, you could give them a hug and say 'Hey, you took your plate into the kitchen – that's great team work!' When they leave the playground when you ask, you simply say, 'You stopped playing on the swing when I told you to – fantastic! I'm going to race you to the car!'

Make it unpredictable and maybe a little silly and enjoyable for all. They'll have a great time and remember it was their positive or appropriate behaviour which gave them the resulting fun. Don't do the same thing every time: mix it up and they will start to do the right thing because they are eager to see the outcome and what you will do next.

Be descriptive in your praise

Re-read the examples above and you'll see I'm suggesting that every time you give your child praise, you state exactly what it is that they did. This is always preferable to 'Good girl' or 'Good boy' or 'Great job'. *Good* behaviour is a very abstract concept for a child. If you describe what they did, then they will know what it was you were pleased with and will start to form a clear picture of socially appropriate behaviour, and which behaviours are a good idea to repeat.

Adjust your praise as your child grows older

Go to town with your animated and unpredictable praise – but understand it will only work when they are young and still able to be fooled into thinking you really are excited about their poo in the right receptacle, or their clean room (and you probably are – but not as excited as your dance suggests). They will reach an age when they realise the effort they need to put into making you dance is not worth the dance. That's the stage when you have to pull back on the theatrical effect and go into better reasons for them to do what you are asking (which will include some strategies we will discuss in chapter 13).

The age where animated praise stops working will be different for different children and different tasks, but you'll know because you'll get an eye roll rather than a smile. That's not to say you shouldn't do the super enthusiastic and silly stuff occasionally (heck, it will sometimes work for all ages – including your partner, and even some co-workers), but don't make it your main method of encouragement.

Be aware that praise is only effective for the time you are encouraging them to take on a particular behaviour. Once they are doing an action regularly, you shouldn't necessarily remark on it all the time. Start to reduce your praise for this action because your child has actually internalised the behaviour – it's in their repertoire and they no longer need your encouragement to do it. At this point, it is always a good idea to start to put your effort into promoting another behaviour you would like to see them undertake, which will help them become more mature.

Keep the currency of your praise valuable

These days, parents are used to providing an enormous amount of praise to their children because they want to support them and they think it will build their self-esteem. But you shouldn't be a walking praise factory engaged in constant production of applause for two good reasons. First, you'll grow very tired of it; and second, your child will not value it. It's the second one that is the most important here.

The more praise children hear, the less they value the praise they receive.

This is particularly noticeable in households where hyperinflation of the praise dollar causes parents to need multiple expressions of 'good job' or 'I'm proud of you', just to have their child take out the garbage.

To be most effective with your praise and have your child value it, try to mainly give it for things that truly deserve praise or you want to encourage. When you get to the stage of 'Look at you, breathing in and out, you are so clever', you'll know you've gone too far and the true observations are getting lost in all of the other inconsequential comments.

A good strategy to keep praise meaningful for your child is to think of some skills you would like them to develop, such as cooperativeness or compliance. Make a decision to primarily praise your child when you notice these desired qualities being displayed rather than being enthusiastic about all and sundry good behaviours. Every now and then, take stock of what they are doing well and what they need to work on and adjust your praise focus.

Focus your praise on effort rather than talent

Another method of keeping your praise valuable is to ensure you praise your child for what they do rather than who they are. By this, I mean you should praise them for their efforts rather than their natural talents.

It is very popular these days to tell a child lovely things, such as how beautiful or clever they are, to build their confidence. It sounds like loving parenting and is always done with the best of intentions, but it does not always have the desired result.

Let's look at something like praising a child for being intelligent or clever, which is a strategy many parents and teachers use to boost their children's or students' academic confidence. Researchers Carol Dweck and Claudia Mueller found that praising a child for their scholastic ability can have adverse effects. In a series of studies, they gave children an academic task and then gave them feedback. They praised one group for their ability and the other for their effort. Both groups were then offered the opportunity to undertake other tasks and also to reflect on their experience.

There were key differences in the outcomes of the different praise techniques. The students who were praised for their ability tended to become highly focused on their scores. They became performance driven in areas such as wanting to know their scores in relation to others', and only wanting to do the sorts of problems they were sure they would do well in. The students praised for effort tended to become much more focused toward learning and becoming more skilled at tasks. They asked for ways to improve their performance in preference to receiving information about how they fared compared to others. They also wanted to try more problems to become better at the task. In short, those praised for effort appeared to want to continue to put in effort. They related their performance more to their endeavours than to some fixed and potentially unchangeable skill set they possessed.

By praising a child for their intelligence rather than noticing their labours, it seems we unintentionally reduce their potential. Praise for being smart can inadvertently result in what psychologists call *perfectionistic thinking*. This may cause a child to abandon tasks they suspect they won't do very well because they are afraid they won't score perfect marks or demonstrate their cleverness. It can also make them less likely to take on educational challenges which will give them opportunities to genuinely improve their performance. Dweck and Mueller concluded that this may explain why so many bright girls, who show early academic promise and are encouraged with high praise for their skills, tend to go on to demonstrate reduced motivation and performance in their later years. It seems we unintentionally burden them with performance expectations when we label them as *smart* or *outstanding*.

Is this where the perfectionism we see in our highly praised children has come from? Is it why I treat so many children for fear about their academic and sporting tasks? Is it the reason why some children won't try something if they perceive it to be in any way difficult? Is it behind the feeling of despondency when they don't do very well? I suspect the answer is yes.

The principle doesn't apply only to academic work because parental praise for natural skill and ability is not just directed at their academic prowess. Think about how many parents now praise their children, particularly daughters, for their beauty and looks, in an effort to increase their confidence and self-esteem. If this produces the same impact as being told they are intelligent, is it putting the same pressure on them to be beautiful or causing perfectionistic thinking about their looks and their weight? What about the children being told over and over they are fantastic soccer players, accomplished artists, persuasive public speakers, or potentially worse, *gifted and talented*?

Are we, through excessive praise, reducing children's motivation to improve themselves? Are we encouraging reluctance to get on a sports field and fear of not doing perfectly in assignments? Are we prompting children to choose a narrower life where they only try the things they know they will be good at and obsess about their academic results and sporting performances? Are we inadvertently creating their obsession with the perfect selfie? Again, I'm going to answer in the affirmative.

Given the research, I believe the safest way to praise your child is to praise them for their efforts.

Focus on the verbs – what they are doing – rather than the nouns or adjectives that describe who they are. Tell your child that you can see they tried their best, that they are working hard at that painting, that they have put an interesting outfit together. This is not decreeing that they continue to be perfect. Instead it gives them permission to pursue their interests, and enables them to embrace the spirit of improvement that will give them enthusiasm for tomorrow's tasks. It gives them your approval to just be themselves. Of course you can occasionally praise them for their beauty and talent – but make sure you put emphasis on what they do rather than a judgement of who they are.

Don't pre-praise

Avoid pre-praising as a means of developing your child's confidence. Pre-praise is when you make positive statements about future events, such as 'Don't worry about the test – I'm sure you are going to do very well' or 'I'm sure you are going to make a friend on your first day'. Parents use pre-praise with good intentions but it backfires. Research confirms that children told these things expect them to happen automatically, and become distressed when the parent-predicted outcome doesn't eventuate. Unless parents can actually see into the future, their predictions are just that – predictions.

It is better not to be so definitive about what will happen. Discuss what they are about to do as an adventure, remind them of the coping skills they have shown previously, and get them comfortable with ambiguity.

Reflect the truth in your praise

I strongly recommend that the praise you give your child should reflect the truth.

Have you ever done, say, a presentation and mucked it up a little or a lot? When you sit down afterwards and your colleague, with an almost manic grin on their face, turns to you and says, 'That was really super!' are you going to be reassured and relieved? Well, unless you are in the five per cent or so of people in the world who are narcissists, your colleague's statement is going to make you feel even worse, because the fact that they had to reassure you as if they were the Joker suggests that you were really, really bad. It would almost be better if they said nothing, or something like, 'Gosh I've had those days too. Don't worry.'

Insincere praise often makes us feel worse. Over-the-top praise can have the same negative impact. Indeed, there is research showing that people perceive extremely effusive praise as likely to be untrue.

You can probably get away with praise that operates as general encouragement in your child's early years with slightly exaggerated statements such as 'You are very good at cleaning up your room,' or 'That was a fantastic kick!' However, if an older child perceives you to be giving the praise for their self-esteem rather than the job they have done, they will know it.

Psychologists believe that children over the age of seven tend to know when the praise is insincere. When they perceive their parent is praising skills they don't believe they actually have, they then question their own ability. The effect is the opposite of the parent's intention because it makes the children doubt themselves.

Indeed, giving a child permission to seem average does them a great favour: it allows them to *be* average and occasionally not good at things. A parent who says, 'No, you weren't totally on your best form, but that's okay, everyone has a bad day' is making a supportive statement for a child, which is more beneficial to them than lavish and untrue praise.

Avoid the praise sandwich

The *praise sandwich* became very popular in the eighties and nineties, when it was felt any negative feedback would impact poorly on people's self esteem. The addition of some pleasant statements was thought to lessen the blow of the hard, cold wind of truth. So, when negative feedback was given it was often in the form of a praise sandwich – negative feedback sandwiched between two bits of praise.

The trouble is that the addition of the nice statements can be confusing to a person, particularly if they have been raised in a bonsai manner and are only used to high praise. Unfortunately, many people retain the positive statements and disregard the negative component. The result? They never improve.

The other problem with the praise sandwich is the bits of praise often make the criticism sound unwarranted because it is outranked by a ratio of 2:1. 'You run well; you didn't make the hockey team; you pass well.' It can even be pointless and patronising, 'I like your shoes; you didn't get the promotion; what a lovely dress.' You can see how a narcissistic person would see the kind words as the truth and the criticism as unmerited.

When you praise, make sure it is with truth and purpose.

Remember, the more praise sandwiches you make, the more stale the bread will become.

Don't allow your feelings to trump your child's achievement

They come home and tell you about their success that day, and you are so pleased. It is not a piece of paper with one of those nonsense awards that schools now hand out as a matter of course each week. (You know the ones I am talking about, where a weekly prize is given out on a rostered basis to every member of the class and comes packaged as 'Best use of a pencil in question 10' or 'Best listening to the instructions about the lunchtime rules.') No, the award your child has brought home, or the achievement they are excitedly telling you about, is for a real accomplishment: they got a place on the team they have been practising regularly for; they did well on the book review they struggled with so much; or they managed to walk away and not take the bait of the bully at lunchtime.

At this moment many – actually strike that, let's say *almost all* – parents would say 'I'm proud of you'. And I'm sure you are, but let's look at what the statement implies.

When parents tell children they are proud of them, I understand that they are letting their child know they support and love the person their child is. But I can't help but think that very regular expressions of parental pride can start to suggest a high level of ego involvement for the parent. For proof, how many parents race to their Facebook page and upload the details of their child's achievements? How many parents regularly share this information with their friends in front of their child? What does that suggest to your child about how important their achievement is to you?

If you *always* tell your child you are proud of them when they achieve something, what might it start indicate to them? It could imply that you make the judgement on their achievements and that they need to look to you for approval. They could become somewhat dependent on your appreciation and not reliant on their grasp of their success. They may be unable to revel in their own pride.

It is actually better to show your child your happiness through your joy at their pride in their success, and your acknowledgement of the work they have put in to achieve it.

Ideally, when they come home with their success, you say, 'Wow, you must be so pleased, you worked really hard on the assignment/to get on the team', or 'You must feel really good about that, I know how tricky it would have been to walk away from Johnny/Mary', or even 'Gosh! That is a great achievement, how did you do it?'

Never be in any doubt that your child will know you are proud of them in these statements. However, your sense of achievement in having a child who accomplishes these feats is not eclipsing their own hard-earned achievement in any way. While you have expressed delight for them, they are still fully aware that the ultimate approval lies within them. In times when they may achieve without any cheerleaders around them, they will realise pride can come from the person who is most responsible for their success – themselves. Of course you can occasionally tell them how proud you are of them, but never let your pride eclipse the pride of the person who actually made it happen – your child.

Never be more excited than they are about an achievement

On the same lines, I encourage you never to be more excited than your child about an achievement. I advise you to keep your excitement level equal to or less than theirs.

Why? It's actually something I learned very early as a clinical psychologist: 'Never be more excited than the client'. We were told that when we are more animated than the client, it suggests to them that the task was for us, not them.

So if my client says they have done their homework, and I whoop it up while they are tepid, it suggests they are less invested in the task than I am. This implies I am more devoted to their improvement than they are, and that is a fraught place for therapy to continue. This is because the person who cares least about a thing is the person who controls it. Alongside that, I will be the person trying to convince my client to change, while they might start to become uncommitted.

I see this all the time when parents discuss school results with their children. As parents become more enthusiastic about school grades, over time children start to become nonchalant about their results in the face of their parent's extreme level of enthusiasm. After a while, the student starts to believe they are achieving at school for their parent, not for themselves. This is often reinforced by the parent's passion for high marks and their eagerness for their child to achieve.

Clever kids can start to manipulate this. By acting nonchalantly, they almost automatically press their parent's *whoopee!* and *yahoo!* buttons. But this level of parental enthusiasm potentially has a negative effect. Over time you can easily see why children might believe subtle pressure is being placed on them to do well at school, due to their parents' over-the-top enthusiasm. Sometimes, in their parents' gusto, the student's personal excitement for the task slips and their achievement is perceived to be more at the point of telling the tale to others than in the personal reward of preparing for and doing the task successfully.

Don't thank them in praise or reward

Again, in the same vein, don't thank your child for doing something they have done for themselves. Going to school, making friends, scholastic and sporting achievements – these are all *their* achievements. Helping you to work out how to program your phone, helping you to carry your work things to the car, or picking up your glasses from the floor – these are things above and beyond that they can be thanked for, because these actions are primarily for your benefit, not theirs.

Also, avoid rewarding them for achievements *they* should be proud of. Steer clear of paying for or buying presents when they score a goal or do well at school or you risk them losing their intrinsic (internal) motivation.

Research shows that rewards provided for the completion of a task reduce a child's intrinsic motivation because they start to think they are doing the task for the extrinsic/external reward rather than the fact they enjoy it or want to do it. So give them five dollars for scoring a goal and they start to think they are playing for money, rather than because they love soccer. This also happens when you tell children to eat their vegetables in order to get their dessert. You think they are learning to love vegetables, but they don't think of it in the same way. Your child is simply asserting their love of dessert and what they will do to get dessert – even eating horrid vegetables! It's only a short-term encouragement for your child and isn't likely to alter their dietary choices.

Avoid the running commentary

When on earth did we start to think we had to provide a running commentary on everything our child does? Why do we feel it is necessary to always observe and judge and praise and make some sort of statement about children and their day-to-day experiences? Is our relationship with them so tenuous, we need to annotate their every action and inject our commentary in their lives to maintain it? Do we believe their confidence is so fragile that we need to constantly re-pump their ego through high praise for essentially ambiguous achievements?

If we do believe this, then what are we suggesting to our children? That they need constant praise to be able put one foot in front of another to face life? Are we suggesting that our love for them is always on the line and is only as good as our last statement of praise or appreciation?

Is that really true in your household? Or have you just taught your child to expect to be at the centre of your attention at all times? Have you inadvertently taught your child that love can't be intrinsically relied on and has to be shown through constant attention and insincere flattery? Have your responses unintentionally taught them to rely on you as the sole arbiter of all achievements? Have you not provided them with the tools to judge their own performance? Have your constant statements of their success accidentally made them fearful of failing or being average, and led them to always seek your approval and the reassurance of others?

If this is the case, I urge you to reduce your praise, pull back on the running commentary, and be sometimes nonchalant about some of the things they do, whether they are successful or unsuccessful. Remember, a little nonchalance does not show them you don't care about them. It shows them that you don't value their achievements more than you value them. This will reduce the pressure on them. You want your children to accept themselves for who they are and take more responsibility for the things they want to improve.

Warm parenting is not constant praise.
Warm parenting is often accepting them for who they are
and trusting them to become the people they were meant to be.

It's also being confident in yourself that by spending time with them, being there for them, and being yourself, warts and all, that they will love and accept you as their parent.

That's a lot of information to take in so let me give you a précis. Here are some scenarios and some ideal parental responses.

'Hey, look at this picture I just drew!'

'Wow, how did you make all of those colours?'

'Hey, look at that! What's your favourite bit?'

'Jeepers, that's a lot of work! How long did that take you?'

'You've shown some great imagination there. Tell me what you've drawn.'

'I got on the team!'

'Wow, all of that work paid off. You must be so proud!'

'Gee whiz! How do you feel?'

'Gosh, you certainly worked hard for that. Well done!'

'I didn't get on the team.'

'That's a shame, but you certainly can be proud of putting all of that effort into it.'

'That's disappointing, but you certainly tried your best.'

'Oh, what a shame! What are you going to do now?'

'I'm hopeless at swimming.'

'Well you can't expect to be good at everything and everyone finds a new skill tricky at first.'

'I could see you were trying your best.'

'Well I could see that you gave up pretty early in that lesson, do you think if you kept trying you would have done a little better?'

'Remember that time you learnt to ride your bike, you didn't get it first go either. It's all about keeping on trying.'

'I'm just not good at riding my bike.'

'No, not yet. You're still learning.'

'Here's my report card.'

'How did you think you went?'

'Ooh! Tell me what things in it you are proud of . . . Why are you so pleased with that? . . . Great, is there anything that you are not so happy with? . . . Do you want to do better in that subject? How do you plan to do that?'

Your child is trying to put a toy together and they can't quite get it right and might be getting frustrated. . .

(You don't have to say anything; give them time to let them work it out.)

'What do you think of my outfit?'

'Do you like it?'

'What do you think?'

(Head nod, slight smile.)

Now, clearly these responses aren't set in stone. But I recommend you consider the following when responding to your children and adolescents.

If you are over the top with your praise, or tend to thank them, or tell them you are so proud of them, or tell them how intelligent they are – it's not the end of the world. But I urge you to intersperse these responses regularly with the approaches I have suggested in this chapter. This will ensure that your children will know they are loved, feel secure about facing the world, and continue their good relationship with you. And these things will not come at the expense of their self-assurance, particularly when they are away from your guidance or reassurance. That's true confidence and can't easily be taken away from them at the whim of someone else. When your child has this confidence, they are truly poised to step out of their bonsai pot and go out into the world.

Summary

While it is important to be loving and caring to your child, it is also important to ensure your well-meant loving actions don't impair your child's confidence or ability to take personal pride in their achievements. Strategies we have discussed in this chapter include:

- Bond with your child by spending time together and giving them affection
- Ensure your time together is more about quality than quantity
- Schedule time to be together with your older children
- Use your praise effectively
- Adjust your praise to suit the age of your child
- Ensure your praise is truthful and given when their actions warrant it
- Praise their efforts rather than their achievements
- Make sure they express their own pride in their achievements.

CHAPTER 11

Help your child become good company

Many parents worry about their children's popularity and ability to make friends. I can't take away all of the challenges of the classroom or the playground, but I will give you strategies to assist your child to be someone other kids like hanging around.

Parents who worry about their child's popularity often put a lot of effort into trying to ensure the child's social success. Based on a popular idea that confidence encourages popularity, today's parents think that if children like themselves a lot, then others will like them too.

Without a doubt, your child is going to feel more secure when they go out into the world when they feel loved and important to those closest to them. However, I'm not sure that pumping up your child too much with love and attention is going to get the desired effect in the world beyond your home. Indeed, being the complete apple of their parent's eye can sometimes make it more difficult for children to assimilate with others.

Social success is assisted by confidence, but it is primarily due to other virtues. Think about your friends and their qualities for a moment. I am sure many of your pals possess some or all of the following: an ability to comfortably fit in with the needs of the group; basic respect and kindness toward others; a positive demeanour which makes them good to be around; and, possibly, a tendency to not take themselves too seriously. This chapter is about developing these qualities.

When you help your child to be someone other children like hanging around, a big bonus is that they will also be more pleasant for you to hang around. Given a lot of adult children now live in the family home until they are 25 or even 30, that's going to make your future housemate much more agreeable.

Help your child learn to fit in with others

Let's look at some practical ways you can help your child learn to get along with others.

Don't always make them special

Making children feel special is certainly a popular pastime. There are now whole books written to give parents ideas about how to make their children feel special in almost every moment of every day. Some parents put huge canvases of their children up on their walls; some have tattoos of their children's names and faces permanently inked on their body to show the children how much they are loved and wanted. Jeepers, we can even buy books where we can make sure our child is the superstar by printing their name throughout the book. We used to have heroes like Angelina Ballerina and Max from *Where the Wild Things Are*; now your children's heroes can be . . . themselves!

Without a doubt your child is always going to be special to you and loved by you (regardless of what they may do sometimes). But I'm not sure that constantly treating them as *special* is doing them any favours. If they become used to it, they may have difficulty coping in situations where others don't treat them as an important, special person.

Let's look at an example. Clinically, when working with adults, I notice an interesting thing when people begin a new relationship with someone who worships the ground they walk on: they often start to quarrel with others. Now, I am not convinced it is the relationship that is making them disagree with their friends; I believe it is the nature of that new relationship that prompts their difficult behaviour. If Sally is used to her boyfriend constantly adjusting his needs to completely suit hers, when Sally meets her friends, who have their own agendas and opinions, I'm not sure Sally is going to be willing to adjust to the consensus of the group. That's because she is getting used to an alternative universe where she is always the star. Sally is likely to start thinking her friends are mean to her or don't listen to her as much as they should. Have Sally's friends changed? No. But her day-to-day reality has changed. Enjoying the company of her good friends in Everybody Matters Land now pales in comparison to living in the Land of Sally.

When a bonsai child becomes used to others (read: their family) adjusting everything to suit their needs, the child is not going to cope well outside the home.

Bonsai children whose families always cater to their needs often don't fit in well with others.

The trouble is, we forget that feeling good is often about being part of a group. Indeed, feeling unique and special can also feel lonely when compared to the joys of being part of something bigger.

Don't always make them the centre of attention

It is really important for you to get your child used to being one of many – not always the most important person in the room. Start to pay attention to others when your child is around, or pay attention to your own needs in the presence of your child. When you meet up with other parents or your friends, bring along something for your child to amuse themself with, and then focus on the adult conversation, without regular input from your child. Check in with them, or comment on their activity or good behaviour, but not too much. Avoid making your entire conversation about your child or to your child. When with your partner, talk about yourselves as adults, not only as parents, in your child's presence. Talk about things that are not to do with your children. This will assist them to learn to amuse themselves. That is going to be a very useful skill when they go into a playground where they don't know anyone, and they have to be able to play by themselves.

Make sure you are not inadvertently making your child into the princess or emperor of your home by greeting them first with great joy and then snarling a question at your partner. Make greetings and farewells to your partner or friends equally enthusiastic and loving as those you give your child. Regularly choose to talk to your partner in the presence of your child. If you are a single parent, pick up the phone and spend time talking to a friend in the presence of your child. You can also read a magazine or book in their presence, or watch a favourite TV program while they play in the same room.

And while we are on the subject, when was the last time you had a date with your partner? Seriously, when? And going to the hospital together to have the baby was not a date; it was the birth! Get your diaries now and organise a date and a babysitter. Get your child used to their parents making each other a priority. For single or separated parents, get on the phone and organise a night out with friends. You have to start cultivating your LAFP (Life Away From Parenting); social engagements with other adults are an excellent way to start.

Get them used to being in the chorus

My first career was as a high-school drama teacher. Sometimes I taught a few weekly lessons in the primary school part of the campus. It was a great job to have the pleasure of working with the beautiful imaginations of young children. In girls' schools, the fairytale scenario was a very popular one played out in my classroom. Someone had to be the princess and assigning this role was where my dream job became a little tricky. About 20 per cent of girls wanted (actually no, expected) the princess role. I faced a diplomatic mission to appease the bruised egos of those who weren't chosen and had to be members of the chorus or less important characters. The same difficulties ensued when choosing a person for the lead role in a musical or play. And that was back in the early nineties when things were easier. I imagine drama teachers now need their lawyers on speed dial to deal with the fallout from the cast list and the resulting complaints from children and parents.

There is more chorus work than there are lead roles in life; people who are comfortable not always being the star are better able to cope with this.

To help your child get used to this reality, it is a good idea to get them involved in things where they are part of a group. Team sports and interests are great for this. Activities such as soccer, basketball, netball, football, cheerleading, hockey, and baseball are all about working together with no particular person being a superstar. I recommend parents make it a rule that their child has to play some sort of team sport because of the many benefits of learning how to work in a team and how to accept occasional mistakes among peers, such as bungled catches or off-target goal attempts. More importantly, they are going to win or lose with others. This will ensure your child is not unduly affected by either the glare or loss of the spotlight.

Help your child learn respect for others and their needs

To be a 'people person', you need to care about others and be respectful of their needs. How can you teach your child to be respectful toward others? Here's what I recommend.

Don't always take the burnt bit of toast

Have you ever got into an elevator with a group of people and hit the button for a floor to suddenly hear a howl of protest coming from a child and an animated apology from a parent? Yep, you suddenly realise you are a truly evil person who has hit the button when everyone knows children own the sole right to pushing elevator buttons. You turn around and apologise but the child cries all the way to the fifth floor, proving that while you might be going up in an elevator you have officially descended as a human being.

Well, I'm here to tell you that adults pressing elevator buttons should not feel like it's the end of the world for a child, and apologies by parents or elevator button pushers should not occur. The apology suggests to the child that they own all elevator buttons and they don't. Sure, children might like to push the button, but they have to get used to not getting their way all of the time. Children who recognise that there are other people with other needs make better companions, now and in the future.

I'm also going to dare to say that the burnt bit of toast is not automatically the parent's – nor is the big bit of the cake, or the last slice of pizza, automatically the child's. Get your child used to compromising their wishes by recognising the wishes of others, occasionally and then regularly. Make sure you teach them to ask before they take the last piece, and sometimes grab that big piece yourself without apology.

Further to that, parents – reclaim your TV! Occasionally sit down and take the remote from your child and watch a program you want to see. Or choose a TV show with your child that you both genuinely want to watch. Develop your child's compromising skills in a whole bunch of ways, such as not always letting them decide the choice of music in the car, the Friday night movie you download, the takeaway meal, or the game you play. Don't always let your child win in everything; get them used to coming second, third, or last.

Make them used to going along with others' wishes and coping when other people win.

When they become older, include them as part of the family team that decides who does what chore, what your holiday plans are, or which theme park you all go to. But make them part of the negotiation team, not the sole decider.

Teach them respect for others

You are a major role model for your child. They will tend to emulate your values and beliefs. So try to avoid being critical of others in front of your children; particularly try to show respect for authority figures, consideration for your friends, and a high regard for the needs of others. Little things will send this message. Return the shopping trolley to the place for the shopping trolleys, and tell your child you are doing this for others. Take your child on a few trips on public transport and teach them they should offer their seat to older people, pregnant women or those with a disability. Teach your child to wait until people get out of the lift or off the bus or train before they get on, and teach them to let the other person go through a doorway before they go through. Teach them to look other people in the eye when they greet them; teach them how to shake the other person's hand. As they become older, encourage them to ask polite questions of other people, and how to show genuine interest in them. Teach them dinner-table etiquette, particularly things such as not starting until everyone has been served their meal, no technology at or on the table, and what to do with their napkin.

Are these things likely to be a little old fashioned? Perhaps, but their value lies in what they teach your child about the importance of others and being respectful to them. Etiquette is about ensuring your needs don't sit above others. A person who is considerate of others is typically very pleasant company; make sure your child has this quality.

Teach them empathy

Good friends understand the person we are, empathise with our emotions and recognise our needs. You can teach your child how to be empathic to others by encouraging their awareness of the experiences and emotions of others, rather than the two of you focusing always on yourselves.

When watching TV programs or reading books together, comment on how characters might be feeling about what is happening. Encourage your child to speculate on the feelings of people based on their facial expressions or their situation. Start telling them work stories about a time your co-worker was in a bad mood or had a bad day, and you showed understanding by leaving them alone or doing something nice for them. Children who can see things from other people's point of view are less likely to take things personally; they may attribute some unkind words from a peer to a low mood or challenging circumstances. This is far better for them than taking every slight to heart.

Often by understanding things from other people's points of view, we don't take minor things so personally.

To help them understand and cope when people around them are not feeling great, occasionally tell your child if you are in a bad mood. There is nothing wrong with saying, 'I'm feeling a bit cranky and I am just going to go and dig in the garden for a little to feel better.' When your child makes a choice that adversely affects others, you might want to talk about how it might affect the other person and what your child might do to make it better. (Don't make that discussion the only consequence; more on this in chapter 13.)

Help your child develop a positive demeanour

Happy people are good to be around and there is nothing worse than the whiny co-worker or friend. I had one early in my career who would regularly tell us over our coffee break how difficult her life was: 'Three! Three loads of washing I did before work this morning!' She could make any lovely story you told into a negative, 'Well you might think it would be a nice day at the beach, but think of the sharks!' She was exhausting and I never left her company without feeling a little worse. Trying to make her feel better depleted me, and agreeing with her made me feel negative about the world. (Sigh.)

Some of you will have bonsai children who are starting to take on similar characteristics: demanding attention by whining and complaining, taking everything personally, and always on the lookout for someone doing them wrong. At first you might cater to their moods, but after a while, being the Minister for Reassurance and Geeing Up will wear you out. Some parents come to almost dread long, wearying exchanges with their child. How can you start to alter their approach to life? Try these strategies . . .

Give equal or more attention to good experiences

Parents love to help their children and often feel most useful when they can assist them. If your child comes home reporting a good day, many parents tend to smile and say something brief such as, 'Great' or 'That's fantastic'. They believe the report of a good day means their child is coping well and doesn't need their intervention or assistance. Nothing to do there.

But when your child comes in and reports something difficult, such as another child being mean to them, or a teacher not liking them, that's when you are *needed* and you can become . . . Superparent! Able to hug out all worries and soothe all ills. Purposefully you stride over, sweep up your child, urge them to take you through the situation blow by blow, and then reassure and support them until they feel better. Maybe you even dip into the freezer or biscuit jar for some extra comfort to take away their sadness, or maybe you offer to call the school or the other child's parent.

Now, a clever kid works out pretty quickly that the report of a good day gets little attention and the report of a bad day gets a lot of attention. They might start to regularly look for some wrongdoing committed against them in order to get some Superparent action. Trouble is, you are turning your child into a Negative Nancy or a Melancholic Max and you become a Pooped Parent.

Start giving your child equal or more attention when they report a good day; ask them to tell you about what made it so great. Give more enthusiasm to the good reports and less to the whiny, complainy ones about minor incidents, particularly things you judge to be insignificant in the Big Deal-o-Meter of Life. Try to refocus your child on the good things that have happened to them: 'Oh, that's a shame, but I'm sure your whole day wasn't so bad. What was the best thing about your day?' Then give more attention to their happy reports. Over time they will seek your attention by being positive, not negative.

Ignore non-verbal bellyaching

Have you ever worked with Mr or Mrs Non-Verbal? You know – the sort of co-worker whose main form of communication is a long sigh or a slammed drawer or a pursed lip. They are a clever family, the Non-Verbals, because they tend to keep up their noises and facial expressions until someone asks them what is wrong. Then they can tell their problem to someone who has officially expressed an interest in their issues. This makes it much more difficult for the person to reject their tale or not listen to or respond to what they say next.

The level of attention directed to bonsai children and adolescents means they come to expect their every facial expression will be noted and acted on by their parents. A slight frown and a parent races over to check what is wrong; a sigh and the parent adjusts the circumstances to suit their child. Indeed, a lot of parents actually judge their own performance on the facial expressions of their child. So clever children pout and bellyache as a matter of course because their conditions often improve immediately.

The trouble is that we are creating a generation of grumblers and moaners who don't even need to put their complaints into words. If you have one of these, you need to get to work to banish the young Non-Verbal who seems to have taken up residence in your home. Here's how to do it.

If your child regularly gains attention through non-verbal behaviour for minor problems, gradually start to ignore their non-verbal expressions: the sighs, the frowns, the whimpers, the moans, the door slams, the hands on hips, and the snorts. Keep on doing whatever you are doing without asking them what is wrong, or enquiring whether they are okay. You'll know they are attention seeking because they will make the sound even louder or the face more animated. Keep ignoring until they approach you and ask you to do something – using actual words.

If they start to do something harmful to show their displeasure – to themself, another person or property – then give them a consequence (ideas for consequences are in chapter 13). Don't ask them why they slammed the door or kicked the sofa, because you will just hear some justification based on their *terribly hard life*. Just say something like, 'You deliberately tried to kick the cat. That is awful behaviour and you're going into Time Out.'

You are trying to teach your child that for them to improve their situation, they need to actually approach you and ask you for something. Asking will force them to think about what is really bothering them, and prompt them to put their request in a manner that you can respond to positively. If their request is about a minor issue, they will have to make it sound compelling, and be reasonable about it. When they verbalise their problems, they will be more pleasant to be around than when they use whining, whimpering, or a displeased or angry face as their regular form of communication.

Ignore whining

If your child takes on a whiny sound when they speak, start to ignore them. You can say something like, 'I can hear someone, but there's so much whining I can't understand what they are saying,' or 'Oh no, did I put Whiny Omari in the car today? I wish Happy Omari was here so I could talk to him.'

Again, you are teaching your child to take on a pleasant tone in their voice. That skill will make them much better company for you and for the rest of the world.

Be clever with your questions

This *being a parent* thing is a fraught business. There are many days when we sit at the office or at home, away from our child, and worry about them. On their first day at a new school, we worry if they are getting on well with their new classmates; when they have expressed concern about one of their peers or a teacher, we worry if they are sorting it out. In short, anything they are worried about, we worry about too – and because our cognitive capacity is much better than theirs, our worry can take on epic proportions.

It is no surprise, when we first see our children after our day of worrying, the first thing we ask about is the thing we most fear. So you get parents asking questions like 'How was your first day – did you make any friends?' or 'Hi, Freya, was Mrs Smith nice today?' or 'Hey, Julius, did Hugo play with you today?' Parents, in their attempt to reassure themselves that their most feared outcome didn't happen, inadvertently emphasise the potential difficulties in their child's life. Because we want to be quickly comforted by the knowledge that our child was socially successful, we unintentionally put pressure on them to be socially successful. And we potentially remind them of the worst part of their day with our initial greeting.

Try to avoid making their difficulties the focus of your conversation with them.

Be assured that your child is likely to communicate any difficulties with you if you chat with them regularly. Start with broad questions – 'How was school?' or 'How was your day?' – to get them to consider the day as a whole, instead of focusing on the individual challenges they faced. This encourages them to be more positive in their outlook on life. This has a double benefit; it makes them better company and is likely to garner them more friends. (And if difficulties they faced come up in conversation? I'll talk more about helping them face those difficulties in chapter 12.)

Show a good sense of humour

For children to cope well with different personalities and social situations, it is important that they don't take themselves or things in their lives too seriously. Having a good sense of humour about events in their lives will keep them much happier than if they treat everything as if it is a life or death scenario, particularly when it is not a life or death scenario: i.e. most things.

If you visit playgrounds or childcare centres, you will notice that kids are generally good at letting things go quickly. Children are naturally inclined to feel happy and light hearted.

Somewhere along the way, we teach them to hold on to their issues longer than is good for them.

Somehow we have categorised teasing and joking as bullying, when often we kid around with the people with whom we are most comfortable.

Try to laugh regularly as a family. Show your child you all have a good sense of humour about things. Demonstrate to them that life is not always meant to be serious and that there is often joy to be found, even in tricky situations. Demonstrate enjoyment in the small things, make silly jokes, and kid around with them and tease them a little. This will help them become used to not taking themselves too seriously and they will be better able to cope with any kidding around in the playground.

I'll touch on bullying in chapter 16, but I can pretty much guarantee your child will be more able to cope with social difficulty if they don't expect others to always notice them, continually make a big deal of them, and treat all of their little issues as big issues. They'll also have a much happier life.

What to do if your child seems to have difficulty making friends

As a clinician in private practice and a parenting educator, I often meet parents who are concerned about their child's ability to make friends. Maybe your child has started at a new school recently and you worry whether they are fitting in. Or perhaps they are in a new class with students they do not know. Your child should put in the effort to make friends, but there are some strategies parents can use to assist them to become confident and capable in social situations.

Teach them how to cope when things don't go their way

Many bonsai children, used to getting their own way at home, find it challenging to go out into the playgrounds of the world and cope with the normal give and take of most social situations.

Help them practise not always getting their way. Teach them how to cope with frustration by allowing them to experience a little frustration. Don't always fix it for them. Don't agree with them that it's outrageous things haven't worked out exactly as they wished. You have to let them know, through your actions, that not always getting their way is normal. This is easier if you keep your relationship with them as one of parent and child, not friends; you also encourage them to find friends of their own age outside the family dynamic.

Teach them how to entertain themselves

Don't stage-manage all of your child's activities. Let them learn to play independently at home so they know how to entertain themselves. This will ensure that even if they are at a loss for friendship in their early days at a new school, they will be able to amuse themselves.

When you catch up with adult friends in the presence of your child, don't make your child the centre of the conversation – teach them to be comfortable without constant reassurance and attention from others. Bring some toys or books to keep them amused while you have conversation not centred on them. Indeed, seeing you with your friends teaches your child the value of friendships. You model for them the give and take of conversation, showing interest in other people, and politeness. This will be a great help for them in future.

Teach them how to make friends

While many children naturally work out how to make friends, some find this difficult.

Teach your child the simplest way to make friends is to ask another child if they can play with them, and then copy what they do.

So if they are digging in the sand – your child should too. If the child who has agreed to play with them starts running to the other side of the playground – they should run with them. Teach your child skills to ensure they are good company, such as how to appear confident, look people in the eye when they meet them, and say their name.

One of the best ways parents can help their child learn how to make friends is to give them lots of opportunities to practise. For young children, take them to the park and let them introduce themselves to children already playing or simply start to play with other children without an introduction or a request to play. When you visit friends who have children, don't do all of the work to get them playing together. Let your child practise independently starting conversations with other children or approaching them to play.

If your child is at a school they will attend for their entire schooling life (i.e. a Prep to Year 12 school), it is a good idea to polish their friend-making skills and social confidence by enrolling them in outside activities or sporting clubs. Encourage them to take part-time jobs when they are adolescents to meet other teenagers and be comfortable in new settings. Children, like adults, can forget their friendship-making techniques unless they regularly practise them.

Teach them how to fix their friendship problems

These days, parents often step in early whenever their children experience challenges or difficulties with their friends. Unfortunately, their children don't learn how to resolve their own issues and sort things out with peers.

Research suggests that children are fairer and more sporting in their behaviour when they play sport without adult supervision. Every now and then it is a good idea to sit back and see if your child can sort out issues they encounter in the playground or with their sibling. Friendship difficulties at school? Instead of calling the teacher or the parent of the other child, brainstorm some solutions with your child to coach them to solve the issue themselves.

Watch your own worry and expectations

Don't let your own fears about your child's social skills affect their confidence. It is unlikely that they will form close friendships in their first few months of school, particularly in the younger years. While they may have a few regular playmates, it is rare for children to be able to name someone as their best friend in early primary school. If your child is slow at making friends, don't start worrying unnecessarily; some kids just take a little longer to work out the social mores.

Ensure your questions to them do not worry them unnecessarily. 'Did you make any friends today?' might focus unhelpfully on their lack of friend-making skill that day. Best to keep your questions broad – 'How was your day today?' or 'What was the best part of your day?' Encourage them to ask the same questions of other members of the family to build their interest in others, not just themselves.

If these strategies don't work, or you continue to be concerned your child is socially anxious, then get some professional assistance. A clinical psychologist can assist them, assist you to assist them, or let you know that they are actually travelling well.

In an ideal world we would all get invited to every party, get every job we applied for and every friend or partner we set our sights on. But this is not going to happen. It's unfair to your child if your expectations for their popularity place pressure on them when it is likely they will not always be the most popular child in the class. Gregariousness is not everyone's skill – what a noisy world it would be if it were! While you can support your child in their quest to make friends, sometimes your support is best expressed by accepting them for the person they are; don't pressure a shy child to be the gregarious person you would like them to be.

Summary

Help your child develop into someone who can face the world as it is, not a bonsai child who requires constant care and consideration from everyone they meet. Develop their social skills by helping them get used to the environment they will face when away from your care.

- Don't always make them the centre of attention
- Teach them to be respectful of other people
- Give attention to the positive parts of their day
- Discourage whining and non-verbal expression of problems
- Encourage them to consider their issues with a sense of humour
- Teach them social skills
- Watch your own tendency to worry.

CHAPTER 12

Help your child develop resilience

Resilience is the ability to bounce back from adversity. It is assisted by a degree of confidence and the perception of support from loved ones, but it is primarily cultivated through facing challenging times and learning how to cope.

One of the great misunderstandings of modern parenting is the belief that children need perfect, unblemished childhoods for them to develop confidence, self-esteem and resilience. As a result we create bonsai children who are only able to face ideal conditions. These children's charmed lives prepare them for future delight, but they don't prepare them for future challenge.

If we don't allow our children to experience struggles, we don't equip them to deal with difficulty.

Without facing anything taxing, children will never acquire confidence in their skills to overcome occasional hard times.

I am going to give you skills to help your child build their resilience in the only way possible. I will show you how to coach your child to cope with and overcome challenges they face in their day-to-day life, i.e. a normal day.

What makes a normal day?

Before we look at how to help your children cope with life's hard times, let's establish what makes a normal day for most people.

- While we all have good days, most of our days are combinations of successes and failures; a few days are not good at all and some days are downright horrible
- Of the people we meet through the day, many will like us, some will really like us, and some won't like us at all
- We will sometimes try our best at tasks and sometimes not, yet the outcomes of our efforts will be relatively unpredictable: sometimes we will win without trying; sometimes we will put in enormous effort and not achieve success
- No matter which rules and regulations are in place, sometimes things won't be fair and some things just won't work in our favour
- We will see others get away with things we haven't been able to get away with, but occasionally we will get a lucky break that is denied to someone else
- We will sometimes drop our ice-cream on the ground, occasionally smash our favourite vase, and get a heavy cold on our holidays
- There is no one to blame – this is just life, and we will always win some and lose some.

Your child is going to be much better prepared for life if they understand these are the realities of living. By protecting your bonsai child from facing disappointment or unfairness, you give them unrealistic expectations of a future where everything is just, everyone gets rewards when they deserve them, and everyone is loved by all. Your child will be ill prepared to cope with challenge if they have been brought up always to expect success. They will not only have to learn to expect occasional difficulty, they will also need to learn how to overcome it or accept it as part of life. To do this, they will need the skills to cope with their emotions when things don't work out for them.

What to do when they are emotional

Thinking about our children's emotions has become a very important part of parenting – and for good reason. Emotions are central to being human and they serve an important purpose. They can motivate us to do something important, like studying for an exam or getting away from a situation in which we feel unsafe. They can help us understand others and be understood in social situations.

We are so emotionally aware these days, that we now have a term to describe the skill of understanding and recognising emotions: emotional intelligence. People who are considered emotionally intelligent are aware and thoughtful about others' emotions and mindful of their own. This usually enables them to be better company and improves their effectiveness in any sort of situation involving other humans. But, like most things, there is a limit to the usefulness of emotional awareness, and nowhere is this seen more than in a parenting context.

These days, many modern, educated parents are not only mindful of their child's emotions, they also undertake more parenting actions either as a direct result of their child's mood, or to deliberately encourage an emotional reaction in their child. The gold-standard emotion parents want to produce in their child is happiness. My research and clinical work has shown that many parents these days choose to undertake actions with the primary goal of keeping their child happy.

To want your child to be happy is completely understandable; heck, to want yourself to be happy all the time is just as understandable. I would certainly have a hard time convincing parents this is not a good general parenting goal.

But I continue to be uneasy about the sorts of actions parents undertake to create constant contentment in their child. My main concern is that the parental approach adopted often succeeds in producing short-term happiness for children, but fails to build any long-term satisfaction or improve their resilience. Indeed, harm may result from some of the parenting techniques used to make children happy.

These days, many ways of making bonsai children happy can make them much more vulnerable to wellbeing issues likely to impact on their future success and contentment.

So, let's examine a typical situation where parents are putting in the hard yards to help their child cope with difficulty. In this, we will see some of the classic ways parents respond when their child encounters difficulty.

Let's imagine Lucinda comes home from school in tears. Despite her very best efforts, her many days of practice, and her private singing lessons, she has failed for the first time to be given the lead in the school play. A new girl to the school, Eleanor, has been given the role, and Lucinda has been relegated to the chorus. Lucinda's mother, Karen, stands in front of her distraught daughter and her heart melts. She draws her daughter to her, gives her a big hug and gently wipes her tears. But hugs can only go on for so long and words have to come. Here are some things the mother might say. Do they sound familiar to you? Which response would you choose?

'Oh honey, I am so sorry.'
'Let's go and get some ice-cream to help you feel better.'
'Do you want me to call Ms Johnston, and see if there is a bigger role she can find for you?'
'I can't believe you didn't get it; they shouldn't be allowed to give new girls such important roles.'
'Oh that must be so disappointing – after all the work you did. No wonder you're upset.'

Okay. Made your choice? Let's examine each one, because there are good reasons parents make statements like these, and it is important to see the motivation behind each one and the message each sends to the child.

'Oh honey, I am so sorry'

This is an apology. But why did Karen apologise? I'd guess Karen has decided one of her main parenting goals is to make her daughter constantly happy. I imagine Karen has undertaken many activities throughout Lucinda's life to reach this goal. I suspect Lucinda would often only have to express a passing interest in something for Karen to take it on as her parental duty to make it happen. Karen may have translated statements like 'Mummy, look at the pretty ballerina' into a clear message, 'Get me into a toddler ballet class fast, Mummy, or you are not doing your job of giving me a super happy childhood.' And as a result of all her effort, I have no doubt Lucinda's life is indeed a good one.

But life happens to our children in ways sometimes out of our control. Occasionally bad, difficult, and disappointing things can happen to our children when they are away from our presence. So when we apologise to our child, we are saying sorry for failing them in some way. I have no doubt Lucinda's mother, later that night, is questioning her choice of school for her daughter. 'Should I have put her in the smaller school down the road with fewer talented children, so she would shine?' Or questioning her actions, 'Should I have enrolled her in singing classes a year earlier?' or 'Should I be volunteering more at school?' And, very late in the night, when the crazy thoughts take hold, 'Has this happened because I went back to work earlier than I wanted? Has that affected her ability to be successful?' Or, 'Would breastfeeding six months more have given her a better ability to sing?' Or, 'Eleanor's parents are still together. Is Lucinda suffering because of my divorce?' In all of these thoughts, Karen is taking the majority of blame for her daughter's failure to get the part. She is probably saying sorry to her daughter because she believes it might be, in some way, her fault, and that her parenting choices have set her daughter up for failure and unhappiness.

If a parent regularly expresses contrition when their bonsai child experiences a difficult or sad event, what message is it sending?

If the child hears 'sorry' from their parent often enough, it suggests to them that anything negative happening to them is their parent's fault.

A child can start to believe that any situation in which they don't get their desired outcome is not their doing, and that it is the responsibility of someone else to make it better for them. This leads us to the next response.

'Let's go and get some ice-cream to help you feel better'

Seeing your much-loved child teary, disappointed and upset can break your heart. You've read the books and you know that self-esteem is the be all and end all of outcomes and, heaven help us, her self-esteem is crumbling in front of your eyes. So what is a parent to do?

You might not be able to change the outcome but you can try to turn that frown upside down, and you can definitely show them they are loved. So now's the time to bring out some treats to make it feel better. Take them shopping, buy an ice-cream or their favourite takeaway . . . the options are endless. If the disappointment is great, you could provide a few things over the next few days. The best bonus? Not only will they feel better, but you will feel better too, because you have made things right again!

To want to feel better is human. To want loved ones to feel better is ultimately a loving act. But the message this type of well-intended action sends is, perhaps, not the one intended – especially if this is the response every time life serves them difficulty or heartache.

The first message you might be sending to your child is that you can't cope when they experience difficult feelings, and neither can, nor should, they. As soon as those negative, unpleasant feelings are present in them, your actions suggest they should immediately be erased through doing things to make them feel good. An occasional treat on a particularly bad day is fine, but if presented every time, you could be setting up some dangerous precedents. A tub of ice-cream every time life gets tricky, retail therapy when melancholy strikes, a bottle of wine at the end of long days? You can see we are getting into dangerous habits here.

Not only that, it's unlikely that someone will immediately make things better when disappointment strikes outside your home or when you are not around. Hands up if in the face of bad news, you always immediately receive offers of good news? Who has heard, 'I don't love you any more. I want a divorce, but here is another partner I found for you who is better looking and will be nicer to you.' Or 'We don't want you to work for us any longer, but here is another well-paid job we have found for you. Congratulations, you start tomorrow.'

Sure, one door closes and another might open, but this can take some time, if it happens at all. By setting up the expectation that sadness always turns into happiness in a matter of minutes, you are suggesting life will be a lot better than it usually is, and tricky situations and difficult emotions will quickly disappear. Therefore, you are not readying your bonsai child for the real world. The first time things don't work out for them, they won't be prepared, and it may take them a long time to recover.

For a variation of this approach, let's look at the next response.

'Do you want me to call Ms Johnston, and see if there is a bigger role she can find for you?'

Again, this response suggests every bad feeling needs to be, and can be, immediately resolved. Not only does it suggest bad feelings can be improved by the right phone call to the right people, it also implies the very act of improving the situation is not in the capacity of your child – it needs to be resolved by you.

It is completely understandable that parents want to stand up for their children, but taking on their child's issues and solving them suggests the child is incapable of coping with a negative feeling, and incapable of improving their situation.

By making things better,
parents are not teaching their bonsai children
to manage or solve the issue themselves.

Am I suggesting that speaking to the teacher is the wrong thing? I don't think it is an ideal response. Being a member of the chorus is not the end of the world for Lucinda; it will teach her she can cope with being one of many. She will experience the teamwork inherent in chorus work rather than always expecting the glory of being the superstar. Every now and then all superstars need to take a back seat because it assists them to become better performers and good team members.

Do I think the teacher should not be approached at all? Well, ideally, the teacher's decisions should be accepted and the teacher treated like a professional and left alone by meddling parents. But a parent can encourage their child to have a conversation with the teacher. This way they show their child how to solve their own problems. Karen could coach Lucinda to thank the teacher for the opportunity to be in the chorus, tell the teacher how happy she is to be in the show, but she is keen to have a part, so if any come up she would be happy to audition for them.

Ideally, Karen could encourage Lucinda, in the next 24 hours, to give Eleanor hearty and genuine congratulations for getting the role. By coaching her to be generous in defeat, she would teach Lucinda how to get the positive feelings of being a good sport and a genuine team member. And if she still quietly hopes Eleanor gets glandular fever and Lucinda gets her rightful spotlight on the stage, for goodness sake, she should keep it to herself!

'I can't believe you didn't get it; they shouldn't be allowed to give new girls such important roles'

The desire to make someone out to be the enemy or the sole cause of a bad situation is human. When distressed, we love to blame someone else for our misfortunes, because it reduces our own role in them. By blaming another, rather than just bad luck or a bad day, we suggest that with the right effort and surrounding ourselves with the right people, we can always be happy and control the future. Unfortunately, the sense of control we think we gain is actually very flimsy and rarely backed up by our real experience.

Why do we do this? Well, we often turn sadness or disappointment into anger because anger can help you feel comfortable and in control, instead of the vulnerability of feeling sad. The problem arises when, as a parent, you always make a negative event in your child's life to be someone else's fault, because you encourage a learned helplessness in your child. You lead them to believe that their life is dictated by their environment and they are at the whim of other people's actions, which means there is not a lot they can do to make it better. This encourages bonsai-like reliance on others to treat them well, rather than confidence in themselves to improve their situation.

Learned helplessness has been implicated in depression because it gives rise to a belief that the world has got it in for you and there is nothing you can do about it. In other words, you've learnt you are helpless to effect change in your life. Planting the seed of that feeling in your child will not be good for their confidence to face the world.

'Oh that must be so disappointing – after all the work you did. No wonder you are upset'

This is my preferred response. I really like this one for a few reasons. The first is that it names the emotion the child is feeling, and acknowledges the feeling, which is really helpful for them. The second is that it also shows the child that the parent understands the disappointment because of all of the work done, and confirms the emotion is valid in this situation. But it doesn't stop the child from experiencing the emotion by immediately taking it away, or changing it into anger toward an imagined terrible third party, or providing happiness through a distraction. The parent does not take on the responsibility of fixing the situation, nor do they magnify the emotion for the child by ruminating on it with them. This response acknowledges their feeling as okay and understandable given the circumstances.

This type of response can pretty much be used in any situation where your child is highly emotional.

What to do when they experience bad events

This is the strategy:

1. You listen to the situation
2. You state the emotion and validate it, if it is understandable in the circumstances
3. That's it. No more to do.

Let's look at some more situations.

The rain, the park, and other things

So you promised them they could go to the park and now it is raining. You say, 'Oh, it's raining now, we won't be able to go to the park.' They become angry or start to cry. You say, 'You are angry/upset because you can't go to the park and that's understandable.' They keep grumbling, so you demonstrate your acknowledgement. You nod your head to the side and do a screwed-up mouth with the face to match, which is the non-verbal equivalent of 'Yes, I understand it's a tricky one for you.' But no more words.

I need to point out a few things. You explain once only the reason for the decision about the park. You don't go into lengthy detail, because the facts are the facts, and lots of justification sounds like parental guilt to kids. And you don't apologise, because unless you went out in the yard and did your best rain dance, it was not your fault it rained, even if you prayed for rain so you wouldn't have to go to that stupid park again this weekend.

Parents are powerful influences in their child's life, but they can't make it rain. So don't apologise, and don't suggest to your child every time disappointment strikes, it may somehow be your fault. You don't need to say anything more to them because what could be said has been said, and now they have to deal with the emotion and accept a situation they have no control over.

The right icing

There are two cupcakes left, one with pink icing and one with butter-yellow icing. There is one child ahead of you in the line and your child has already decided on their choice. (You are ahead of me on this one, aren't you?) The child ahead picks the clearly superior cupcake. Your child is devastated.

Let's look at this. Your child is devastated about getting a cupcake with the wrong icing. *Your child is getting a cupcake and they are upset about it.* We've landed in a parallel universe here, and you've got a bit of work to do. Better start now.

Don't apologise to your child and don't offer the other child money for their cupcake. In fact, don't do anything that keeps your child in the enchanted Land of Entitlement. Just say, 'The only cupcake is this colour,' in a very nonchalant manner. If your child keeps making a loud fuss, you could cancel your coffee and walk out of the cafe or at least indicate to them that their behaviour is inappropriate and you will not be buying any cupcake for them. And, if this has been happening quite a lot recently, you will need to make a mental note to yourself, 'Oops, somehow I have given my child the idea that life will always go their way. That's something I am going to have to change gently but quickly, or real life is going to be very, very hard for them.'

iWant

So your teenager asked you for a new piece of technology last night. You have explained you won't buy it now but they can earn the money to buy it themself, starting with a few jobs you have around the house. Your adolescent, who was convinced you would race them to the shop that very minute to get it, surprisingly does not take this news well. They have been in a bad mood ever since. They come home from school and start the teenage slam dance - slam their bag on the table and slam the door to the beat of the house band, Grunt and Sigh. What do you do?

Well, you don't ask, 'What's wrong?' Your teenager is communicating their emotion in an extremely unsocial manner, and non-verbal displays of anger or frustration are horrible childish traits in anyone. Don't pay the behaviour by asking what's wrong, because it will teach them to communicate through childish tantrum techniques rather than to actually say what they are feeling. So if their slam dance is not harming anything - themself, your property or another person – ignore it. If your child really wants to go into round two with you on this matter, they are actually going to have to come and speak to you to let you know their disappointment at the outcome of the conversation last night.

So, after a bit more of the dance, they say 'I can't believe you won't buy it for me, everyone else has it!' And your response, cool as a cucumber? 'You're upset because you can't get what you want immediately.' I'd even leave out justifying the emotion bit in this instance, because they are getting petulant here. They know you are not buying it for them, they have a way to obtain it, but they are remaining in Wallow Land rather than taking a trip out of there on the Make-It-Happen Express, and there is no reason for you to reward their choice of location.

What if your words have made them even angrier? They may start on a variation of make-my-parent-angry-or-guilty-so-they-are-going-to-keep-this-argument-going-so-I-can-yell-some-more-and-make-myself-feel-a-bit-better. Let's say they choose something like, 'You never do what I want! How come every other kid has better parents than I do?' or 'Nothing has been good ever since we moved here. I hate my life!'

Aren't they clever? Bless them, they have managed to say something that, depending on your own emotions about your parenting or recent events, will have you guilty, angry or both. And that advantages them, because guilt will soften you and possibly make things go their way again. Anger will keep it all a bit shouty and allow them to put their efforts into yelling rather than accepting their situation.

The worst thing you can do is respond emotionally to their line of defence, 'I love you! I always have! We feel terrible about moving but we had to!' or 'How could you say that, after all I've done for you?' Why? Because your teenager will argue the point even further because they have provoked an emotional response in you. That means to them, 'Bingo, I am onto something here, let's keep this going.' And adolescents always have superior debating skills than their parents, particularly when the topic is 'Gosh my teenage life is hard' and, as always, they have chosen the affirmative position.

Your best response is to repeat what you have already said. If they remain angry, you state the pointlessness of continuing the conversation. And there is no point. It has all been said and done. It is time for them to accept and move on, or wallow alone.

So the whole scenario would go something like this:

Slam slam
(No response from you)

Slam slam
(No response from you)

SLAM SLAM
(No response from you)

Finally your teenager comes over to you, sighing. 'I can't believe you won't buy it for me. I need it now. You don't care about me.'

You: 'You are angry because you can't get it right away.'

Them: 'Every other kid at school has one and their parents bought it for them. Why did I get the worst parents who never do anything for me?'

You, with a little shrug: 'You are angry because you can't get it right away.'

Them: 'You have one – how come you get one and I don't? Where is the fairness in that? You only think about yourself.'

You: 'There is no point in discussing this any further, you know my decision.' And you leave the room or ask them to go elsewhere. You might give them a consequence if they keep going on about it despite you telling them the conversation is over.

Done.

So, here is the strategy again, including what to do if they labour the point . . .

1. You listen to the situation
2. You state the emotion they are experiencing and validate it, if it is understandable in the circumstances
3. You listen again, if they want to keep discussing it
4. You state the emotion, again, and validate it, if it is understandable in the circumstances
5. If they keep going, you confirm the conversation is over and walk away
6. If they persist, you give a consequence
7. That's it, no more to do.

These are the days of their lives

Your child comes home very upset: their friend talked to another friend at lunch and their friend said yesterday they didn't even like the other friend but now they are hanging out with that friend, and that friend has been nasty to your child before, and they haven't liked them from day one, and you should have seen the message they texted to Zelda . . . It's exhausting, isn't it?

Well let's be discriminating on this one, and determine our reaction based on how big a deal this is on the alarm-o-meter. As parents, it is important to remember not every issue your child brings home is 10/10 in importance. Apparently, when James Cameron was advising his extras on the set of *Titanic*, he explained it would be implausible for the crowd to be absolutely terrified in every scene of the movie; the level of terror shown needed to be appropriate to the state the ship seemed to be in. So he would say, 'Right, now you are all five out of ten terrified,' when the ship was at a 30 degree angle, and 'Now you are ten out of ten terrified!' when the ship was at a 90 degree angle.

As parents, we should not react
as if each friendship bump in the road
is the worst thing we have ever heard.

When your child's story describes a relatively minor issue, allot the time and the reaction appropriate to a minor situation. This starts gently guiding them away from the drama queen's or king's throne they appear to be walking towards. Sometimes a facial expression or a quick 'that's a shame' is sufficient for minor issues they report.

Vent or problem-solve

A good strategy in trickier situations is *vent or problem-solve*. This one is really useful for children over the age of eight or so, particularly if your child has a tendency to dissect every social situation they have been in, and appears to be automatically putting on a white lab coat as they walk in the door each afternoon.

When your child comes to you with an issue that is a genuine challenge for them, first determine when you can give them time to discuss it. While you can listen to their situation there and then, I would recommend you sometimes tell them you don't have time to listen to it now, but maybe in an hour when you have dinner simmering, or after their shower. This is beneficial for your child because they occasionally resolve the issue by themselves in the meantime, or they just let it go. To be really sneaky, sometimes set up the time to talk about it when their favourite TV show is on.

By doing this, you'll start to help them discern which issues they really need your ear for and what they are prepared to forgo to get your sage advice. This action is not unnecessarily harsh when done occasionally, because in real life we don't always get a calm listening ear exactly when we want it. Sometimes we have to wait before we can receive counsel from our manager, friend or partner, and have to cope in the meantime without support, or have to rely on our own judgement. Therefore, learning how to cope with minor issues is a great skill for children to develop.

So, at the predetermined time, your child comes to you to talk to you about something that has provoked anger or sadness in them. They describe it briefly (hopefully!) and you ask them whether they want to vent or problem-solve. Venting is complaining about the situation without attempting to resolve it. When they vent, you listen but try not to allow the venting to turn into rumination, because too much going over and over a tricky issue without resolving it is a bad habit associated with depression.

If they decide they want to vent, give them an amount of time, or ask them how long they need to vent about the issue – typically maybe three or five minutes, after which you will do something else. 'Okay, let's talk about it for five minutes before we watch our favourite TV show together,' or 'Let's walk to the shop to get the milk and we can discuss it on the way,' (double points for setting up an activity that's good for their health and wellbeing). As the listener, you respond by listening, naming the emotion, and validating it, if their emotional response seems reasonable and helpful to them.

You might employ some Socratic questions in this conversation if you see your child becoming more emotional than is beneficial to them. Socratic questions help them clarify their thinking, e.g. 'Why did you feel that way?' and 'Are you sure they meant that, or could there be another reason they said it?' Psychologists use these questions all the time to enable our clients to get greater insight into their situation without telling them what to think. This is because teaching a person how to find their own insight into their situation is much more useful to them than teaching them to be reliant on others' counsel all of the time.

Your child can vent about an issue up to three separate times, but . . . *three strikes and they're out.* You have completely discussed it together, and they must now problem-solve. 'Diego, three times this week you have come home complaining about this friendship group. I think it is time for you to problem-solve the situation so it doesn't affect you so much.'

Problem-solving is done after the problem is briefly discussed. Your child has to come up with some potential solutions, list the good and bad elements of those solutions, and then choose a course of action. Note the entire to-do list is their responsibility. You can coach, but leave most of the problem-solving to your child or adolescent. Certainly leave the majority of the responsibility for the actions in the plan to them. You teach them to fish with this strategy; you don't wrap it up in newspaper for them.

About 70 per cent of problem-solving is working out ways to accept the situation and change your thinking or actions to make reality suit you more. If your child is upset when a particular friendship group won't include them, there is often nothing they can do to change the situation. Often the best thing is to accept it and then work out a way to feel better, such as establishing another friendship group.

Is it fair that some children don't want to be friends with your child? No – but that's life. George Clooney didn't return my calls; it's time to move on.

Don't let them take it out on others

Our children and teens need to experience the full range of emotions. Having said that, while they have permission to be in a bad mood, they have no permission to take it out on others. Indeed, I would encourage you to make this a rule of the household – *we all have the right to be in a bad mood, and we have the responsibility of not taking it out on others.* Children should be responsible for removing themselves if they are not feeling social; and they should be able to manage their moods in front of others when they are obliged to stay. We all have to swallow our bad or sad mood when we are at work or talking to Aunty Margaret, and our children need to learn this skill. Your child's mood gives them no permission to be rude to you or others; if they behave appallingly, they need to get the same consequences as at any other time.

The approaches to your child's or adolescent's emotional challenges discussed in this chapter might seem unkind to some parents. In reality, they are a loving act. It is not helpful for us to allow our children to wallow and ruminate on their temporary difficulties and setbacks. As their parents, we shouldn't use these situations to bond excessively with them over the unfairness of the world. If we immediately erase the bad feelings, we do not allow our children to feel the emotion, accept it, and use it in a way to teach them an important lesson, motivate them to put in further work, or give them the satisfaction of eventually learning to cope with something difficult or out of their control.

By letting them experience all emotions, including difficult ones,
we give them the confidence to face tricky events
and develop the resilience to bounce back
from the difficult issues in their lives.

Children need to learn how to face occasional emotional winds and storms to develop the confidence to step out their door every day, assured they can face both the good and the not-so-good things the world is going to bring them. As their parent, you can empathise with them when they face occasional headwinds, but you do them no favours by always sheltering your bonsai child from life's weather.

How to deal with your emotions in front of them

Of course, children and teens are not the only ones who face difficult events and have negative reactions to things. Parents will face challenges and be emotional in front of their children. What is the best thing to do?

It is not the end of the world to be emotional in front of your children. You also have permission to have all emotions, not only the positive ones.

Children can cope with emotional parents
but they can't cope with parents who look like they are not coping.

Even though you may be crying about the loss of someone dear, you need to show your children you are going to muddle through. When something major occurs to you, you need to reassure your children things will be okay and they should not be anxious about your wellbeing or the family's safety or security. Indeed, I suggest you should take your children to a funeral only if you believe you can broadly keep it together. If you can't, it is better not to let them see you completely break down, as it will really worry your children if they are young. Tell them difficult things only when you think you can stay in control of yourself in front of them. If you lose your composure, reassure them you will eventually be fine and they should not worry.

Fighting in front of them

Disagreements between parents are okay. You can certainly have healthy debate, but big fights involving name-calling and screaming should never occur in front of children. Research shows that adolescents who have been exposed to family fights have more mental health issues than those who haven't. When discussing the sorts of issues that invariably come up between partners, you need to keep your voices calm. Avoid aggressive tones to ensure the disagreement remains rational and your children don't become scared. If you find you are fighting more with your partner then you should, seek some professional therapeutic support before it starts to impact on your relationship and on your children.

Not the whole truth

Now I need to address an important issue I notice clinically: the idea that you should tell your child everything and be totally honest with them. I can't tell you the number of parents I have treated who have let their child know things they should not be sharing with them because the child is too young to understand, or, more importantly, too young to be able to cope with such news. I have had clients tell their young children that Mummy and Daddy are breaking up because Daddy wants to date boys, or share the details of their bipolar issues or their clinical depression.

Now I am not suggesting you don't tell them the truth at some point, but try to tell them the complete truth only when you genuinely believe they can cope with the news. Until then, give them only the information they really need, made into something palatable. You don't need to talk about a parent's depression; you can talk about 'not feeling well'. You don't have to give any details about why you are separating. Save the truly adult talk until your child has maturity and well-tuned coping skills.

Don't look to them for comfort

Today some parents look primarily to their child for comfort, hugs and reassurance when the parent is upset. This is a worrying trend. It is fine occasionally, but if a parent looks for this reassurance too often, it starts to put pressure on the child to support the parent. Expecting reciprocal support from your child is called *parentification*. It means you are making the child into a parent figure who is caring for you. Research suggests that parents who seek this support from their child lack sensitivity to their needs. Research also shows that youths who experience parentification, particularly from their mothers, may be at greater risk of internalising issues such as anxiety or depression, and externalising behavioural problems.

To ensure you don't lean on your children, I would use the mantra 'Never complain or explain' when dealing with big issues in their presence. I suggest you find any support you need from adult peers or seek therapy rather than confide in or obtain emotional support from your children.

Summary

Normal life is not always happy. Parents' reactions to children's difficulties can inadvertently discourage them from overcoming challenges. Ways to help our children get used to life's ups and downs include:

- Let your child experience all emotions, including difficult ones, and you will give them the skills and confidence to face their challenges

- The best response to your child is to listen briefly, identify the emotion, and then empathise, if their reactions are understandable
- Use the *vent or problem-solve* technique when they are emotional about something
- You can show your child you are feeling sad or cranky; however, always stay relatively composed to make them aware you can cope with these emotions
- Avoid arguing or name-calling with your partner and keep calm in disagreements
- Only tell your child information they can handle; often they won't be able to cope with the complete truth
- Avoid relying on your child for comfort; get same-aged peers or a professional to help you with your adult issues.

CHAPTER 13

Help your child learn self-regulation

Self-regulation is a person's ability to act in their best interests and choose constructive, appropriate behaviours. Children don't possess self-regulation in their early years, and adults need to assist them to develop it.

Although not often discussed, self-regulation is a very important skill. A toddler who can self-regulate will be able to stop playing and start cleaning up at their parent's request; a child who can self-regulate will be able to stop talking to their friend and listen to the teacher; an adolescent who can self-regulate will be able to forgo watching TV to study for their exam on Monday. Their choices respond more purposefully to their environment than just wanting to have fun all of the time. They regulate their current desire for the purpose of their future benefit.

Parents who have developmentally appropriate expectations of their child's behaviour can assist their child to develop self-regulation by modelling good behaviour and cueing the child to do tasks such as taking their plate to the kitchen or listening to others. Over time, children will internalise these adult expectations of suitable behaviour into their own behavioural repertoire and will not need to be reminded of them by the parent or teacher. As they become capable of facing new tasks and challenges, the adults in their lives can increase their expectations of them. In this way, children become responsible and able to contribute to their family and community for the good of themselves and others.

Bonsai children are often not good at self-regulation because it is primarily the efforts of others that give them their individual successes, not their own efforts.

Bonsai children don't learn the discipline of self-management, or develop the incentive to choose appropriate behaviours, because their parents (and, sometimes even their teachers) mould their environment to ensure these children are always triumphant and happy.

In this chapter we will look at ways to develop self-regulation in your child. We will look at why it is important for parents to be in charge, and the benefits of rules, routines, and chores. We will talk about ways you can encourage your children to do tasks by giving instructions effectively. Finally – and this is the bit I'm sure you have been waiting for – we will look at what to do when they behave inappropriately or don't do what you ask. Together, these actions provide essential scaffolding for your child to develop behaviours that will stand them in good stead for future success.

It's important to understand that it takes consistent application of all three components – rules, routines and chores; effective instructions; and predictable consequences for defiance – to develop your child's self-regulation. The good news is that once they have it, your child (and you) will reap the benefits for the rest of their life.

How to tell if your child is developing self-regulation skills

Children who aren't developing adequate self-regulation skills are often challenging to live with. Because they can't adapt their own wishes to adjust to the demands of their environment, they don't react appropriately to others' requests of them, even when these requests are for their own good. These children are often reckless and tend to have poor impulse control, meaning they choose immediate satisfaction (continuing to play) over what their parent wants them to do (have a bath). These children are usually not socially competent because they choose their own interests over the consensus of the group: they may not play according to the rules of the game, and may have difficulty sharing, both of which make them unpopular with their peers.

Self-regulation helps children manage their emotions and express their feelings in ways that others can respond to. Children with good self-regulation skills are often able to soothe themselves when distressed, and are not as dependent on other people's help or attention all of the time. Conversely, children with poor self-regulation are reliant on others to help them and make things better for them so they can cope. When upset, children with poor self-regulation may express their emotions in harmful or extreme ways.

Your child should start to show some self-regulation skills between the ages of two and four years. Experts think the critical period to develop these skills is between three and seven years old. In these years they should start to adapt their behaviours to the demands of their environment. If your child has not begun to do this by the age of six or seven, you can still set up structures in the home to support their development of self-regulation. However, at this age, it will always be more difficult.

Problem signs

Many of the children's issues I treat are the result of poorly developed self-regulation skills. Clear signs to me are when the child is unable to comply with the instructions of adults or follow the rules of the household or classroom. They might have difficulty fitting in with peers and be bossy with other children or choose the most disruptive peers as their pals. Poorly self-regulated children often overreact to minor events, such as not getting their way; or they might randomly say hurtful things to others in a deliberate attempt to upset them. They also tend to have extreme reactions when challenged and are difficult to calm down.

When I treat a child with these issues, I determine whether their environment is encouraging them to develop self-regulation. I check to see if there are clear rules in place, and whether there are family routines that establish a structured environment where the child feels safe and capable of following plans. I find out if they have an overly pleasant and resource-rich life, and if this wonderful life is dependent on the child behaving appropriately, or if the parents give them a charmed life as a matter of course. I enquire about the child's chores, whether they are paid or unpaid, and whether the child actually does them. I assess the parent's confidence in giving instructions to the child and delivering consequences when the child or adolescent makes bad choices or fails to do what is asked of them.

I am looking for *consistency* in all of these areas. Nearly all parents have rules, chores and consequences, such as Time Out or grounding a child, but I find that many parents are very poor at being unvarying in the delivery of these strategies.

> *Consistency of delivery is always the key to successful parenting strategies, particularly when managing challenging behaviour.*

Inconsistent responses will keep your child gambling on bad behaviour because they can't predict with certainty what will happen as a result of their naughty choice, so they figure they might get away with it. Uniform application of rules and consequences will make the outcome predictable for your child and they will be less likely to indulge in bad behaviour.

How to treat poor self-regulation

Implement all strategies

If you are having issues with your child's ability to self-regulate, I urge you to take on everything I suggest in this book. If you haven't read the earlier chapters on developing your child's confidence, social skills and resilience, I strongly suggest you go back and read those before reading this chapter. Bonsai children often don't behave appropriately because the adults in their lives adjust their expectations to suit their child. The earlier chapters provide the essential foundation for the work you are about to do in this chapter.

Be persistent

It is essential that you persist. Most parents tell me they have tried setting rules and giving Time Out, but many then say, 'it didn't work'.

Typically, nothing works perfectly the first time, particularly if your child is used to getting their own way.

You have to persist with applying these strategies. Understand that it may take weeks or even months to see a result. It is important for you to know that the time it takes will reflect the extent of the problem in your child's behaviour, previous behavioural expectations in the home, and whether consequences have been delivered effectively to date. If it takes longer than you expect, it is not because there is a problem with the strategies I provide. These strategies are based on extensive research and clinical experience, and they *will* be effective; but if you have been locked into some bad patterns, it might take significant effort and a consistent approach to produce a better situation in your home.

Don't let difficulty allow you to lose your resolve. If you don't address this matter now, it is likely to become even more difficult to manage your child's or adolescent's behaviour and teach them the skills to get on in the world. Their self-regulation problems are going to make the home environment unpleasant for the family, and, more importantly, make your child's life far more challenging. So, by addressing this now, you start to turn the situation around. Again, please don't expect instant miracles. It might take a while.

Take charge

Parents must be the ones in charge. Children who don't respect the authority of adults have difficulty developing self-regulation because they don't allow anyone to guide their behaviour. Indeed, one of the easiest ways to start compliance problems in your child is to give them the impression they are in charge, or that they at least hold an influential position on the board of directors of the household.

Many parents have in mind the relationship they eventually want to have with their child – one of being equals and friends. This relationship is fine when your child becomes an adult but if you start out this way, it's not going to work. As the adult, you have higher status and better ability to steer your child in the right direction. It is going to be very difficult for you to give instructions and establish rules and give consequences, if you are also trying to be friends with your child.

In my clinical experience, when adults say they are friends with their children, the child is typically more in charge than the adult. That's because the parents' desire to be liked by their child comes at the cost of establishing common-sense rules and insisting on age-appropriate behaviours. It also comes at the cost of the child learning any sort of self-discipline in the home environment.

If you have to remind your child you are in charge,
*you are **not** in charge.*

Things that are accepted don't need to be said. You should be able to give instructions and make rules without reminding your child of your position as chief policymaker. Likewise, if you regularly have to tell them they should respect you or treat you better, then they *don't* respect you and they *don't* think they need to treat you well. Again, if they respect you, they would not call you names, would be considerate of you, and would acquiesce to your wishes, with only occasional lapses. If lapses regularly occur in your home, you need to quickly gain back their respect and get yourself into the position of higher status, pronto.

You must re-establish yourself as the chief decision-maker. You are the key authority figure in their childhood and adolescent years, after which you can relax into a more adult type of relationship with them. During their childhood and adolescence, they should have no doubt as to who is in charge, and who has the final say on what goes on.

If your child doesn't accept your authority, it will be problematic for you to accomplish the techniques in this chapter. You will need to be unfailingly consistent in your use of the strategies. If you are in a two-parent family it is ideal for both of you to adopt the same approach, even if you are separated. If you are the only parent to adopt this approach, it can eventually work, but it will be trickier than if you were both to adopt it.

If you have not been in charge in the past, you have some hard yards coming up. You can do it, but be aware you are starting the race on a handicap. Don't worry – you can catch up.

So, grab your most comfortable shoes, your backpack, your packed lunch and water bottle. Let's commence our journey.

The combination code for developing self-regulation

You need to employ three essential components to assist your child to develop self-regulation. I think of them as a combination code: you must use all three for the mechanism to click into place and produce the desired result. If you neglect to apply any one of the three, you won't get the outcome you want and your child needs.

The combination code is:

1. Rules, routines and chores
2. Effective instructions
3. Predictable consequences for defiance.

Now, let's go through each component of the code.

Rules, routines and chores

Rules help everyone

Life is busy. Rules simplify our lives and make things easier in the home. They set the standard for satisfactory behaviour. They help parents, who won't have to constantly re-think what is acceptable behaviour and what is not. They help children, who will be clear about the limits. In short, rules and guidelines make everyone feel safer and more confident in most situations. Yay rules!

Set the rules

Parents should set the basic rules for their household. Some of the big ones would be about movement through the house, voices, bedtimes and basic respect for others. Rules should ideally be expressed in a positive way so they state *what to do* rather than *what not to do*; but this isn't always possible. Some obvious ones for a younger child would be:

'Walk in the house.'
'Use your "inside voice" inside the house.' (i.e. no shouting or yelling)
'Bedtime is 7.30.'
'Treat others and their things with respect.'

When they are older, you can set other rules, such as 'social events only on the weekend' or 'TV after homework is finished'. The rules you design will act as a shorthand and minimise the need for you to re-create guidelines. So when they ask to go to their friend's place on a Wednesday night, you say, 'It's a school night,' which should be a sufficient response for them to understand that it isn't allowed. This stops you from having to enter into G20- or UN-type policy discussions with your child every time they ask for something outside the rules.

Ideally your child will be able to reel off the rules. It is a good idea to post them up somewhere, such as the fridge door. If your child can't read, you might use pictures to convey the rules. Even if your child can't understand language yet, it is important for you to establish some rules in your mind, such as 'bottom always on chair'. This will help you and your partner to be on the same page.

Once children know the basic house rules, you shouldn't need to remind them all the time about appropriate behaviour. If they forget, you can gently remind them with a question, 'Hey, what's our rule about the way we talk in the house?' You are looking for your child to self-correct here through your calm question. It also means you don't have to nag ('What did I tell you about yelling?') or break the rule yourself ('STOP YELLING!').

When you go out, it is a good idea to re-state the rules of the space: 'Now, we are going to a restaurant. Remember – inside voices, stay on your chairs reading your books, and don't forget to say *excuse me* when interrupting adults.' You might ask them to repeat the rules back to you, or you could ask them what they think is appropriate behaviour in the environment you are about to enter.

Enforce the rules

Setting the rules doesn't mean your child will follow them if you don't enforce them.

The most important part about the rules is that they have to be consistently enforced.

Remember, you teach people how to treat you. This means that the onus remains on you to enforce the rules, not your child. If your child speaks to you with disrespect and you don't pull them up on it, then it is not your child who is at fault; the greater mistake is you allowing this situation to occur. You will only ever teach your child to self-regulate their behaviour through your actions and consequences for their poor choices.

Revise the rules as they grow older

You need to revise the rules as your children grow older. With increasing maturity, children should become part of a negotiation process. When they commence high school or university or work, sit down with them and together agree on new house rules. This is important when they become teenagers or adults and start to enjoy new freedoms.

In these discussions, remember it remains your house and, as such, all occupants remain under your rules. The person who should compromise most is the one who is not paying the mortgage or rent. I suggest the greater their contribution to the household (through chores or financial input), the more you allow them adult freedoms. Having new freedoms outside the home shouldn't automatically mean they have them in your home: you need to be comfortable in your own space. And take note – the more sovereignty they have in your space, the less likely they will move out during the next decade, and the less likely you will ever get the spare bedroom, billiards or Pilates room that you desire.

Establish routines

In busy lives, routines help keep family life sane and sensible. Your basic routine should allow you to get through your days effectively, managing to do all the jobs required in a way which keeps things moving and all family members relatively calm.

The greatest benefit of a routine is its impact on children's behaviour.

When children and teens know what to expect, they are not going to fight you as much or feel their day is open to debate.

With routines, children feel safe and secure: they know what is coming up and what they need to do. A night-time routine helps them set their body clock and lets their body set itself up for sleep. A morning routine helps them know which tasks to do and in what order they need to do them for everyone to get to their day's activity on time with a minimum of drama. Children who have established routines can often start to do things themselves and not rely on their parents to remind them at every step. Adolescents who have routines for important study tasks are less likely to forget assessment items or fall behind schedule.

Routines can also be set up for adolescents for how often and when they bathe, change their sheets, or have their clothes washed. This is essential in the sticky years when for some inexplicable reason, teens don't want to get in a shower or clean their teeth. Parents should be very explicit about their expectations and prepared to enforce them with rules, such as access to the computer only after the adolescent has showered that day.

Putting some fun elements at the end of routines is also beneficial. It gives young children something to look forward to, such as a reading a story with their mother or father at night after cleaning their teeth, or being able to watch TV or play outside after homework. It can give older children a light at the end of the tunnel, such as watching TV or playing a computer game if they finish their homework on time.

Critical times for routines are just before the start and finish of work, day care, or school hours, to ensure these stressful times don't become even more so. Ideally, sit down and work out the order of tasks that need to be done for you to get them to school or day care on time; or bathed, fed, and to bed in the evening. And then do those tasks in that order as a matter of routine.

Use behavioural reward charts

I often recommend parents become explicit with their child about the morning or evening routine by writing it down or putting pictures on a chart. Sometimes you can create behavioural reward charts out of these routines. Younger children who have eaten their breakfast, got dressed and cleaned their teeth by a certain time or without being reminded, might get a sticker, or a chance to do something fun after school. Teens may not require this level of organisation but they should know what needs to be done and finish their tasks on time.

Ensure it is in your child's interest to complete things on time in the morning. For example, rather than nag your adolescent to be at the car at a particular time every day so you get to work on time, make it in their interest to be there so they are not required to take public transport, arrive late to school, and perhaps have to speak to the principal about their tardiness. This will only work if you are prepared to carry it out and can cope with them catching the bus or train and being late. In the same vein, I strongly recommend that you make it your teen's responsibility to wake themselves up in the morning as part of their routine.

It should be their alarm clock that gets them out of bed – not your threats.

Routines are not only useful for busy morning and evening times. You can also develop routines and rewards for other activities, such as going grocery shopping with your young child. You might start a sticker or point system for every aisle where they do what you request and don't ask for presents or chocolate. You can also schedule pleasant outings after difficult events, such as going to the park after they see the dentist, or going to a café for a brownie after they have their immunisation shots.

While you can continue to use motivational rewards with particularly non-compliant children or teens, it is always best to simply expect this behaviour from your child without reward. Behavioural reward charts shouldn't go on forever. Once the child has internalised the behaviour, the incentive of a chart should not be needed. There are other things you can do to keep them interested in a task, particularly when they are young. For example, keep grocery shopping exciting for them by getting them to help you find their cereal in the aisle, locate the bananas, or pick up a certain number of fruit or vegetables – 'Help me choose three red apples'.

Rewards, such as an extra story if they are prepared for bed by a certain time, or a sticker for their collection if they are ready in the morning, are best given immediately. However, as they grow older, you may wish to alter this to enable them to develop their ability to delay gratification.

Make 'em wait

Putting off current pleasure for future gain (aka delayed gratification) is a fundamentally important skill for a child to develop in order for them to achieve and become successful. The ability to stop enjoying an immediate pleasure (watching TV, eating chocolate, spending money) will enable them to engage in activities that ensure future longer-term pleasure (studying and eventually gaining the job they desire, becoming healthy, buying a first bike or car). This is an essential element of self-regulation.

Walter Mischel's famous 1960s marshmallow study is a clever test of a child's ability to delay gratification. In this experiment, he put one marshmallow on the table and told children they could eat it now or, if they waited a short time, they could get another marshmallow, so they would have two marshmallows to eat. Some could wait, some couldn't.

Later research showed that the preschool children who could wait in the presence of the marshmallow with a goal in mind, appeared to do better on cognitive and social tests in their junior and senior high-school years. Their parents also described them as better able to concentrate and cope with frustration and stress. It appears that a child who has the skill of being able to wait with a goal in mind tends to do better in life than a child who wants things immediately without delay.

Bonsai children's charmed lives
often make it difficult for them
to develop their ability to delay gratification.

While this ability seems innate in some children, certain parenting approaches encourage it to develop and others allow it to weaken. Buying everything your child wants, as soon as they express desire, is not giving them the opportunity to learn the typical process of gaining desirable things – namely, you have to wait and work for them.

So how do you ensure your child develops their ability to delay gratification?

Delay behaviour chart rewards

While reward charts can be about immediate reward in your child's early years, as they become older you should start to delay the reward. Perhaps your child or adolescent could earn points toward getting a larger benefit, such as going to a movie, buying an electronic game, or investing in an expensive piece of technology. The older they get, the more they should be able to wait for things and undertake a current activity with a future goal in mind.

Don't make their life too easy

I have started to notice many young adults reluctant to finish university and keen to continue studying well into their twenties or thirties. Only recently has it dawned on me why.

A few months ago, one of my clients was tossing up between getting a job in another city after his four-year degree, or going on to study a postgraduate degree. 'But I am only going to be paid between $40,000 and $50,000 in the job,' he said. 'It isn't a lot and I think I'd prefer to keep studying.'

I thought about this conversation for a long time. I remember how excited I was when I got my first job after my initial teaching degree. After years of doing it tough as a student, attending college in a city away from my small home town and living in particularly basic accommodation, I was going to be able to go out to dinner, buy myself nice things, and live a comfortable life. I couldn't wait to start working! So why was my client so reluctant when I had been so keen?

I started to reflect on his life. He lived with his parents in a very nice house in the inner city. He had his own bedroom and bathroom, a computer and free internet, great clothes, his phone paid for, and a car given to him by his parents. He had all of this without doing any paid work, and his study included four months of holidays a year. I did some quick sums and I worked out that as a student, my client was living a $70,000–$80,000 life. Working in another city would be a step down for him; he would actually be better off living with his parents and going back to university. A paid job at his stage of career just couldn't compete with his life as a student.

I have treated many people in situations where a young adult is living at home and does not really want to go to work or put their best efforts into university. And if I think about it, there is no way a paid job could compete with the sweet life they have living with their parents. Why on earth would they want to grow up, study, get a job and move out of home, when their life at home is the best deal going? In fact, where can I hire some parents for the same fabulous deal?

In our desire to give our children good lives,
we have made things too comfortable for them.

We effectively put our bonsai children on a great salary from a young age, so they get used to living a charmed life without effort on their part. This has a huge impact on the child: it makes them unwilling or incapable of moving on to become an independent adult whose conditions and lifestyle may be less charmed. So they stay under their parents' roof and remain on their payroll.

Assess your child's current salary

As an exercise, I want you to think of the life you are giving your child: their accommodation, the quality and abundance of the food in the cupboard and fridge, their life at school, their holidays, their social life, and their transport (i.e. you driving them everywhere, I'm guessing). Now I want you to think of what they need to do in order to earn this life. (Breathing doesn't count.) Do they work – and I am talking about real work like chores at home or a part-time job – for their nice lifestyle? And let me be clear, going to school or studying isn't a job which benefits parents or pays students; it is part of growing up and gaining the education a child needs to give themselves a great future life.

If your child leads a charmed existence without earning it then I am going to be the bearer of bad news: you have inadvertently put them on the sort of salary that will be hard for them to match in the real world at their age. This runs the risk of making the rest of their life feel like a let-down from the wonderful existence they lead now. There is also another effect to be considered when making their life too easy.

A child whose charmed existence requires no effort on their part
is actually denied a powerful means of developing
self-esteem and confidence.

If you ask any adult what they are most proud of in their life, they will often talk about some hardship they went through, long hours of work and doubts overcome, to ensure their life improved. It is a rare person who will talk with pride about something that came easily to them or was bought for them and required no effort on their part.

Here's the real clincher. Unless your title is Lord or Lady, as their parent, you've most likely worked very hard to give your children their lovely life. You have probably put in some very long hours to be in a good financial position. You might even have worked on yourself to be the kind and loving person you have become. The trouble is, after doing these hard yards, many parents don't teach their child similar methods of creating success, self-esteem and happiness. By giving their bonsai children everything they want without requiring them to do anything, these parents deny their children the opportunity to develop the skills of delaying gratification and self-regulation essential to create and live a good life.

This approach means that children fail to develop the very skills that created the parents' and their family's prosperity. By giving them a sweet life they don't earn in any way, parents give their children a huge dollop of entitlement but hold back on developing their self-regulation skills.

By giving your children the opportunity to learn how to take pride in their efforts and develop a sense of accomplishment, they will reap the rewards now and in future. What do you need to do?

Stop paying them a salary and put them on commission

Putting your child on commission means making them work to earn many of the things they enjoy. The essential elements include doing paid and unpaid chores, being pleasant to be around, and being aware of, and undertaking, their responsibilities.

Behaviour charts with incentives can help young children understand that it is their efforts which earn them special things. Older children can have part-time jobs, or do chores such as cleaning the car or mowing the lawn, to earn them the extra, 'special' things. These chores should be on top of the basic ones they do as as contributing members of a family (washing up, cleaning up their mess). If you allow your child to enjoy the good parts of the weekend (watching TV, seeing friends) only after they have done the tiresome parts (cleaning their room, doing their homework), you will assist them to understand the way the world actually works. Start as soon as you can, before they take up a permanent position on your sofa.

Let's talk about some specific ways you can re-develop their work ethic. We'll start with chores.

Use chores to develop their work ethic

Unless you are so affluent that you can hire help to pick up your socks from the floor and clean the fridge, I imagine you have to do quite a bit of extra work on top of your actual job. Indeed, the large range of chores involving a child and others in the household may even make up your primary job as a full-time parent. These chores don't make your situation unusual. It's a rare person who doesn't have to do all of the chores of modern life, such as cooking, cleaning, washing, sorting and tidying up.

Make your children used to this fact of life early on. Get your child to do chores from a young age to give them an opportunity to contribute to the family, and make them as aware of their responsibilities as they are of their rights. There is no point in being a martyr by doing everything for your child; they won't appreciate it, you will give them a sense of entitlement rather than teach them accountability, and it will just contribute to your stress.

> *Insisting your children have responsibilities and do chores in the home is one the best ways of improving their self-esteem.*

This is shown time and time again in my clinical experience. I believe it is because they build a real sense of self-respect through the jobs they do, their contribution to the family, and the pleasure of working to earn the good things in their life. They get the opportunity to feel pride and satisfaction rather than expectation and entitlement.

How to get them to do chores

First of all, remember it is actually your responsibility to create the environment where your child does chores. If they are not doing them, you need to alter the circumstances to successfully persuade your child to contribute. Here are some ideas to help you set up this environment.

Start young. Children should do chores from an early age. They can start with taking their plate to the kitchen, helping to set the table, and helping their parent clean – in the special way kids 'help'! Increase their responsibilities as they become older.

Make most chores unpaid. Children should contribute regularly to the things that have to be done in the family, such as food preparation and cleaning, as a matter of course.

Set up a list and allocate chores. Write a list of all of the chores involved in your household. Be sure to include meal preparation tasks such as setting the table and cleaning up, re-tidying the kitchen and wiping down benches, taking out the garbage and recycling. Include bathroom tasks such as cleaning sinks, showers, baths and toilets; bedroom tasks such as making beds and changing sheets; laundry duties such as gathering, washing, hanging out, collecting, folding, ironing, and distributing clothes. Don't forget taking care of your pets, giving them food, water and cleaning up after them. Include indoor tasks such as tidying, vacuuming and dusting; and seasonal tasks such as sweeping, raking and other duties in and outside the house.

Once you have the entire list, start allocating the easier chores to your children. They can have a regular set of chores, or tasks can be rotated among children. Start this at a young age and simply expect it. Increase their chores and the complexity of their tasks as they become older.

Make laundry their domain. Keep increasing their responsibilities for laundry. At a young age, give them a basket where they put clothes they have worn; later make it their responsibility to drop it off to the laundry room. Teach them how to do the laundry at least by their adolescent years, and make it a chore they can be responsible for, including hanging it out, bringing it in, and folding, ironing, and distributing.

Don't give them a break from chores. Don't stop their chore responsibilities when they are in exam times or particularly busy. They will always have to do chores for the rest of their lives, so don't encourage them to expect any other reality. More importantly, during stressful exam times, doing relatively mindless chores is a great way to put their brain into virtual rest mode, allowing them to come back to their study energised and with increased cognitive capacity.

Adult children must do an equal share of your chores. If they haven't done chores in the past, they need to start to do chores in your home or find other living arrangements. Don't allow them to act like children while living as adults in your home.

Consider a cleaner. Many of the 'couple' issues I treat are often about the distribution of household chores. For these couples I often suggest that hiring a cleaner would be more beneficial than coming to see me to complain about the allocation of cleaning (and probably cheaper). If your adult children live with you, consider hiring a cleaner and sharing the cost among all adult family members, including your working children. Alternatively, your children may opt to do the household chores as payment for their board. If so, you should write an explicit list of the chores you require them to do. Either way, it will save you a lot of disagreements over whose turn it is to clean the toilet.

Teach them the value of money through paid chores

I recommend children do most basic chores without payment. Having said that, they need to learn the value of money and doing paid chores will assist them to gain some financial understanding.

Introduce paid chores when they start to ask for games and technological devices, when they want to go out to movies with their friends, or when they begin to request particular clothes. At this stage you can advise them that they can earn money to buy these extra things by doing additional chores. Ideally, the paid chores are 'above and beyond' normal chores. They might include washing the car or doing the gardening, or taking responsibility for some household tasks usually undertaken by their parents. Paid chores should ideally make your life a little easier.

The key is that your child should be very keen to do paid chores, because they are looking for the money. If you have to remind them to do these chores then one of two things is happening. Their life might be so charmed they don't think they need money; if so, you need to pull back on buying them everything and force them to start earning things. Or, they may be confident that if they have not earned the money, they will be able to sweet-talk you into giving them the funds they need. You must be resolute: make 'no chores, no money and never any credit' your mantra.

Encourage them to get a part-time job

Another way for your child to earn money to pay for things they want is to get a part-time job. Indeed, I recommend all adolescents get a part-time job at some point in their high-school life. The benefits of part-time jobs are many: adolescents learn the sense of responsibility that accompanies paid work, and the complexity of working for an organisation that won't put up with excuses or off days (like parents or teachers might); they learn how to manage their time more efficiently; they start to experience what the world of work might be like and begin to consider the sort of career they might be interested in; they become more employable by adding work experience to their resume; and they experience the pleasure of payday.

Some parents believe a part-time job will interfere with their child's study responsibilities. I argue a balanced life should include activities such as part-time work, sport, socialising and chores. If they put all of their time into study, they risk obtaining an artificially high final school result and may get into a course that could be beyond their natural ability. At the very least, your child should be working part time in their holidays or doing a few extra chores around the house.

What to do when they resist doing chores

If you give chores to your adolescent late in the game, you may have some difficulty persuading them to do their chores. This is because they might be used to having a maid or butler (read: you) who looks after their every need. When you introduce the idea that they need to work a little for their lovely existence by doing a few things around the house, a child who is unused to responsibility will feel very hard done by. They might resist by not doing the chores assigned to them.

We also have to be realistic here: teens just don't make chores a priority. They genuinely can't see dirt, mess, overflowing bins, dusty surfaces, a full-to-the-brim laundry basket, or washing that has been on the line for days. We have to be aware that we care more about this stuff than they do. (Some of us don't really care that much about it ourselves.)

Because of this, you might have to pay children as an incentive to do chores if they are not used to doing them, or if they can't see things in the house that need addressing. This is not ideal, but you have to work with your situation. I'll give you my recommendations.

Stop buying them everything they want. Tell your child they can now earn money by doing chores around the house. Give them a list of things that need to be done and how much money they can make on each activity and then let them choose. Avoid setting the payment too high – they have to have a realistic idea of what their work is worth. Tell them they have to do the chores each day/week to earn this money and let them know there will never be any credit on payment.

Try this for a few weeks and see how it goes. You should not have to nag them at all to do chores. If you have to remind them, it suggests to me that you are paying for too many of the things they want and they don't need to earn money. Reduce your payment contribution to items they desire, to see if their increased need for money reminds them to do the chores. If this doesn't work, I recommend the *chore jar* approach. Indeed, you might decide to start off with this approach.

Adopt the chore jar approach. Get yourself enough jars to have one for each child doing chores and one for the parent/s. After your child has chosen the chores they want to do, explain clearly when they need to have completed the chore to get the payment. You might say, 'The dishwasher has to be unpacked in the morning by 7.15 am for you to make the 50 cents. If it is not done by then and I have to do it, I will earn the 50 cents.' So when it comes around to 7.15 am, if your child has done the chore, you pop 50 cents in their jar to give them at the end of the week. If it is not done, you unpack the dishwasher and you put the 50 cents in your jar. Sometimes to gently remind them, at 7.10 am you might say 'Looks like I am earning some money this morning!' Never let them do it at 7.16 am – you are teaching them responsibility here.

Some children who are not very materialistic may not really want things that cost money. Get creative with what they earn by determining their currency. It might be time watching TV or time on the computer that they earn by doing chores. Perhaps they could swap the money they have earned to buy TV time, computer time or horse-riding lessons. Every child has something they like to spend time doing or spend money on: your job is to find their currency, and then pull back on giving it freely so they have to earn it. Remember your child is on commission to help them feel good about the fact that it is their efforts that give them a good life.

Rules, routines and chores form the first component of the combination code required for your child to develop self-regulation. Now let's talk about the second component – effective instructions.

Effective instructions

As a former teacher, I know the importance of instructions. I know that communication is less about the language in the declaration and more about the timing, tone, confidence in delivery, the expectation of a successful outcome, and assurance in one's ability to deal with whatever happens next.

As an early-career teacher it took some time to figure this out. At first I thought it was all about stating instructions loudly to show I was boss. That didn't work. I tried the obvious threats: 'If this class doesn't behave in this lesson then I am keeping you in for lunch.' That didn't work either. I tried being their pal and being funny when first meeting a new class. That also didn't work.

It took me much frustration and almost all of my first year as a teacher, before I found the perfect 'teacher voice' that worked every time. Then I found I could walk into any new classroom and get the students to behave well and do the work assigned, even if they didn't know me. I could even have a bit of a joke by the end of a 45-minute class. All achieved simply with my teacher voice. I now find I can use my teacher voice in any situation where children or teens who don't know me aren't doing the right thing – at the movies when kids are talking behind me, or when a child is doing something dangerous out of sight of their parent, and I have to step in.

The way you give instructions is actually more than half the battle to get children to comply with your instructions.

I will go through the essential elements of effective instructions. I'll give you the tools to learn how to use your voice to its best advantage to encourage your child to follow your instructions. I'll also explain how to deliver instructions in the most effective manner. Being able to watch the movies in peace without noisy kids in the immediate vicinity will be an added bonus.

Choose your moment

Choosing the right moment to give instructions is essential. As a teacher, I would sometimes stand at the front of the class and wait until they calmed down before telling them what I would like them to do.

There is no point in giving instructions by speaking over your child, or when they are completely absorbed in a task, because their minds are elsewhere and they won't hear you. Likewise there is no point in calling instructions from afar because you'll have to raise your voice, which will reduce your authority. And even then you are not likely to have their attention. If at all possible, choose the moment wisely.

Get their attention

Ideally, get close to your child when giving an important instruction. Be near enough to them that you don't have to shout out the instruction. You can bend down to their level and look them in the eye when you tell them what to do. This way you know they are listening.

Sometimes your first instruction might signal what is about to come: 'In five minutes, you'll have to stop playing because Grandma is coming over,' or 'When Barney finishes, it's time for a bath.' But it's not always essential to provide this signal of what is to come. Children should be able to do what you tell them without five-minute warnings, but occasionally an indication of what is about to happen will suit some situations and some children.

Use a calm stance and voice

Make sure that you deliver your instruction in a calm manner. Your tone should be relatively warm and relaxed, with no sign of tension or fear in your voice. This will be easier to do once you are completely certain of what you will do if they don't comply and you have confidence you can carry out your plan to your satisfaction. Try not to focus too much on what you think your child will do before you give an instruction: you don't want to take on an authoritarian or shouty tone to start with. A yelling parent makes children ill at ease, and this can trigger silly behaviour or make a child more non-complaint. Your calm manner will make your child more composed and capable of following direction.

You are not always the best judge of your tone. In my experience, many parents who think they show no emotion might come across as strident or upset. When they think they are being firm, they might come across as fearful or angry. If you don't think you can judge how you sound, ask for honest feedback from your partner. Or perhaps set your phone to record yourself giving instructions and play it back so you can listen with an objective ear. This will help.

Use statements, not questions

Adults have ways of saying things that children don't understand. For example, at the end of a treatment session I might pose questions to a client to indicate the session is drawing to a close. I might say, 'When would you like the next session?' or 'How would you like to pay?' When I meet a friend and want to leave the cafe, I might say, 'Shall we go?' To an attendant I might say, 'Can I have the bill, please?'

These are questions but their message implies a statement. The queries at the end of the session show my clients that we are finishing up; the question to my friend indicates that I am ready to go; the request to the waiter is actually telling them I want to pay and leave. The use of a question implies I am not telling them what to do – but giving them my preference. It allows them to have an opinion, but states my preference and usually the other person will acquiesce. It would be a rare person who just said 'no' and kept doing what they were doing. Most adults would understand it was a statement disguised as a question, and if they wanted to disagree they would explain why.

Adults can understand and discern this difference much better than children, because we have a fully formed adult brain, and we are better able to notice subtleties. Children can't really pick up such subtleties, particularly if they are really involved in what they are doing. When you ask a child, 'Would you like to have a bath?' they are listening to your request as if it is a genuine question. So they will reply as if you are taking a 'Desire to Have a Bath Survey' around the family. Unfortunately, when they reply 'no', it sounds like they are being defiant, when they are actually answering your question truthfully.

In this age when parents want to be friendly with their children and liked by them, we are in a tricky space when giving instructions.

Bonsai children typically have parents who ask questions rather than give clear instructions.

To these parents, a question sounds like they are treating their child as an equal and not being too authoritarian, while a clear direction might sound unnecessarily harsh. They have good parental intentions, but they do no favours to the child, who won't understand. It will also be frustrating for parents, because they won't get their children to do what they need them to do the first time they ask.

A teacher does not use questions in the early days of establishing authority. We give clear instructions, 'Turn to page 34 in your books' not 'Would you like to . . .' or 'Can you . . .' Once our authority is established, we might adopt a more casual way of speaking, 'Today we are looking at chapter three, so you'll need your books,' but we would only do so when our students respected our authority and would understand this statement as an instruction to get their books out. There are some classes and some times of day when you would know to keep up the habit of clear and direct instructions in order to have the students act in accordance with your requests.

Many of you will have children who need every instruction to be given as a clear statement. You will not be able to let up on that until you are genuinely asking questions of them: 'Would you like the red pen or the blue?'

You might have a compliant child who will carry out what you wish when you ask a question such as 'Would you like to pick up your toys?' However, you might have inadvertently led your child to always expect sweetly delivered, low-key questions, and not crisply delivered statements. When your child comes across a teacher who tells children what to do rather than asking them, your child might find that person 'mean' or feel worried that their teacher may not like them because they are not speaking in a Disney-like, sing-song voice, which sounds very friendly.

Because of this, I urge you to get your child used to responding to clear instructions given as statements. This will prepare them for all types of authority figures in their school and working life.

Speak slowly and use pauses wisely

In busy times, it's understandable why many parents want to bark out instructions to get their child to comply quickly. But I encourage you to think about speaking more slowly and calmly. This will ensure your voice doesn't stress your child and make them less likely to be calm.

Use your pauses wisely. Sometimes after saying their name, wait a little. The solemnity of speaking slowly and calmly will signal to them that the instruction is important and they should act promptly.

Use few words

Parents often make the mistake of using too many words. Research shows that the more reasons we give to someone as to why they should do an action, the more the other person thinks the action is *not* important or essential. This is because the more justification you use, the more it sounds like a dubious plan or that you doubt its veracity or usefulness.

Use few words when telling your child what to do.

This will allow them to focus on your instructions, not on your justifications. Remember, you are the parent and you don't need to defend what you are asking them to do. As the adult you genuinely know best, and if they disagree it is because they can't see the big picture or lack the maturity to make a wise decision, not because you are being unkind.

Avoid complicating your clear message with extra information, such as how much you know they are upset, how bad you feel, or why it is important to do what you ask. Give one reason why – 'You have to have a bath every day' – or none at all.

Tell them clearly what to do

When a child is doing the wrong thing, parents have a tendency to focus on the poor behaviour, not the behaviour they want to see. Make sure your instructions are clear. Words such as 'good' or 'nice' are too vague for a child. Rather than 'Play nicely,' try 'Share your toys.' Rather than 'Be good at Grandma's,' try 'Ask before you touch things.'

When giving instructions, focus on the behaviour you want to see from your child, rather than the things you don't want them to do. Rather than 'Don't jump on the couch,' try 'Bottom on couch.' If you need to tell them what to stop, try to end your statement with what to start, e.g. 'Don't kick the ball near the flowers, come over this way.' Imagine your final words are echoing in their mind, so you should end on the behaviour you want to resonate in their memory.

Avoid asking 'Why did you do that?'

When you see your child do something irrational, I understand why you want to ask why they chose that ridiculous behaviour. Seriously, why would they pour the milk on the couch? Why? So you ask your child why, and – surprise, surprise – the four-year-old can't elucidate a good reason either.

Let's make an assumption at all times with poor or naughty choices made by children. They did it because it felt good, they weren't thinking, they thought they might get away with it, or . . . let's assume that for a moment in time, they wanted to. Maybe it was a moment of boredom and they knew it would get a lot of attention from you. And when you focus on them and ask why they did it, their dumb choice pays off in spades.

Because of this, avoid asking them why. Go straight to an instruction, or, if it is a serious lapse, a consequence. Save precious time by not asking your child an often-unanswerable question. Just assume they did it because they wanted to or had a lapse of common sense, and quickly move on.

Get calmer, not louder, if they defy you

I will discuss precisely what to do when they refuse to do what you ask when I talk about consequences, but in general I encourage you to become calmer rather than louder when they defy you. Many parents fall into the trap of becoming louder to show they mean business. Research suggests this only works a couple of times before it becomes ineffective. Quite simply, the child becomes used to the louder voice and it no longer works.

By staying calm you will keep them focused without making them agitated or edgy as a result of your anger.

More importantly, by yelling when you are frustrated, you teach them to yell when they are frustrated. (Look forward to years with a loud and annoyed teenager – bliss – and, best of all, your actions modelled it!) So, model a calm approach when things don't work out. Indeed, get even calmer the second time you say something.

Don't use threats

If you've ever had a manager who is all about threats, you will know that it is disempowering and disheartening to be treated as if you are going to do the wrong thing all of the time. Don't treat your child the same way.

Let me discuss the danger of using threats when you give instructions. Threats are an antisocial form of communication. They are unnecessarily aggressive when delivered with anger, particularly if the consequence you threaten is harsh. Threats suggest you expect your child not to comply with your instruction, and that you have thought of a consequence already. Threats imply you lack faith in your child's ability to do the right thing.

I am always asked about warnings in my sessions. This might be something like, 'Honey, it's time to leave the park and if you don't come right now then we won't come tomorrow,' or 'If you are not well behaved at lunch, you won't get an ice-cream.' Let me be clear: these are threats, just nicely packaged into warnings. I know many parents justify them by saying they want to warn the child of the consequence; however, the consequences I am going to suggest in the next section are never so bad that you would need to warn a child about them.

You want your child to respond to your authority, not to a threat or a 'warning'.

Remember that your child will learn you mean business by the consequences you give when they don't comply. These consequences are never going to be so harsh that they regret their mistake for days or months or years. So you don't need to warn or threaten them.

Demonstrate poise and confidence

As a teacher I discovered that when you are nervous, it is best to act as if you are very calm. Sometimes it's all in your attitude and you can certainly 'fake it till you make it'. If you become nervous that your child won't follow your instructions and your voice gives this away, then you need to alter your approach.

Try saying confidence-building statements to yourself such as, 'I'm totally in charge here and I can handle anything that happens,' or 'This might take a while, but my child is totally going to have a bath,' or 'This might be temporarily tricky, but I'm in charge; I love them, and I know what's best; my strength of character will prevail.'

Demonstrate authority

If you find it too difficult to pull off the whole poise and confidence thing, or you have a tendency to melt like butter around your much-loved but naughty child, then you might need to pull this trick. Treat your child as if they are your employee, and speak to them as if you are their manager not their parent. Trying this with instructions can work a treat.

Think of the following scenario if your adolescent has started to become disrespectful. Imagine at your workplace where you are the manager, a young person has come into your team. Even though you manage them, they are starting to get above their position and treat you as if you work for them. They are telling you what to do, and sometimes even roll their eyes at you. (You know the type? Of course you do – you probably live with one!)

If this occurred, you would need to gain the upper hand quickly but you could not talk about their disrespectful behaviour or how upset you feel, because it would look like they had got one over you and had hurt your feelings. You would have to be very calm and speak with great authority in your voice to make them aware that you are the boss. In this frame of mind, you would manage your strong emotions and put the upstart back in their place with authority, assertiveness, poise and composure. This is the only way you can reclaim the higher status; anything emotional or loud won't get you anywhere.

Try the same thing with your mouthy teen. Grab a teeny bit of Meryl Streep in *The Devil Wears Prada*; channel the caring but assertive Tim Gunn from *Project Runway*; imitate the tough and inspiring President Obama; or keep in mind a former manager or teacher you admired and respected. Act like them at first and then develop your own style, which might be a close approximation or another equally effective approach.

In short, the instructions you give your child should show assured authority. They should not display the authoritarianism of someone who screams orders; nor should they demonstrate the indulgence of someone who wants to be their friend rather than their parent.

Your instructions to your child represent your judgement of the best course of action for the child you love. Believing this will go a long way toward helping you gain the required authoritative stance and tone.

Okay, so now you know how to set up rules and routines, and what to say and how to say it when you give instructions. You are all set and ready to go.

But hang on . . . your child is not. They are stamping their feet, rolling their eyes and crossing their arms. They are still playing when you have asked them to put their toys away; they have not taken the garbage out despite your request; they are sitting there unwashed for three days. They are clearly not on board with the new system.

What do you do? Simple, dear reader, read on.

Predictable consequences for defiance

Childish tantrums and adolescent defiance typically occur when parents' preferred or requested behaviour is not what the child wants to do. Children can show their disinterest or displeasure in a range of ways, from quiet surliness to a full-blown, lying-on-the-floor, screaming, hollering explosion.

Being defiant or bad tempered is not abnormal. Everyone has their off days and we all occasionally feel in a bad mood, frustrated, or surly and want to do our own thing. But parents have a responsibility to guide their child to appropriate, socially acceptable behaviour. This is in the best interests of the child, the family and society at large.

In this age of emotional, extreme-effort parenting, parents' responses to their child's defiance are sometimes unhelpful. Many parents take disobedience personally and become upset at their child's rejection of their expectations. Some parents are so enmeshed with their child that they become one-eyed about them and unable to see the child's poor choices as anything other than the parent's fault or the fault of other people; this encourages all manner of excuses. A small number of parents almost encourage their child to be defiant, citing the value of 'expressing their own mind' and 'doing things the way they want to'. A few parents expect complete obedience at all times, and take it as a personal affront when their child even expresses a differing opinion. And other parents tend to let the child dictate the terms and adjust their own expectations to suit the child.

Children need to become used to a world that does not revolve around them. As your child moves from an egocentric view of the world, where they are at the centre, to become a fully contributing member of society, they will need to make many adjustments as they learn to choose appropriate, constructive behaviours. As their parent, you will need to provide disciplinary actions if they continue to make poor choices and refuse to change.

If you are teaching your child how to self-regulate their behaviour, you need to model self-regulation in your own behaviour.

This means you have to show restraint and control in your reactions to their conduct and not be too emotional or angry. If you explode back at their angry outbursts, you are simply modelling the same behaviour as theirs. Your calmness in the face of frustration will help them learn the same skill.

Remember the poker machine analogy I presented in chapter 10? I advised you to act like a poker machine – loud and fun when their behaviour is winningly appropriate, but quiet and predictable when they gamble on poor choices. In this section I am going to show you some strategies to tackle defiance and rudeness with calm, predictable behaviour.

I encourage you to implement these strategies *always*. Don't be tempted to occasionally let these behavioural issues go when you can't be bothered. Your consistency will teach your child or adolescent that they can predict what will happen when they make unsuitable choices, and they will learn not to gamble on crimes and misdemeanours which never pay off for them.

The five scenarios of defiance

Generally speaking, there are five basic scenarios in which your child is likely to exhibit defiance or rudeness:

1. When they don't follow a basic rule of the house

2. When they don't complete a task or chore
3. When they don't comply with an instruction you have given them
4. When they behave inappropriately or obnoxiously
5. When they behave very badly or are seriously rude.

I'll go through the principles of what you should do in each situation.

When they don't follow a basic rule of the house. When your child momentarily forgets to follow a basic rule of the house, try to make your reminder low key.

Solution – give a low-key prompt to remind them of the rule.

You could ask a question, 'Hey, what's our rule about speaking?' or 'Whoa, what's this school bag doing in the hallway?' You could make a statement such as 'Someone is speaking, but I can't understand their whiny voice.' You could state the rule explicitly, 'No phones at the table, Leo,' or even just look at the phone on the dinner table and then give Leo a quizzical look.

When they don't complete a task or chore. If you have set up a virtual or actual behaviour chart or payment system, you have an easy consequence ready to go: they don't do the task, therefore they don't get the sticker / money / computer time / TV time / point toward buying a new tech gadget. In this scenario, you don't need to do anything beyond carrying out the consequence, i.e. don't give them the good thing they would have earned.

Solution – don't give the benefit they would have received by doing the chore.

If you have problems here, it might be that your child's life is too charmed or you are not always following through. Perhaps you are caving in and giving them money when they need it, even when they have not completed their chores. If they are not doing chores that aren't paid, consider tying a benefit to doing the chore.

This sort of defiance can be a signal that you are letting them get away with too much. Consider changing your approach: you need to be firmer and more authoritative with your child.

When they don't comply with an instruction you have given them. In this scenario you give them an instruction, such as 'Take your shoes out of the lounge room,' (a pet peeve and ground rule in my home), or 'Put away your phone during dinner.' For some reason your child does not do as you ask. What do you do?

Solution – wait, repeat instruction, wait.
If they still don't do as you say, give a consequence.

Ideally you wait a short time, say five or so seconds. Then you repeat the instruction exactly as you said it the first time. Then if they don't comply after five more seconds, you give them a consequence.

When they behave inappropriately or obnoxiously. This is a sudden gust of noncompliance or rudeness blowing through your house, which you need to quell.

Solution – give an instruction to alter their behaviour, wait.
If they don't do it, give a consequence.

You need to give an instruction to stop the behaviour immediately: 'Keiko, give me back my phone,' or 'Skye, that sounded rude.' You might include a statement about what to do next: 'Harry, don't play near the TV – you can go outside to kick the ball,' or 'You might like to rethink the way you asked me to help you, because it sounded a little demanding. Would you like to try it again?' If they don't do as you ask, or become even ruder, then you need to give a consequence.

When they behave very badly or are seriously rude. This is a cyclone of bad behaviour or rudeness, which you must completely shut the door on before it messes up your whole establishment. In this instance you might have seen your child or adolescent thump their sibling, kick the cat, or call you a b*tch. In this type of instance you need to let them know very briefly that their behaviour is inappropriate and give them a consequence.

Solution – briefly, coolly and calmly
state why the behaviour is inappropriate,
and give a consequence.

You might say, 'You should not kick your sister, our rule is to be respectful of others. You are going into Time Out,' or 'That is incredibly disrespectful, you have a Chore Set and will have to wash the car before you can have your privileges returned.'

Ineffective consequences

Now you know the scenarios of defiance, we can discuss giving consequences. First, I will show you some actions to avoid using as consequences.

Words aren't consequences

Words are not effective consequences. This is because the language parents need to use to have an impact on their child ends up being threatening, hurtful, or induces guilt.

Some parents try to use words to show the child that their actions suggest a poor future for them. They tend to use threats of doom as the consequence, such as 'If you keep doing that you are going to end up a failure,' or 'No one will want to be your friend if you are like that.' Some parents try to use the situation to teach their child a hurtful lesson: 'You never listen to me, and I'm sure you do that at school too - no wonder your teacher doesn't like you.' At times, a parent might use words to make their child feel guilty about what they do: 'After spending all my money sending you to an expensive school, you don't even study, you are such an ungrateful child,' or 'I cried all night about what you said to me yesterday.'

I find many of these parents have to continually up the ante to make their words effective enough consequences to discourage their child from behaving the same way again. Some children, possibly in an attempt to not let their parent's words affect them, show no emotion at these tirades, so their parent uses increasingly hurtful words to have an impact on the child.

A few children actually don't hear the words of their parent. Their parent is speaking but the child's head is down and all they hear is *blah blah blah* while they think, 'Just endure this and it will stop.' Other children become distressed at the parent's words, which makes the parent guilty, which makes them overindulge their child afterward, which makes the child more likely to behave inappropriately, which angers the parent, so they yell at them, and so the cycle continues.

Saying sorry is not a consequence

Go to any playground these days and you will see parents insisting their children apologise. As they might say in *Zoolander*: 'Apologies – they're so hot right now'.

Parents like to believe that making children apologise shows them that their actions hurt another person, so they won't do it again. Apologies have the added benefit of being great public relations for the other parent whose child has been wronged, because the forced apology demonstrates that you know their kid is a victim of your child and that you are a good parent who tells your offspring to apologise. Great, you are likely to be invited back!

I disagree with the effectiveness of apologies as consequences. I really don't think forcing your child to say sorry does anyone any favours. I don't think their brain has the capacity to understand the word 'sorry' in many instances. We are relying on them to have the insight of a fully formed brain capable of judging the effects of their actions on others. But their young brain doesn't work like that. Most won't fully develop empathy and higher judgement until they are at least 25.

Remember that saying sorry as an adult is more of a consequence than it is to a child. As adults, we are admitting that we did wrong, we worry whether the other person will accept our apology, and we know our apology shows our vulnerability and embarrasses us when we publicly admit our mistake. Children, and many teens, typically don't have this understanding and their apology is not really a big deal for them.

When you force a child to say sorry, they are likely to say it with a snarly or resentful tone, which makes it seem more of an insult than an apology. Some children say it happily because they really don't know what it means; you might as well get them to say 'elephant'. These children might pour their cereal on the floor and say 'sorry' very quickly to their parent because the word really doesn't mean anything to them. It's no skin off their nose and might avert a real consequence from their parent.

A note or hug of apology is not a consequence

The other issue I worry about with the whole *sorry* craze is the note of apology that comes back to parents. Clinically, I find many parents report the same sequence of events: when their child gets into trouble for doing the wrong thing, their behaviour becomes angry, loud and stubborn; the parent sends the child to their room; then, at some point in the next hour or so, the child emerges from the room with a note. And that note is as emotive as you can get. Hearts and kisses all over it, along with heartfelt words of apology and declarations of love to the parent. No parent who receives a note like this fails to be moved, particularly after the drama and anger of the scene an hour ago. They typically pick the child up, smother them with kisses and hugs, and all is well again. The apologies are not always notes; sometimes the child comes out and says, 'I'm sorry!' with arms outstretched and tears in their eyes, and parents can't help but hug them again and tell them how much they love them.

These parents come to see me to talk about their child's behavioural issues but then they mention how loving their child is at times.

The problem is that these apologies are all on the child's terms. Your child has not learnt to be repentant; they have learnt the art of emotional manipulation. These notes get them an enormous amount of attention that comes at no real cost to them. By not complying with their parent's wishes, the child remains in charge of the household, and regains the parent's affection at their say-so. Well done to the child for manipulating the circumstances – clearly they are clever – but it is not good to encourage the emotionally manipulative side of them at the expense of their self-regulation.

When these notes and big apologetic hugs come to you, respond only a little; occasionally be somewhat nonchalant about them. Try to not give your child what they crave at that point, which is the reassurance of being in charge again and confident of their ability to manipulate you into doing things according to their will.

I am not suggesting that all notes and hugs from your child are similarly designed. Sometimes it is a wonderful surprise to receive such expressions of love, but I am questioning the veracity of the message when delivered after a huge tantrum by your child. Particularly I want you to examine whether the notes or statements of contrition from your child result in actual behaviour change the next time round. If that's not happening, well then, dear reader, you are probably being played for a mug.

I am not suggesting they should never apologise; however, never use an apology as the main consequence for poor behaviour.

Sometimes you could explain the impact of their actions on another child or adult, and then ask your child what they think would be the right thing to do. They might come up with apologising as a way to demonstrate to the other person they know they did the wrong thing. Make sure their demonstration of remorse comes at some cost to them, such as allowing their playmate to use their toy for the rest of the playtime.

Asking *them* to think of what action they need to take will assist them to develop empathy, but the forced apology or their note or hug will not change their long-term behaviour.

Effective consequences

Okay, now we know what not to do or rely on, let's talk about effective consequences for children of different ages.

Take something away

Taking something away is one of the most effective consequences for toddlers. Imagine your toddler is playing with a toy in a way that might break it. First you tell them firmly 'no' and even shake your head. You might then show them how to play with it appropriately. If they smack it against the concrete again, you take it from them for just a few minutes, then give it back to them. You are giving them a consequence that shows them that if they play inappropriately, they have things taken from them. You take it away for a minute or two only – enough time for them to miss it, but not so long that they forget it even existed – and then you return it to them.

You are looking to see that when their toy is returned to them, they are able to show you they can play with it in an appropriate manner. You praise them or smile when they do the right thing with it. If they start to play with it forcefully again, you might take it from them for a little longer, say five minutes. If when you return it to them, they don't show you they can play with it appropriately, you take it away for maybe ten minutes to see if they can play with it suitably when you return it again.

This strategy also works for other ages. If you tell your 11-year-old to turn down the TV twice, but they don't act on your instruction, turn the TV off for five minutes.

Sometimes it might not be a physical thing that you take away: it might be something such as their freedom or independence. If you are walking through a shopping centre with your four-year-old and they keep running away, you might grab their hand so they can't get away or put them back in the stroller. You are effectively limiting their freedom to do as they please.

Use Time Out

Children often make inappropriate behaviour choices when they are overstimulated. They can become too keyed up when having visitors or overexcited when a parent comes home. They might be worked up because they haven't got what they wanted, so they throw a major tantrum and their screaming and stamping serves to fire them up even more. Sometimes there is no logical reason why they are agitated; it comes out of the blue, and you don't even know what they want.

As a means of managing overstimulation and extreme anger in children there is nothing better than Time Out. It regularly gets a bad rap, but I am here to sing its praises as one of the most effective ways of managing an overstimulated or out-of-control toddler or child.

Let me get one thing straight about Time Out.

Time Out is not punishment by isolation;
it is a way to calm an overexcited child.

Time Out is not about putting them in a prison; it is about putting them in a place where they will be better able to compose themselves and then be able to return to whatever they were doing. It is not about children sitting there and thinking about their 'sins'; it is primarily putting them in a non-stimulating place where they can just gather themselves together. It is like the child's version of adults counting to ten to calm themselves down so they don't feel the need to scream.

Because kids don't have the ability to see when they are too angry or agitated, parents have to step in and calm them down, just like our friends sometimes encourage us to relax. If we don't help our children become calm, they run the risk of hurting themselves or others, and we run the risk of our temper getting the better of us and scaring or hurting our child.

Time Out can be called anything – Time Out, Calm Time, Time Away – whatever you want. The point is your child should know what the name means. So if you have given them an instruction to alter their behaviour and they haven't, or if they have suddenly thrown their cup on the ground in a fit of anger, you can evenly tell them that their behaviour is inappropriate and they are going to Time Out/Calm Time/Time Away and they will know what you mean.

Time Out is an effective consequence for children aged from 18 months to eight to ten years, depending on their development and maturity. It is probably best suited to children aged from two to ten years.

How to do Time Out

The place. Find a place in the home that is relatively boring and safe. A great place might be on the bottom step, on a mat in the hallway, in the laundry, or on a particular chair.

You are not restricted to using one place only. It is possible to set up a Time Out space anywhere – on an upturned suitcase at the airport, or on a seat at a shopping centre or mall. When your child understands what a Time Out instruction means, you can implement the strategy anywhere. In the home, the Time Out space should be apart from the action – for example, if the family is watching TV, ideally it won't be in the same room. The child needs to be away from the stimulation and attention of others so they can calm down. I imagine their room is not too boring either, so it is not usually a suitable place for Time Out.

When giving Time Out to a toddler, you might use a playpen or cot as the quiet space. Their cot can be ideal because it is the space where they calm themselves to go to sleep. Placing them in their cot is a really useful strategy for times when you are fearful of losing your temper with them. By putting them in the cot, you calm them and you ensure they are in a safe place while you regain your composure. Once you are both composed, you take them out again. Don't worry that they will associate their cot with a negative consequence; remember Time Out is about calming them down, not punishing them. You can remain in the room while they are calming down and while you also might be collecting yourself a little.

The time. Ask them to sit in the place for anywhere between one and three minutes, with no noise or activity from them. You choose the time based on their age and how long you think it might take to calm them down; make it a shorter time for younger children and a longer time for older children. This isn't an exact thing – you might look at your watch – but your child's serenity or lack thereof will indicate whether they need to sit longer to become relatively peaceful again.

The process. When they have not followed an instruction you have given them, or they have done a very naughty thing, or they are out of control, you explain to them briefly and in an unflustered manner what they have done. You then tell them they have to go to Time Out. 'Aarav, you have not done what I said and you have to go to Time Out.' You might take them by the hand and lead them over to the step or the chair and put them on it. You then tell them, 'Time Out goes for two minutes and it starts when you are quiet.' You might stand near them – but not too close – and don't focus too much on them or stare with any emotion.

The key here is for you to be very calm. This encourages them to become composed. Sometimes I recommend looking busy while close to them; you could stack some papers, or file your nails to help them believe that you are not flustered by them being in Time Out. This will encourage them to feel less emotional.

What to do when they resist Time Out

If your child gets off the chair or step and runs away, you go and get them and bring them back. Don't hold them down on the chair with your hands as they will simply resist and might hurt themself or you. If you have to hold them in the place, it is not teaching them to be calm.

They might run away a few times (or many, many times) but this does not mean the strategy is not working. It is simply is a sign of your child's extreme agitation. The more your child runs away from Time Out, the more they are failing to respect your authority and demonstrating that they don't possess enough self-regulation of their emotions and behaviour to even stay in a spot when instructed. This means Time Out is going to be very helpful for them in the long run. However, it may take some time for them to be able to use it effectively, so be patient at first.

A Time Out session might last for a while. I have seen Time Outs go for as long as two hours, during which a parent puts a child on a step, the child runs away, the parent puts them back on the step, the child runs away and so on.

When it goes for a very long time, it is a clear indication to me that the child has not at all accepted the authority of the parent. In these situations, the parent should keep bringing the child back until they start to accept the instructions given by the parent, and learn how to calm themself down and sit there. Parents have to keep going until it works, no matter how long it takes.

The good news is that the strategy does eventually work; and the better news is that once your child is able to sit still for a few minutes, they have accepted your authority, and have been able to compose themselves successfully. This means the next occasion of using Time Out should take a shorter time, and the next occasion an even shorter time.

Your child might use various strategies to get out of Time Out and reclaim their alpha status in the household. They might keep asking you how much longer they need to sit for. Advise them they have to stay quiet. Repeat your mantra: 'Time Out goes for three minutes and it starts when you are quiet.'

They might ask to go to the toilet, or say they need a drink of water. How tough you are here is your decision. You could refuse and make them stay until they are quiet for the specified time and then allow them to go to the bathroom or get a drink. If that sounds too cruel, you might let them go to the toilet or bring them a drink of water, and then start the Time Out minutes again.

Anything they do in Time Out is usually an attempt to regain control. I have heard of children urinating on themselves or even defecating. This is not because they are in Time Out for so long that they can't help it, but because they are seeing it as a way to regain the upper hand. The hardline approach is to ignore it and keep going, but if that is too difficult, clean them up and return them to the place to start the time again. Remember their response to Time Out is caused by their distress at the thought of losing power and you being the boss of them, or their extreme agitation at the time; it is not the strategy itself that causes this reaction. Keep in mind: you are there, they are safe, and there is nothing harmful about the strategy.

How to finish Time Out

When your child has managed to be quiet for the time you have allotted and they actually look calm, then you can finish the strategy. You can say 'Mia, Time Out is over now, you can come off the step.' If Mia refuses to leave the spot, then just shrug and walk away, but note it as an indication she is probably still high on her own power, and likely to get all dictator'y again at any moment. Perhaps you need to increase the time a little on the next occasion or be more authoritative generally to improve her cooperation skills.

If you put your child in Time Out because they did a really naughty thing out of the blue, then you should simply let them get back to normal again. But if you gave them an instruction they did not follow, you have two choices. The less time-consuming option is to simply give them the instruction again when they are coming out of Time Out. The other option is to allow them to go back to the same situation that caused the problem, such as playing with their toys. After letting them play for a few minutes, give them the same instruction as you did before. If they don't follow your instruction the first or second time you say it, take them into Time Out again.

The second option is the better choice because it is teaching them to do as they are told, despite what they prefer to do. It also demonstrates to you that they have learnt how to comply with important instructions. But hey, I understand that sometimes you are busy and need to get things done quickly.

No apology after Time Out

Many parents ask their child for an apology at the point of finishing Time Out. Or they try to explain again why the child had to sit in Time Out. I believe they do this because they want to reconnect with the child or confirm that their child knows what they did and understands their parent wasn't being unnecessarily cruel. Neither of these actions are a good idea because they are unwarranted. Your child will know what they did because you said it at the beginning of Time Out. Your actions weren't cruel: you asked them to be quiet and sit still for a few minutes. You weren't being heartless; you were teaching your child how to calm themself when irrationally upset or behaving inappropriately. Teaching them this important skill is ultimately a loving action.

Remember, Time Out is simply an activity to calm them down. You are nearby; they are safe. It is not an onerous task, and their distress is not because you are being cruel – it is because they are horrified at not getting their own way and unused to a situation where they feel you are in charge. It is also because they find it difficult to calm themself down. Practice will make this easier for them.

Time Out when you are away from home

You can do a lesser version of Time Out away from home, e.g. when at the park or at a party with children. If your child is playing in a sandpit and they throw sand at other children, first you could say, 'No throwing sand.' If they don't follow your instruction, you could take them out of the sandpit and make them sit with you on the bench for a few minutes. Then return them to the sandpit and see if they play without throwing sand. If they throw it again, take them out for a longer period of time. If, on return, they still throw sand, then you might take them away from the park. This strategy allows them to calm down away from the sandpit and the other children and also shows them that when they play inappropriately, they will be removed from the fun.

Before you begin to give Time Out

At first, before you use Time Out, it might be beneficial to explain the technique to your child. Say, 'Theo, I am going to show you something which will happen when you are too angry or you don't do what I say. If that happens, I am going to put you in something called Time Out. In our house, Time Out will be on the bottom step in the hallway, but if we are at other places, it might be somewhere like a bench at the playground. You will have to sit there for two minutes being completely quiet. Do you want to see what two minutes feels like? Let's have you sit there and I will tell you when it is two minutes . . . that's two minutes. Then I will tell you that you can go back and play. Do you understand? Do you have any questions?'

Ideally you won't need to use Time Out too often. Over time you should need to use it less and less. Keep a record of how long it takes for your child to become calm and how regularly you have to implement it. You should see a gradual decline in need over a couple of weeks, after which it should rarely be needed. If you don't see this reduction, I suggest you check you are doing Time Out correctly by re-reading this section.

If you are a two-parent family, you might try it first when both of you are there and can help each other out. If you are a single-parent family, then you might like to first try it on the weekend when you have a bit of time. If your child always refuses to do an element of the morning or evening routine, you might start that routine a little earlier to allow extra time for a likely Time Out. So if your child always refuses to put their shoes on in the morning, you might have to wake up 15 or 30 minutes early to ensure that a Time Out will not make you late to work. It's painful, I know, but the eventual long-term benefits of the technique will more than make up for the temporary loss of sleep.

What to do if Time Out is not working for you

When I recommend Time Out to parents I see at my clinic, most tell me they have used Time Out and it has not worked. They typically make some rookie mistakes, so let me go through some classic errors.

Many parents say they use Time Out by sending their child to their room and saying, 'Stay there until you feel like being better behaved,' or similar. They often have to lock the door on their child (awful!) and their child screams and kicks the door until they eventually become composed again. The trouble with this type of Time Out is that it *is* a form of isolation, which I don't think is helpful. Also, allowing them to come back out when they feel like it may mean they return when they are still angry, so there is greater potential for issues to flare again.

Other parents use Time Out inconsistently. Sometimes the strategy is employed only when the parents are very angry, instead of every time the child's behaviour warrants it. At times, some parents are aggressive in their instructions to go to Time Out, or rough with their child when they are moving them to the space, which is not helpful for calming their child. Some parents occasionally revert to yelling at their child as the consequence, or just let things go occasionally. Remember, to teach your child self-regulation, you have to show evenness in your emotions and as much consistency in your approach as is possible.

Many parents expect Time Out to work quickly. When they ask their child to calm down by sitting still for three minutes, they expect the child to magically be calm after three minutes of chair or step sitting. The parents are disappointed when it doesn't work immediately the first time their child is placed in the Time Out spot, so they decide it won't work for their child.

Let me be clear, when your child is extremely distressed, angry, or behaving in an out-of-control fashion, there is no alternative to Time Out.

I know there are some people who say that when your child is distressed you should hug them until they feel calm again. This solution is not an effective long-term strategy because it relies on your affection to pacify them. The time will come when your older children or teens won't accept your hugs. And what about times of distress when you are not present? It is highly unlikely that when they are screaming at the dry cleaner because their shirt is not ready, the dry cleaner is going to lean over the counter and give them a big bear hug. Nor is their teacher or manager allowed to or likely to hug them when their behaviour is inappropriate or out of control. You are simply not equipping your child to face the world if you permit them to expect all of their bad days to be hugged out or soothed away by other people. They need to learn to manage their temper and frustration themself.

I know this sounds like A. Lot. Of. Effort. But remember, if your child learns self-regulation and follows your instructions, your relationship with your child will be better, your child will be happier, you will be happier, and your relationship with your partner and friendships with other people will also be better because your child can behave in their company. Not to mention the savings on your time, stress, heartache, psychologist's bills (and wine or chocolate)!

Chore Sets – Time Out for teens

Your child will reach an age when they are too old for Time Out. For most children this will be anywhere between eight and ten years of age. So what do you do when they are suddenly rude to you or deliberately don't do something you have asked them to do? I'm suggesting you use something called a *Chore Set.*

A Chore Set is a strategy where they lose privileges until they have completed a chore you have nominated. They will lose all good things, such as watching the TV, using their computer or being able to go to their friend's place, until they complete a job you set.

The chore you set them should reflect the gravity of their misdemeanour. It could range from taking in or folding the washing, doing the ironing in the basket, sweeping the front deck, washing the car, picking up what the dog has left in the yard, washing the windows, cleaning the blinds, or cleaning the gutters. You should always have a few chores up your sleeve ready to go, but heck – the car can be cleaned every weekend! Indeed, you may want your teen to swear at you next weekend to get those darned windows washed.

When you tell a child or teen they have a Chore Set, you must be composed even if you are very angry or upset about what they have said or done. You say, 'Mario, what you just said is incredibly rude. You now have a Chore Set. All privileges are stopped until you wash the car.' You might add, 'That means no TV, computer, phone, or going to Charlie's place until you have washed the car.' Then you leave it.

The beauty of the Chore Set is that your teen can stew in their own I'm-so-hard-done-by juice until their emotions are more regulated and they are capable and willing to do the chore. The thing is, they will have to do the chore to get back the privileges they want, so there is some incentive but no imperative.

The other advantage is that you don't have to use words or emotions to make your teen understand they have done the wrong thing. You don't have to make them feel guilty about what they said, be nasty to pay them back, or show them how upset you are to make them reconsider their actions. By telling them they have a Chore Set, you stay calm and you model restraint. This will stop the matter escalating into a full-blown argument with your teen. You demonstrate that you believe their actions or words to be so inappropriate they need a consequence, but you don't show them that they have upset you; this helps you to keep the upper hand and continue to be the calm adult.

If they take a long time before tackling the chore, you might sometimes do it yourself but up the ante by giving them a more difficult chore. This might occur when you have to get the washing in now or if you feel they are setting up a *Game of Thrones* power grab that you want to nip in the bud. Just let them know that the chore is now something else because you have done the one you set them. Set them the new chore – one that's a little dirtier and more time intensive.

To be successful in this strategy,
you have to be able to take technology and privileges
away from your child.

Technology in the home, from the moment it is introduced, should be under your control. Your teen should never get the sense that they are in charge of a particular item, such as a TV. If you believe you cannot withdraw your teen's privileges successfully, you really need to work on what I say in Part A to regain authority in your home. If that doesn't work, I strongly recommend you seek assistance. I describe how to do that in chapter 17.

Your teen's occasional rudeness is nothing to worry about if it is relatively infrequent. They have teen hormones raging through their body, setting their emotionality to high. They are also becoming independent from you, which is developmentally appropriate. Sometimes, in their quest to individuate from you and become their own person independent of your influence, they may go a little too far. That's okay; you are there to let them know when they have crossed the line. There is no sense in taking this personally. Just deal with it as it happens, quickly and coolly, because you are the adult. Once it is dealt with, you can all go back to being a happy family again.

Summary

Self-regulation enables children to choose actions that contribute to their future wellbeing, not just their current desires. When they develop self-regulation, they are able to manage their emotions, behave appropriately, and fit in with others.

Remember that it takes all three components of the combination code – rules, routines and chores; effective instructions; and predictable consequences for defiance – to successfully develop your child's self-regulation.

Follow these strategies:

- Ensure you are always in charge
- Develop and consistently enforce basic house rules
- Develop morning and night-time routines for your child to follow
- Put your child on commission to earn the good things they enjoy
- Give your child paid and unpaid chores
- Encourage them to work part time when they are old enough
- Reduce the things you pay for and introduce the chore jar technique when chores aren't done
- Give clear, concise and confident instructions
- Tell (don't ask) them to do things and avoid threats and warnings
- Remind them of the rules and give a consequence when they are defiant
- Give effective consequences, such as taking something away from them for a short time, Time Out, or a Chore Set
- Once they complete the consequences for their inappropriate behaviour, return to being a happy household.

CHAPTER 14

Step back – so they step up

Parents can help their children develop responsibility and maturity by allowing them to become gradually less dependent on the adults in their lives and more capable and confident in themselves. In short, parents need to step back to allow their child to step up.

As I start to write this chapter, it's 'Schoolies Week' in Australia, when thousands of teenagers flock to the Gold Coast and other beachside cities to partake in a week-long summer party to celebrate the end of their schooling.

It is almost every teen's dream to go to Schoolies and almost every parent's worst nightmare. Send their precious 17- or 18-year-old to a party for a week where they stay with their friends in hotels and are exposed to alcohol, sex, drugs, and ~~rock'n'roll~~ hip-hop? Are you mad? No wonder it is estimated that a third of parents forbid their teen to attend.

The week is certainly one the media lap up. Parents are terrified by images of drunk, scantily clad, amorous or violent teens splashed across the papers – even though the majority of teens are well behaved and safe.

I understand parents feel concerned about what will happen to their child when exposed to such revelry. But I find their paranoia remarkable when, in a few weeks or months, their child will become an adult and be exposed to all of the supposed dangers present at Schoolies on any weekend, weeknight or even weekday of the year.

I also find it intriguing that parents appear to believe Schoolies to be their child's first encounter with these opportunities and pressures, and by avoiding Schoolies, their child will remain unchallenged by such dangers. I think this simplification ignores the reality of the world our children face from a much younger age than parents want to believe.

Without a doubt, the bonsai parenting approach attempts to protect children from the risks of the outside world, but in an ironic twist, it also leaves them unprepared to successfully face these risks when they step out the front door.

By protecting your bonsai child too much, you don't prepare them to be able to face any potential risk.

To be ready to face challenging and alluring but risky lifestyle choices, your child needs to be responsible and mature. In this chapter, I'll show you how to draw up a game plan to build their independence, sense of responsibility, and maturity so they will be equipped to face risky situations. The strategies in this chapter encourage your child to take on more responsibilities as they become older, and to gain the benefits of the rights that come with those responsibilities, such as more freedom and autonomy. I'll also give you ways to develop your own independence alongside theirs, so that your enjoyment of life is not entirely invested in their presence and company.

Determine a game plan

I want you to get a large piece of paper and draw a graph. On the X-axis (the horizontal one) I want you to write two numbers – on the far left, write the age your child is now; and then, on the far right, write the age they are going to be when they face adult things, and to all intents and purposes, will *be* an adult. Most of you will choose the age they finish school, start full-time employment or university – maybe 17 or 18 years old. Give this axis the label *Age*. Now I want you to label the Y-axis (the vertical one) *Independence/Maturity* and number it starting from 0 at the bottom to 100 at the top.

Your graph should look like the one on the top of the opposite page, with your child's age written on the left hand side of the X-axis.

Now I want you to think of a future event in your child's life which will be their first truly adult experience. They will require high levels of maturity and responsibility to successfully negotiate the challenges this event will present. It could be starting university or their first full-time job. Typically these require

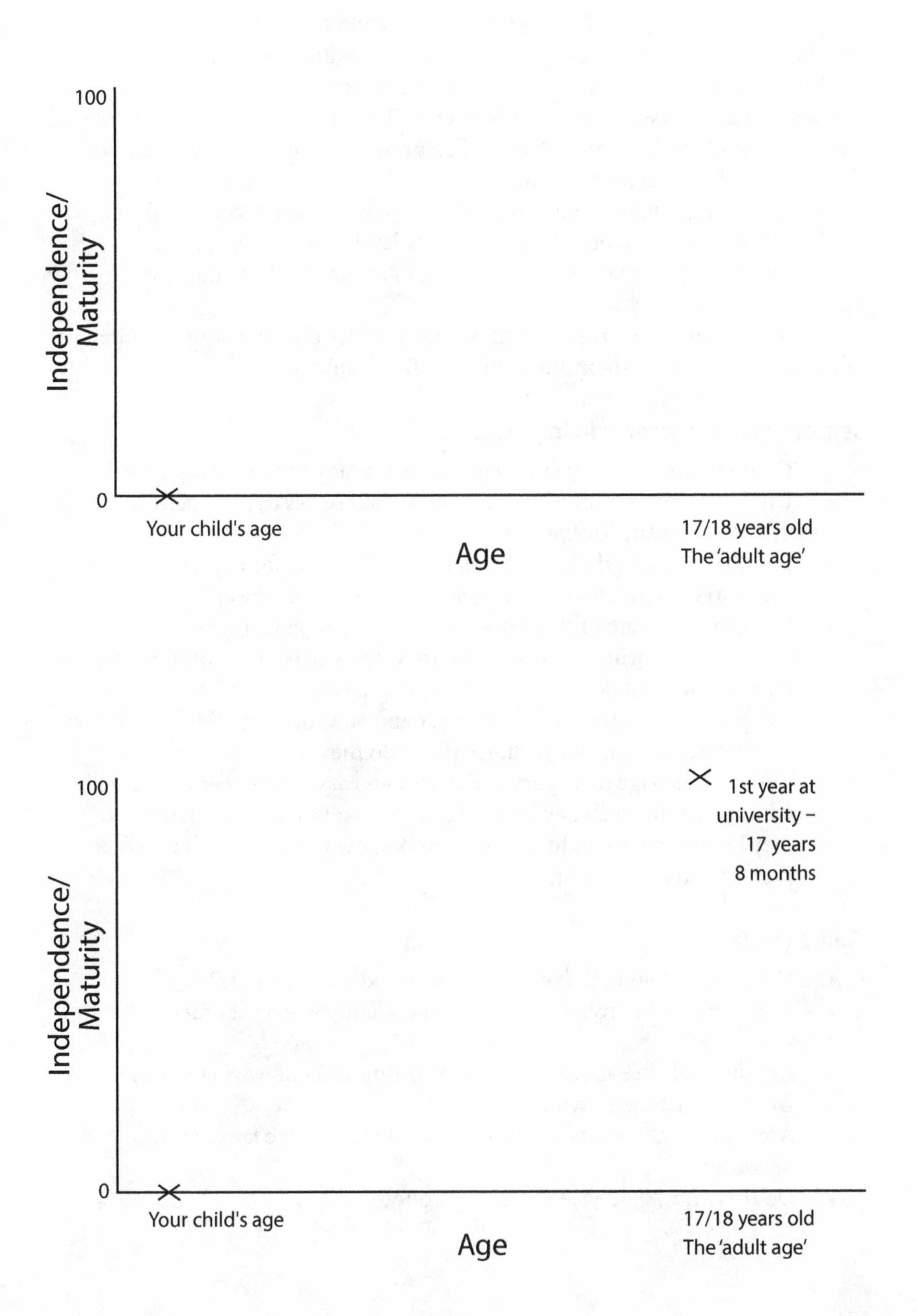
100
Independence/
Maturity
0
Your child's age
Age
17/18 years old
The 'adult age'
100
1st year at
university –
17 years
8 months
Independence/
Maturity
0
Your child's age
Age
17/18 years old
The 'adult age'

considerable maturity, but if you plan for your child to continue to live with you during these experiences and remain primarily under your guidance, you might choose another event when they are away from home for a time, such as Schoolies or an overseas holiday with friends. I want you to mark that event with a cross on your graph at the 100 level of responsibility and at the age you noted they will be when that event occurs.

Now your graph might look like the bottom one on the preceding page.

Given the event will require a responsibility level of 100, where are they now? How would you rate their present sense of responsibility, maturity and independence out of 100?

When thinking about this, I want you to consider the following combination of factors to determine their independence and maturity.

Self-motivated personal living skills

- Do they shower and clean their teeth without you reminding them?
- Do they take responsibility for waking themselves up, and getting themselves ready for the day?
- Can they manage their meals, including shopping for food, preparing appropriate nutritional choices, and cleaning up afterward?
- Can they take care of their clothes, including organising, washing, sorting, and storing garments? Do they know when they need new items?
- Can they use public transport and work out ways to get from A to B independent of your advice, your car and your driving? If they have a car, are they responsible for its upkeep and do they take care of it?
- Can they manage their personal health and assess whether they are ill, take care of themselves when sick, or get themselves to a doctor? Do they know what to do to get better and know when to pull back on social events for their wellbeing?

Self-confidence

- Do they have good judgement in large and small matters?
- Are they able to problem-solve independently when they face difficult situations?
- Are they able to evaluate right from wrong and know what to do?
- Do they trust their own judgement?
- Are they capable of making their own choices in the face of peer pressure?
- Do they show evidence of a moral code?

Organisational skills

- Are they completely responsible for their studies and schedule?
- Are they organised in their schoolwork without adult reminders?
- Are they capable of prioritising their work?
- Can they successfully juggle competing tasks like a part-time job, home chores, their studies, and their social life?

Self-sufficiency

- Do they understand the value of money?
- Can they budget to meet the requirements of their responsibilities and schedule?
- Do they live within their means without a parent bailing them out regularly?
- Have you seen them forgo opportunities because they decide they can't afford them, rather than you pointing this out?
- Will their current expectations of their lifestyle allow them to live within their means when at university or in their first year of work?

Respect for others

- Do they respect authority and accept guidance from authority figures?
- Do they accept responsibility for their actions?
- Are they respectful of others in the community?
- Do they have community spirit?
- Are they willing to help others with no expectation of praise or glory for their assistance?

Personal motivation

- Is the adult experience noted on your graph (going to university, or getting a full-time job) fulfilling their dream? Or is it your dream?
- Are they doing it for themselves? Or are they doing it for your approval or the admiration of others?
- Are they committed to this new experience? Do they show passion for it? Or are they doing it just because it is 'the next step' or what their friends are doing?
- Are they prepared to work to achieve this goal? Would they be prepared to support themselves financially through the process of achieving it, even if you have offered to do this?

Sexuality and self-respect

- Do they have all of the information they need about sex and sexuality?

- Do they know the difference between good and bad relationships?
- Do they demonstrate good relationship choices in their friendship circles and romantic attachments?
- Do they have a sense of proportion when in a relationship and maintain their other friendships? Or are they easily besotted, dropping everything else for a new relationship?

Drugs and alcohol

- Do they have all of the information they need about drugs and alcohol?
- Do they show evidence of making wise choices about drugs and alcohol?
- Are they confident about their ability to make good decisions in situations where drugs and alcohol are present?

When you have considered the entire list, rate your child's current level of independence and maturity out of 100. Mark that figure with a cross in line with their current age. So, if you believe your 15-year-old child is currently 50 out of 100 on the responsibility scale, your graph will look like the top one on the opposite page.

Now I want you to note the difference in height between the two crosses. This difference indicates the amount of work you are going to have to put into developing your child's independence and maturity. The greater the height difference, the more work you will need to do to ensure your child is prepared to face their adult challenges within the time available.

This is critical if your child is already a teenager. Parents who fail to develop their teen's maturity to match the tasks they face, do their child a great disservice. Indeed, I can guarantee the graphs of many adolescents and young adults who get into trouble in their first year at university or work look like the bottom one on the opposite page.

In this graph, the child's level of maturity has not developed to meet 100 on the scale by the time they must face adult challenges. Instead, it has scarcely reached beyond half way. In this scenario the parents have continued to do pretty much everything for their child. This leaves the child unprepared to face their adult experience and responsibilities. They risk dropping out of university, losing their job, or even getting into danger in some situations.

This child faces these risks because of the wide gap between the maturity level they need to face their challenges and the maturity level they actually possess. Because they don't have the resources to cope with their adult situation, they may not even face the challenge and they may reject their adult responsibilities altogether. The bonsai child might retreat to their parents' home where they take up a position back in their pot and get their daily to-do list from the TV guide.

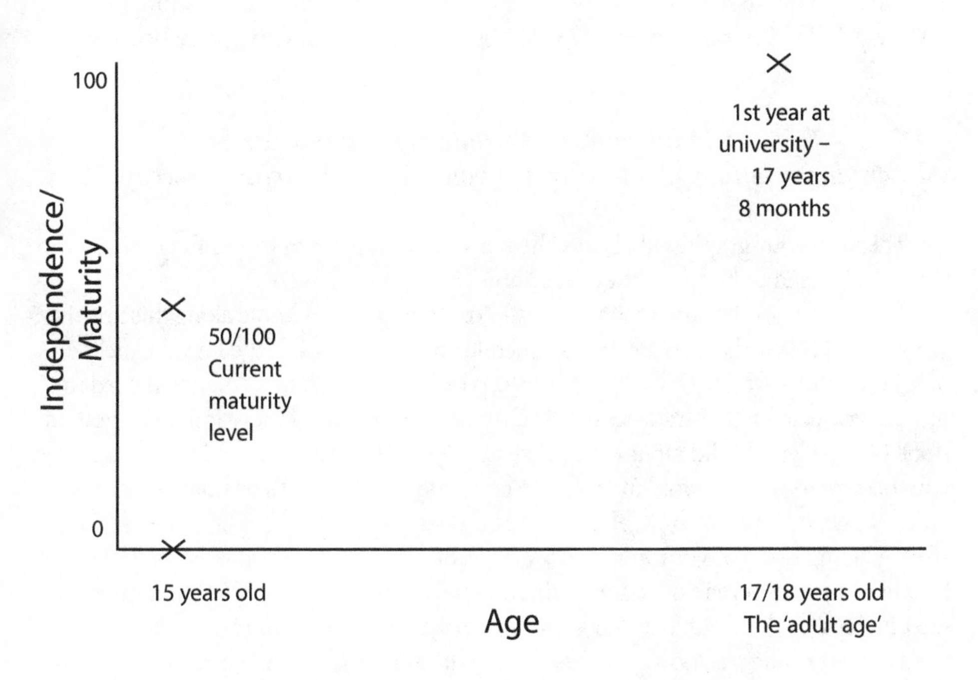
100
0
Independence/
Maturity
50/100
Current
maturity
level
1st year at
university –
17 years
8 months
15 years old
Age
17/18 years old
The 'adult age'

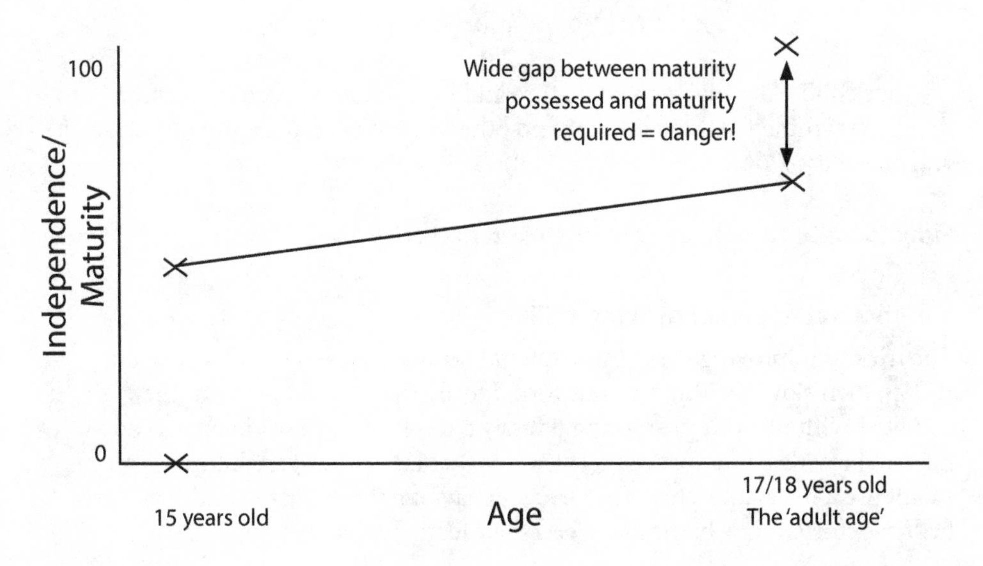
100
0
Independence/
Maturity
Wide gap between maturity
possessed and maturity
required = danger!
15 years old
Age
17/18 years old
The 'adult age'

The best way to develop a child's maturity, independence and responsibility is slowly and deliberately over the years between now and when they become an adult.

Slowly build your child's maturity and independence by gradually letting go and allowing your child to increase their capability.

This way your graph will always show a straight line from where they are now to where they need to be when they face adult challenges.

Draw a line now between the two crosses on your graph and note along this line the amount of time you have to increase your child's maturity. Look at the line, the incline of it, and the time you both have. If it is a steep incline and little time, then you need to move quickly to put the strategies in this chapter into practice. If there is a more gradual slope because your child already possesses a degree of maturity, then I encourage you to keep doing what you are doing to continue developing their maturity and independence. Take on some of the strategies I suggest in this chapter if you are not already doing them. If your graph shows a gradual incline and you have a lot of time between your child's age now and their adult years, then you have plenty of time to start increasing their independence and maturity. However, make no mistake, you need to start doing this now, whether your child is in kindergarten, primary or high school.

How should you do this? I suggest with great care and deliberation. Use the strategies suggested in this chapter, which build on the information in previous chapters.

You need to step back for your child to step up.

Your child will only become mature and independent because you stop doing everything for them. There is no other way to encourage them to develop responsibility.

How to build their independence and maturity

Self-motivated personal living skills

The trick to improving these fundamental skills is to teach them how to do things, then slowly withdraw your help. Ideally they should perform the activities without your prompting or assistance. If this doesn't happen, you need to provide some sort of incentive for them. For younger children, you might use a behaviour chart (or virtual behaviour chart) that includes an extra bedtime story if they bathe and clean their teeth by a certain time. In their teens, make having a shower necessary before they even think about using the computer, watching TV or having dinner. Because of these incentives, showering and cleaning their teeth will enter their normal routine, and soon become an unquestioned part of their day. Re-read the section on rules, routines and chores in chapter 13 to help with establishing routines, particularly morning routines.

Slowly withdraw your assistance with things like waking them up for school. By late junior school it should be their job to wake themselves up. Give them an alarm clock and tell them they need to be ready at the car by a certain time, or they will have to get public transport. Don't make it your job to get them out the door in time, and let them face the consequence of being late to school.

Teach them how to perform tasks such as cooking and washing, and start expecting them to make dinner or organise the washing when they are in high school. You could put washing or cooking on their chore list. When they are around 14 years old, involve them in grocery shopping. Show them how to budget and make wise choices and then sometimes give them the shopping list. Increase their opportunities to earn money and start allowing them to choose and buy their new clothes.

To help them learn how to get around, gradually reduce your offers to drive them places. Encourage them to work out how they could get to their friend's house or their training sessions. You might need to take them on public transport a few times to show them how to do it.

When your child is in high school, let them make their own way to school (unless you live in a remote area). There are usually many public transport options and it is useful for them to be able to get themself from home to school and back. You might have a few rules, such as not visiting the mall or shopping centre after school and being home by a particular time. Mobile or cell phones help parents and children feel comfortable and confident with this sort of independent activity.

You can prepare your child to venture out in the world on their own or with their friends. Teach them how to problem-solve: pose some difficult situations that might arise and ask them to come up with solutions. For example, what if they got on the wrong bus, or they lost the money for the fare?

Avoid buying them a car because it is better to give them opportunities to earn the money to buy a car. Buying their own car is a real achievement that will significantly boost their confidence. Even if you give them lots of paid chores, they still earn the money to buy their car. If you really want to give them a car, make sure they earn the money for petrol and servicing so at least they can be proud that their mobility is the result of their efforts.

Encourage them to take some responsibility for their health. When they feel sick, ask them what they think they need to do rather than immediately booking a doctor's appointment for them. Let them start to book their own appointments; it is ridiculous that some parents of university students book their appointments with medical professionals, rather than getting their young adults to do it for themselves. When they are in senior school, let them get themselves to appointments sometimes.

Self-confidence

If you continue to do everything for your child as they grow older, you will increase their dependence, not their confidence.

The only way you can develop your child's ability to judge risk and problem-solve is to give them opportunities to make their own decisions.

Gradually start to ask them what they think they should do, rather than telling them what to do. In the early stages, begin with minor decisions and build their skill over the years by allowing them to decide more of their actions. Ideally, start to sit back and let them make the occasional mistake, accept the consequences, and learn from the whole experience.

Coach your child to make decisions from an early age. You can guide their decision-making process by making suggestions, and occasionally you can share how you came to particular decisions. You can do this at all ages. A good opportunity is when you are watching a show together and a character has to make a difficult choice. Discuss their options by looking at their situation in a more nuanced way than simple right and wrong; start this when your child is capable of understanding this level of complexity. Discuss the motives and actions of ambiguous characters like the teacher Severus Snape in *Harry Potter*; Carl Fredricksen, the elderly widower in the film *Up*; or the Wizard in *The Wizard of Oz*. These characters are not straightforward 'goodies' or 'baddies'; nor are most people your child will encounter. These discussions about the complexity of human nature will help your child start to look at things with more maturity.

Before they begin to go to parties or events where risks or danger may be present, coach them on what to do in situations involving peer pressure to participate in adult behaviours, intimacy, alcohol and drugs, or general high jinks. Talk to them about the sorts of things likely to arise and ask them what they would do in each circumstance. If they are unsure or their answers are not helpful to them, coach them on wise choices they can make. Again, use opportunities presented in movies, TV shows and books to build confident decision-making skills in their younger and older years.

Start to encourage them to have their own opinions. Even if you disagree with them, it is good to show them that having their own outlook on life is okay and they don't need to always follow the herd. Do they have good judgement in large and small matters? Coach them to develop this skill and the confidence to take a stand when necessary.

Organisational skills

Parents need to reduce their involvement in schoolwork so their children increase their sense of responsibility for it. Let them start to remember their homework and assignments without your constant reminders and nagging. Show them how to organise themselves, and then start to reduce your assistance. Remember to make this process gradual, and make sure you start early enough to ensure they are responsible for completing their schoolwork by the early high school years.

Adult life presents multiple responsibilities. Make sure your child starts learning to prioritise and juggle competing tasks by ensuring they continue to do a range of activities, such as a part-time job, sports and fitness activities, seeing family and friends, and having some downtime. Children and teens who have learnt to organise themselves across different activities will be well prepared to succeed at university and in the workplace.

Self-sufficiency

By putting your child on commission at an early age, as discussed in chapter 13, they will learn that rights come with responsibilities and they need to earn a good life, not simply expect it. From the moment you first give them pocket money, you need to make them responsible for paying for things. In the early days you can remind them of upcoming events they need to save for, but gradually stop reminding them to improve their own planning and budgeting skills.

Before times such as Christmas or other cultural events where gifts are part of the norm, give your child the opportunity to earn money to buy gifts for the family and their friends. Paying for these gifts themselves will teach them the value of money and the pleasures and associated costs of generosity.

Respect for others

Start to let your child take responsibility for their relationships with other important adults in their lives. Be explicit about appropriate behaviour toward authority figures. Don't smooth the waters with adults at school: if their teacher gives them a detention, they need to do it; if their coach makes them sit out a game for rudeness, they need to endure it. Let them manage their relationships with other family members with your guidance. Teach them how to be a team player and let them experience the consequences when they don't behave appropriately toward others.

Help your child to realise they are not always the most important person in the room. Teach them to cope with a range of personalities and conversations so that when crotchety Great Aunt Elsie lectures them about their hair, they can respond in a respectful way without your assistance. Insist that when Grandpa tells them that long story about his childhood again, they show deference to his age and listen politely or work out a gracious way to change the subject.

Part-time jobs are excellent for building your child's maturity, particularly if they occasionally work with difficult customers or need to cope with demanding managers. Ideally your child should get their job through their own efforts. I have lost count of the number of clients who tell me they have organised a job for their child. While that is okay, it would be even better if teens could be proud of finding a job for themselves, without parental assistance.

If something comes easily to your child, they are less likely to value and continue to work hard for it.

If they are too young to work, you might like to start them doing some sort of volunteer work – primarily for the benefit of others, not so they might win a fundraiser award. Many schools organise opportunities for their students to do volunteer and charity work.

Personal motivation

Start to let your child make decisions early in their academic lives. Let them choose their subjects, including which language they study at school. You can coach them with some ideas but allow them to decide. You might ask them to present clear reasons for their choices to show they have thought about it sufficiently. When the stakes become higher, such as their choice of university course, apprenticeship, or first part- or full-time job, you can make sure their arguments show pragmatism about the demands of the course or role, and recognise the benefits and costs of their choice.

Sexuality and self-respect

Start talking about sex to your child at an early age to ensure they are well informed and unlikely to be at risk of harm due to ignorance. Most parents consider they need to talk to their child about sex by at least late primary school but this will depend on your beliefs. Answer their questions as honestly as you can, in language appropriate for their age and maturity. If they have not asked, you will need to start giving them age-appropriate information in the early primary school years; you don't want their sex education to come from someone who is ill informed, an inappropriate role model, or from untrustworthy or pornographic websites. You might want to tackle the subject in stages: as they become more mature, initiate conversations that give them more information. (In chapter 18, I include a reference to a useful guide by Dr Laura Berman to talking to your children about sex. It gives guidelines on what to discuss and when to discuss it, with handy suggestions for phrases you can use. I recommend it.)

Younger children of early primary age and under are likely to ask questions about their bodies, the physical differences between genders, and making babies. At a later age they will need to know more about feeling comfortable in their own body, sexual feelings, and what it means to have a sexual relationship with another person. Don't just talk about the stark facts; discuss feelings as well. Ensure you discuss important issues such as respect for themselves and other people.

While your conversation will naturally reflect your own and your family's values, don't let your beliefs contribute to their ignorance. If you believe there are appropriate ages for people to experience particular sexual milestones, state these as your own beliefs and say why you feel that way. Do not make threats to your child about consequences should their choices differ from your beliefs.

You want to make your relationship with your child open so they are comfortable to talk to you and seek your counsel.

This will not happen if you treat them as if they are younger than they are, or as if they have no permission to make independent decisions.

Don't leave the 'big talk' about sex until a certain older age. Children develop differently and often parents leave the serious discussion until it is too late. And make sure you have this conversation several times, not once. Research shows that many children don't think their parents have discussed sex with them, even though parents believe they have had 'the discussion'. Make sure your conversations show a non-judgemental attitude; some children believe these discussions show whether a parent will be supportive of their sexual orientation.

Ensure you stay calm in these conversations, and open to their questions. Don't make a big deal about things they ask: inquisitive children ask a lot of questions. Encourage them to talk at least as much as you do, if not more.

You are likely to be more nervous about these conversations than they are, but don't stress. Don't get too hung up on your 'performance' in this chat, the more relaxed you are the better it will be for them. If you think it is beyond you, or you haven't been clear or helpful in previous discussions, consider asking for help from a trusted adult, such as an aunt or uncle they get on well with, or a close family friend.

Don't just tell them 'the rules'. When they are in late childhood and early teens, these conversations should always include information about pregnancy and information about STDs, but make sure you also discuss the pleasures of exploring their body with another person and on their own. You do not want to raise them to be passive or hesitant to insist on their experience being as pleasurable as it is for the other person. This is especially important for daughters.

On a related topic, make sure you always model good relationships. If you are partnered, ensure you show respect to each other. Don't always be angry with each other, and never demonstrate abusive or controlling behaviour or indicate you are willing to put up with any type of abusive behaviour. If such a negative situation occurs between you and your partner, consider whether remaining a two-parent family will model an unhappy relationship as the norm for your child. Relationships are complex; get professional help if yours is in a mess.

Your child should learn that a good relationship is based on mutual respect where partners prioritise each other's needs, although not at the expense of their own basic satisfaction. Happy partners typically feel contented and comfortable in their relationship. They allow time for family, friends, work and study, as well as time together and alone. They enjoy good communication and occasional fun together. Ideally parents' own relationships are role models for these important qualities. I would always counsel that two happy parents, even if separated, are better for your child than two unhappy partnered parents.

Drugs and alcohol

I have similar recommendations about the importance of good communication with your child about drugs and alcohol. You need to talk with your child and answer their questions about drugs and alcohol to the best of your knowledge and with their maturity in mind. Your child is in a better position to make wise choices when they are well informed about the potential effects of drugs and alcohol.

Drug-related news stories present opportunities for you to discuss the topic. Remember drugs aren't just sold on street corners: your conversations need to include discussions about painkillers and medications.

Your lack of knowledge about drugs may make these conversations difficult for you. As a professional working with teens, I know it is difficult to keep up with changes in the popularity of certain drugs and the names they are called. If you need assistance here, Paul Dillon has written an excellent book: *Teenagers, Alcohol and Drugs*. Dillon answers questions parents commonly ask about young people and drugs; he also reminds us that there are many teens who *don't* drink alcohol or take drugs. Indeed, recent research suggests that rates of alcohol consumption in Australian teens are actually declining. Don't be under the misapprehension that excessive alcohol use is an inevitable part of a teenager's life.

Assist your child to face situations involving alcohol and drugs by improving their confidence to stand up for themselves, and encouraging them to make decisions in their best interest.

Developing their confidence (chapter 10), social skills (chapter 11), and ability to self-regulate (chapter 13) will help here, as well as using the techniques I talk about in this chapter to encourage their strength of character and maturity. You may also need to coach them on ways to cope if their peers pressure them to drink or take drugs. You might talk to them about your responses when unwanted drink or drugs were offered to you when you were young, if you are comfortable with the conversation. A prepared child is better able to cope with challenges.

Facing risky situations

If you adopt the strategies I have given, you will be more confident to allow your child to go to parties and participate in activities on their own. However, I understand many parents will continue to feel hesitant and nervous about this. Let's go through some fundamental procedures to enable your child to take part gradually in more independent and grown-up activities, and allow you to be comfortable to let them do this. An essential prerequisite for the following strategies is that you are already developing their maturity, independence and responsibility in the techniques I have discussed so far.

Plan it out

First think about the activities your child is likely to want to do as they start to mature and begin to expand their social life. You might put together a list of activities: things they will do on their own; movies and concerts with their friends; visits to their friends' places at increasingly later times; dates; part-time jobs; using public transport, walking, or cycling to school with friends or on their own; staying the night at friends' places; and trips away.

Then rank the activities on your list in order of the degree of maturity and independence required to navigate them successfully. Something like going to the corner shop on the same block as your house might come first, because it requires a low degree of maturity; going to a party without adults present, or going away for the weekend with friends, might come last because a high degree of maturity is required.

Then consider the age you think your child would need to be to do each activity. Write this age alongside each one. Aim to ensure these activities represent a gradual development of confidence and independence, which allows them to slowly mature and become independent at a rate that doesn't overwhelm their capabilities.

If you wish, you can make this plan with your child or teen. You might sit down with them and talk about your desire for them to slowly become more independent and begin to do more grown-up activities. You could write down the major activities and put them in the order you agree on together. This will allow your child to let you know what they feel confident about facing, and what they see as the degree of difficulty involved in each activity.

Once you have established the hierarchy, you can begin to allow your child to face these situations in order of difficulty.

With each activity you might like to go through the following strategies to ensure they are ready to face its challenges.

Discuss the activity together

Schedule a time to sit with your child or teen and discuss the activity they are about to undertake. Good times are when you are driving somewhere, when you are walking, or doing an activity together such as gardening. Try to ensure that others are not around; you both want to feel comfortable.

In the discussion, talk about what they will be doing and what you expect will happen. Don't dictate the conversation or talk at them; you want to discuss the event openly.

Help them develop a plan

They will need to be aware of what they must organise in order to do the activity successfully. To get themselves to a concert, they may need to take public transport, organise a lift or have you drive them there. You might ask them to look up the transport timetable and then come to you with a plan. You might give them a few tips, such as suggesting they get an earlier bus or train than absolutely necessary to be sure of arriving on time. This way you increase their skill in being well prepared.

Of course, not everything is always going to go perfectly to plan. Give them tips on what to do if they miss their bus or train, lose their friend at the concert, or find out their designated driver is late. Think of some unusual things which might occur and get them to think what they would do in these situations. You are checking their maturity and problem-solving skills to see if they are ready to face the activity. Depending on their responses, you may need to coach them further or insert a few more preliminary activities for them to develop the required skills.

State your expectations and rules about the event

Communicate to your child or teen your requirements as to how the event should happen, such as the day and time you will allow them to go to the shopping mall or the movies; your expectations of their behaviour, such as the time you expect them home by; and your rules in regard to the event, such as whether you allow them to drink alcohol. You might also want to meet the friends they are going out with, or their date; or you might call the parents of the child who is having the party.

While you are the one who is setting these requirements according to your beliefs and values, don't dictate the terms in a manner that makes them feel disempowered. Ideally try to gain your teenager's input here. You want them to understand and agree to the rules; you also want them to feel you are treating them as mature and that you trust them to contribute to the discussion and decision-making.

Make sure you are really clear with your child or teen about the benefits of following the rules – for example, if they are home by the time you specify, you will allow them to go to the next event.

It is very important for you to clearly set up and explain the consequences should they not follow the rules. This is not a threat; it is so they know what will happen and can choose their actions fully aware of the consequences. More importantly, by working out what will happen should they get home late, your anger or fear won't make you go overboard on the consequences and ground them until they are 25!

Develop a contingency plan

Of course, your child or teen will not be the only one at these events. They might be subject to peer pressure, or there may be others present who may not be as mature as your child. There is a possibility their friends' behaviour may put your child at risk. Discuss what might happen and help them develop a plan to deal with peer pressure to do silly or dangerous things such as high jinks, drinking or sexual activity they may not be ready for. Other situations may arise: their designated driver may get drunk and be unable to drive or be driving dangerously, or they may find themselves in a place where they don't feel safe. Your job here is to use your knowledge to bring up the sorts of things that might occur and help them develop a contingency plan. You might get them to practise what they would say or do.

Sometimes you may find these conversations uncomfortable. For example, if your teen is going on a date, you may need to talk about what might happen when they are alone with their date and how to stop things if the situation starts to feel uncomfortable or unsafe for them. You may need to teach your teen some clear ways of assertively communicating their expectations and feelings. Depending on the gender of your child, you may need to educate them about arousal and their rights and responsibilities when being intimate with another person.

I strongly recommend you clearly communicate to your child your desire to keep them safe. Make sure they understand that you would always prefer them to call you at any sign of difficulty rather than remain exposed to risk. You don't want them to be fearful of your reaction to a situation and not call you when they are in danger.

Make sure your child is always comfortable to talk to you, even in times of difficulty that may have been caused by their choices or actions.

There is a view that teens of parents who have zero tolerance to drinking, drugs, or sexual activity are more exposed to risk, because when they get into danger they are less likely to seek a parent's help for fear of the parent's reaction to their drug or alcohol consumption. Make sure your child is confident they can speak to you regardless of their circumstances and their choices.

Discuss the event when it is over

Schedule some time the day after the activity to discuss how it went. Broadly talk about what happened and chat about their enjoyment of the activity before you discuss their compliance with the rules. If they broke a rule, such as not being home on time, don't allow your child's creative excuses to let them get away with it. If you become distracted by their clever imagination and ability to stretch the truth, you will not deal with the actual reason which made them late home, or smelling of smoke or alcohol. Think back to your own childhood and remember how you were creative with your explanations of poor choices; if you were a goody-two-shoes, I'm sure you have someone in your family who can clue you into the clever excuses they used.

Remember the consequences for their behaviour are not so bad; they will just miss out on the next activity. Don't ever bend the rules you have set. This will ensure your child understands that all rights come with responsibilities and poor choices come with consequences.

Link their rights to their responsibilities

Your child may be desperate to start taking advantage of their slowly growing rights, but not so keen to undertake their increasing responsibilities.

You must link their rights to successful completion of their responsibilities as they reach particular ages. Set out a plan of the responsibilities you require them to fulfil in each coming year (or six month blocks of time). Let them know that if they carry out these responsibilities as they reach particular ages, they will earn the right to be involved in more mature activities. So, if your 14-year-old completes their homework without a reminder from you, gets their breakfast and lunch ready, and takes full responsibility for organising their own laundry, you will allow them to go to the city or mall on a Saturday afternoon. You may wish to set a couple of weeks 'probation time' when they can show you they are taking on new responsibilities before you allow them to take on new activities.

This is an ongoing contract between you and your child. If you find they begin to neglect their responsibilities, step in and take away their associated rights.

This is not harsh, authoritarian parenting. It can be dangerous to allow an immature child to undertake an activity that requires more reliability and common sense than they possess. When your child can show they are able to take on more responsibility, you will know they are ready for greater independence.

Remember, they need to step up to their responsibilities to step out of the house.

When they are grown up and still under your roof

When adult children live at home, they should become housemates who continue to look to you as the parent figure in their lives. Make them good housemates and they will be pleasant to be around, somewhat independent, and not a burden on you. You will also allow them to respect themselves as contributing members of a household, not entitled adults behaving like children.

Continuing to be the parent figure in their lives has a few pay-offs. It ensures you are still the ultimate authority figure; you remain in charge of the household, and comfortable in your own home. It ensures they keep the house as you want it kept, and (I might whisper this bit), *it actually encourages them, at some point, to leave the nest.* Here's how it's done.

Make them part of the household team

At their age, they should be able to perform most domestic chores and contribute equally as part of the household team that does the cooking, cleaning and chores that are part of every adult's life. Hold them responsible for cleaning spaces such as the living room and kitchen. If they have friends over, they need to clean up the dirty dishes and glasses. Ideally they do their own laundry or, on occasion, do the washing for the whole family. They should do as much cooking and cleaning as you do. Keep encouraging them if they are slow to take on these tasks – sons as well as daughters.

Make them pay board or rent

They need to pay for the space they inhabit. They can give you money or do extra chores to cover their portion of the rent or mortgage for their room. This will teach your child to budget better, and prepare them for life outside the home. It will also ensure that they are not taking for granted the lifestyle you are providing for them.

They should have a part-time job so that they are able to pay for many of their expenses, including at least some of their clothes and all of their entertainment, even if they are at university. Part-time jobs also teach them responsibility and are good inclusions on their CV.

Make them earn or learn

If they are not studying, they should be working full time. It is also a great idea for them to get part-time jobs in between finishing school and starting university, and during their summer breaks. Many people don't cope well with idleness during long holidays; often their mental health suffers, or they may run the risk of involving themselves in far too much celebrating and socialising. A job or internship keeps them on track during these times. If they have no inclination to work, you may need to withdraw your financial support a little to give them an incentive.

Make their academic work entirely their responsibility

Don't remind them about assignments or give them the week off chores in exam time. Don't help them with their assignments, ring their lecturers, or read their textbook to help them.

Make them follow your rules about dinner and coming home at night

Regardless of who prepares the evening meal, if it is a planned family meal they need to be polite and call you beforehand if they are going to be late or not eating at home. If they are going out and are not going to come home afterward, they must call you. This is the same consideration non-related housemates would show to each other. Be very clear on this: you don't want to be up all night worrying. If they become inconsiderate about this, it might be time to re-evaluate whether the living arrangement is working or not.

You decide what they do in your home

You need to be comfortable with their behaviour in your home, whether it be having a few drinks (if they are of age), bringing their friends over at night, or even having their romantic interest in their room. You make these choices according to your rules, your moral code, and the comfort of other members of the household. Make these decisions according to your beliefs, but remember to consider any younger family members, as it is unwise to expose them to certain adult behaviours. Be very clear on what you consider to be okay so they understand and are able to act according to your standards.

I strongly encourage you not to allow them to have their boyfriends or girlfriends over too often. If they want to have an adult relationship, that's great – but let it be on their dollar or under their own roof. If they want time alone, they can go on dates with them or go away for the weekend if they are of the right age. It is hard for a parent (particularly a single parent) to sit on the single seat while their child and their romantic interest sit together on the couch watching television. The higher status is always with the couple and you don't want to be in a situation where your child and their partner are the alpha couple of the house. 'No overnight stays' is a great rule. To be able to have an adult relationship when they are of the right age is a real incentive for them to move out of your home. (Remember? Almost all of us had to leave home to be able to go on to the next, more adult, stage of our lives).

It is a privilege for adult children to live with their parents

The most important point I want to make is that their actions should show they appreciate you allowing them to stay in your home. It is not their right to remain there; it is a privilege. If you are always angry because they don't seem to respect you or your space, you need to think seriously about whether you will allow them to continue to live with you.

If you start a conversation by stating that their attitude is not appropriate, you must end it with what will happen if it doesn't improve. This is not a threat. It is to maintain your happiness, your relationship with them, and their respect for you and your space. It is also about you being strong enough to state the actions you are willing to take to back up what you want.

The qualities of the young adult living under your roof will be the result of the behaviours and respect you demand of them in their childhood and adolescence.

The truly loving parent guides their child to be a good and considerate human being. Sort this out now in their childhood and early teens, to ensure they continue to be a pleasant person in their young adult years and to give you both the best chance of maintaining a wonderful relationship.

Develop your life away from parenting

I have talked about your child facing risky situations and learning how to cope for themself. I've discussed what to do when they are still living with you as a young adult. Now it's time to talk about you facing something that can be quite terrifying to some parents: becoming more independent of your responsibilities to your child. I am talking about you letting go of your parenting role a little and starting to develop your life away from them. It is essential for you to develop your LAFP (Life Away From Parenting).

I am sure some of you became a little upset when drawing up the graph for developing your child's ability to lead an adult life. That's because, for many parents, the prospect of their child becoming more independent and less reliant on them produces feelings of great loss and loneliness.

The post-parental period (a more neutral term than 'empty nest', which is now believed to have sexist and ageist connotations) is something all parents will eventually experience. However, some will be strongly affected by the experience of their child leaving home. You will never stop being a parent, but, eventually, you won't have to do the time-intensive activities involved in raising your child. Parents who have allowed their responsibilities to their children to monopolise their lives can experience loneliness, loss of purpose, and depression once their children no longer need their constant assistance.

Clinically, I notice issues appear when parents whose identity and sense of purpose have been wrapped up in the experiences of their child, suddenly find themselves not as physically or emotionally close to their child. They experience a major void in their lives. Some parents continue to worry about their children out in the world and hold great fears that past parenting mistakes may affect their child's daily experiences, particularly their successes and challenges. If their child calls them and tells them they are having problems at university or in their job, these parents worry that their child's difficulties reflect their poor parenting actions.

When children do not make life choices the parents see as important, such as leaving home, partnering, or having a family, some parents can take it personally, and blame themselves for their child's choices. This means the parent's happiness remains dependent on their child and their child's choices, long after their child becomes an adult.

There are many ways you can reduce your chances of feeling distress when your child or children become adult. Let's examine a few.

Re-establish your independence as they establish theirs

When your child starts to become independent, it is a clear sign to start increasing your activities outside your parenting role. Nurture your interests. This might mean moving to a full-time job, starting a new fitness routine, learning a new skill, or planning travel for when your child leaves home. Maintain interests outside the family unit throughout your parenting, including activities you can undertake in the home, such as reading or gardening.

Maintain other relationships throughout your parenting

Parents should not devote all of their social skills to their child. They should continue to invest in their own friendships and relationships. Parents in two-parent families should continue to spend time together and nurture their relationship. Hire babysitters so you can go on dates. Keep your old friendships alive through phone calls and visits; don't primarily base your friendships on your child's friends' parents. I understand these friendships can be easier when children are young, but these relationships can remain reliant on children being around; some risk disintegrating when children have left home.

Don't only invest in your child's happiness

I have worked with many parents who have sent their children on overseas trips and then, when their children have left home, the parents have no money to travel themselves. Try to ensure that your financial support of your child's lifestyle, schooling and interests is not so extravagant that it affects your own chance of living a good life when they are adults. Remember my advice in chapter 13, and put them on 'commission'.

Understand that your independence is good for your child

While young children might want your constant presence, this will change. As they get older they will want to become more independent. Your own independence and interests outside the family will assist your child to become self-reliant. Clinically I notice many parents report that their children become more capable and autonomous when both parents take on full-time jobs and are suddenly in a position where they no longer have time to micromanage their offspring. Most children enjoy this new-found independence and revel in the confidence and trust their parent places in them to do more things for themselves.

Understand that your child's independence is good for you

The odds are you will be happy when your child leaves home. Daniel Gilbert explains this in his excellent book, *Stumbling on Happiness*. He shows that marital satisfaction increases when the last child leaves home. That's not to say there are no joys in bringing up children, but there are just as many chances of happiness once you've finished the very time-consuming parenting years.

The degree to which you fear you will be bereft away from your child is probably an indication of how much you have given to your parenting. These fears are probably evidence of your devotion as a parent and your love for your child, but they are not necessarily an accurate prediction of how you will feel in future.

You can create the same joy you have found in family life in anything you put your mind to, and you can continue to live a fulfilling and enjoyable life. Develop some hobbies, make new friendships and rediscover some old ones, go back to lost interests and previous pleasures, pursue your passions. Rediscover yourself as you were before children and use your talents to recreate your life after the time-intensive years of raising children.

I'll end this discussion with a very important truth.

They are always more capable than you think or want to believe.
And so are you.

Summary

Don't leave your child's maturity and independence to chance; help them develop responsibility and maturity by allowing them to gradually increase their independence. Step back to allow your child to step up.

- Sketch out a plan that allows them to gradually develop their self-sufficiency
- Assess their current level of maturity and identify the skills they need to develop to become more independent and responsible
- Important factors to consider include their self-motivated personal living skills, self-confidence, organisational skills, self-sufficiency, respect for others and personal motivation
- Improve their personal living skills, organisational ability and personal motivation by deliberate reduction of your role in these areas
- Encourage your child to be respectful and behave appropriately toward authority figures

- Make sure you inform your child of issues around sex and sexuality, and drugs and alcohol; maintain good communication and discuss these topics regularly in ways appropriate to their maturity and understanding
- Help them to face a risky situation by making a plan, allowing for unexpected events, and confirming the rules and the benefits of following those rules
- Make this conversation a negotiation between you and your child, with your wishes taking the lead
- Link their rights to their responsibilities; make this an ongoing contract
- Insist that your adult child is respectful and considerate if they live with you; if they are not behaving appropriately in your home, insist they make other living arrangements
- Don't neglect your independence and life away from parenting while you focus on developing your child's independence
- Have confidence you will be happy after your child leaves home, especially if you cultivate your life and interests beyond parenting as your child grows older.

CHAPTER 15

Frequently asked questions

I present parenting sessions to groups of parents at schools, day care centres and workplaces where the participants' children are of varying ages. At the end I invite questions, and there are some that always come up. Here they are with my short responses.

'What should I do about sibling rivalry? My two don't get along at all.'

Can you give one away? I'm kidding – you'd actually be better to give both away, you'd get more peace.

Sibling rivalry is a ploy children have devised that works for them and has many pay-offs. They often start into each other when they are bored, so any sort of distraction is good. When they start or continue a fight with their brother or sister, they get the chance to have some rough-and-tumble action with the added bonus of whacking the annoying person they are stuck with so often.

The result is usually going to be parental attention: this is the bit they willingly gamble on. There is a chance that once their fracas is brought to their parent's notice, they will have to endure a bit of yelling from their mother or father but, as we know, negative attention is better than no attention at all. There is also a chance they will be able to convince their parent that 'he (or she) started it', providing an added bonus when their sibling gets into trouble while they, as the victim, get rewarded.

Often, the odds of success are in their favour. If you have two children, mathematically each has a 50 per cent chance of convincing you that they are the victim of their sister or brother. Many children use some clever footwork when they constantly complain to you about what the other did to them so you start to form the idea that their sibling is the troublemaker. Bingo, they have won the daily or hourly sibling showdown and, if they repeat the victim story often enough, they will likely have some regular winning form.

The best way to deal with sibling rivalry is to ensure that two things happen. The first is to occasionally reward good behaviour when they are playing cooperatively. Give unpredictable rewards, such as praise, high fives, or joining them in their play. When you give them your attention as a result of their appropriate behaviour, they are less likely to feel they need to attract it through poor behaviour.

The second is to always give both of them the consequence for fighting with each other, such as turning off the TV or taking the toy away, even if it is only one child telling you what their sibling did to them. In this, never become the judge. Sometimes when they come to you with a telltale look on their face and no visible bruises or sign of a scuffle, you might ask, 'Is it worth telling me? You know what is likely to happen.'

Remember the poker machine here – be loud and animated when they play well; stay quiet and give predictable, boring consequences for inappropriate behaviour. I also advise you to strip away all preconceptions of who is the hard-done-by child and who is the perpetrator. Many clever kids make out they are always the golden children, their big, innocent eyes hiding their mischievous intent. Your referee's decision as to who is the victim and who is the perpetrator may not necessarily be accurate.

Don't encourage emotional manipulation – be firm and fair to all.

'My teen is always gaming or on Facebook. What can I do?'

Why are screens so attractive to your child? It's simple: they provide immediate gratification. Anyone who has enjoyed the odd game of Candy Crush, or can even hark back to the Pac-Man days, knows there is a pleasure rush to be had playing video games. The trouble is they can become addictive for children and adults. Research suggests that if your child has a screen – a TV or a computer – in their room, their maths results will worsen over time. Experts believe this is because children, particularly boys, can find it hard to do their homework when they are unable to shut out thoughts of the fun they could have watching a screen. So they tend to choose the screen over the homework.

Social media works in the same addictive way. You put something out to the world in the form of a text or a Facebook update and you feel that your popularity is under review. So you anxiously check the screen for replies, comments or likes. You can easily become addicted to the *ping* of approval or attention, particularly if you are socially anxious.

Limit their time on any of the screens in the home to no more than a total of two hours a day on weekends and one hour a day on school days – even less when children are younger. Introduce a technology curfew: make sure they return laptops, tablets and phones to you before they go to bed so they are not tempted to use them at night.

Have very clear rules about places where technology is not allowed, such as at the dinner table during a meal. Ensure adults also follow these rules. Don't allow your child to multitask between two screens: they are either watching TV or looking at the internet. Again, parents should generally follow the same rules.

Make their screen time dependent on doing other things, such as chores. If you are concerned that your child is choosing to isolate themself with computer games over socialising, ensure they socialise for a certain period of time to get their internet time. A good rule might be that they must spend a specified amount of time playing team sports or exercising before they get on the computer each weekend.

To help with cyber safety, keep all screens in full view in family areas until children show they can use them responsibly. When your child is young, have them do their homework where you can see them; when they are older and do their homework in their room, make sure their door remains open. Be broadly aware of the websites they access.

Many parents insist on having their child's password for their phone and computer. I believe it is better to build their self-regulation and common sense in the years before they start using technology. Children and adolescents need a degree of privacy and I am not a fan of parents snooping on children. Have your child first show their maturity in other tasks to prove to you they have earned the right to more privacy as they become older. High-school children can have a passcode you don't know to ensure their privacy when they give you their phone at night before they go to bed.

Technology is great but don't let it be the boss of your family. Stay in charge and on top of it.

'Can you talk a little more about separation and divorce?'

Some people panic about separation and divorce so I will sort the fact from the fiction. Divorce is clearly a very difficult time for children and parents, but not something that ruins children's lives, and not an event that can't be overcome. Of course your child will be upset because their family circumstances are changing and they will not be able to see their father or mother as regularly as they have. However, research shows us that while the event remains sad for children, its impact on them typically disappears over time if other elements of their life, such as financial security, are not adversely affected.

Separation and divorce are clearly better for children than seeing their parents in an aggressive, abusive or just unhappy situation.

The effects on children of seeing their parents unhappy and regularly fighting, or seeing abuse or violence between their parents are far worse than having parents who divorce.

Although reconciliation may be ideal, if you have done all you can and the relationship is still unmanageable, then you should accept separation as an unfortunate outcome, which has occurred despite your efforts. In the end, it is best for you and your children if it offers a chance at more happiness for both parents. Acceptance of this will minimise any risk that guilt will adversely affect your wellbeing and erode your parenting confidence. It will also minimise any negative influence of your guilty feelings on your child's long-term wellbeing.

When you explain your separation to your children, try to have both parents together, if possible, and show great calmness and clarity. You do not need to go into great detail why: explain it briefly, be clear that the problems are adult problems, and answer their questions according to their age and the information you think they can understand and handle. If you are speaking to the children by yourself, be very respectful of your partner, regardless of what has happened; remember children have two parents and dividing their loyalty is cruel. Assure your children that they are not, in any way, the cause of the separation and both parents still love them; you will need to do this because children's egocentric brains often make them believe things such as 'My parents separated because I never keep my room tidy'. Make sure you are able to tell them what will happen with their living arrangements so you can reassure them. Look relaxed if you need to explain that all of the details are not fully ironed out.

When you are in a shared custody arrangement, make sure you don't set one parent against the other. Try not to be too interested in what happens at the other parent's place, and avoid using your child as a go-between. Some children manipulate information; others find the grilling for detail to be very distressing.

Avoid calling your child too often when they are with their other parent because this can also distress a child who may feel the phone calls are dividing their loyalties to each parent. Within reason, try to fit in with the child's desires for contact, and work with a psychologist if this gets tricky for you. Remember that if your child adjusts well to their new environment and does not miss you too much in the few days you are apart, it shows your success in raising a resilient child. It might break your heart to be apart from them, but to want to be missed by your child is cruel, because it wishes them unhappiness to benefit your ego.

Many parents want to do all of their chores when away from their child so their time with them can be 100 per cent quality time. Avoid this: you don't want your child to get too used to being the centre of attention. It is good for children to develop their ability to amuse themselves while you are busy doing the washing, or you can get them to help you complete the chores. It is not good to make their time with you super fun all of the time – it puts too much pressure on you.

Finally, keep them doing their chores and following their routines; don't bend the rules. When children's behaviour goes haywire following separation, it is often because parents feel guilty about separating and tend to relax or remove the rules in an effort to make it up to their child. This halts their child's development of resilience and self-regulation. Keep their routine essentially the same and you have a better chance of a smooth transition for your child to their new circumstances.

'It takes ages for us to get our child into bed at night. What can we do?'

This is a common complaint amongst parents, particularly those who have not really established their authority with their child. Sleep is important for everyone – so it is essential you get it right. Whole books have been written on the topic, but here is my two minutes' worth.

Be very consistent with bedtime. Follow the same routine every night, in terms of the order in which things are done and the time when they are done (e.g. dinner at 6, bath at 6.30, teeth cleaned, go to the toilet, bedtime story and light out). You might also make a ritual of how you say good night to them so they know what to expect (e.g. big hug and 'I love you'). Say good night and then shut the door. Avoid staying in the room with them, because you will make them reliant on your presence to go to sleep: when they wake up without you there, they will scream blue murder because they are used to you being in the room with them when they are in bed. You have to get them used to being in their bed and build their confidence that they can self-soothe themselves back into sleep.

If they get up and come out to you, simply put them back into bed with a minimum of fuss. Calmly say to them, 'You have to go to sleep now.' Avoid losing your temper. Follow the same process I have suggested for Time Out: just keep putting them back so they know you mean business but don't give them any negative attention and excitement by raising your voice or altering your response. Do the same if they get into your bed: pick them up and take them back to their bed every single time; this will ensure they get the message that you will not allow them to sleep in your bed. I know you are tired and want to keep sleeping, but, if you don't do this, their presence in your bed will reduce your quality of sleep and set up a pattern for their future behaviour.

You might provide a reward when they stay in their bed all night. If they don't come out of their bedroom before morning, give them a sticker when they get up, place something under their pillow or in the room (when you know they are asleep), or award a point on a behaviour chart towards going to a movie, getting a toy, or doing a fun activity the next day. As they start to get better at this, remember to make it slightly harder to get the reward (e.g. two nights in their bed to get the sticker), and phase it out when they can do it on their own.

If these suggestions don't work, consult a professional.

'What should I do about bullying?'

First of all, let's be clear on what bullying is. According to Professor Marilyn Campbell, an expert on bullying, the term has somewhat lost its meaning. She reminds us that behaviour must have three fundamental properties to be correctly called bullying. The bully must intentionally harm their target, not be accidentally hurtful; the behaviour must be repeated, not a one-off incident; and there must be a power imbalance in the relationship.

I certainly don't want to suggest that all children who are bullied have brought it on themselves. They have not. But I encourage parents to ensure their child is more able to handle the occasional slings and arrows of the playground by using the strategies recommended in chapters 11 and 12 to develop their social skills and resilience and prepare them for the ups and downs of friendship.

If your child is experiencing bullying, first coach them on what they can do to deal with it, including strategies to deal with the other child or children. If the bullying continues, encourage them to talk to their teacher. This will empower them to take the initiative in the situation.

If these actions are not sufficient, then I encourage you to get involved and talk to the school. Be careful that your behaviour does not resemble bullying. I have lost count of the number of times I have been told about parents going to schools demanding the principal's PA pull the principal out of a meeting so they can see them 'right now or else!' or insisting in loud, threatening tones to speak to the teacher immediately regardless of the teacher's commitments. Remember you are modelling behaviour for your child to follow; bullying their teachers does not set a good example.

'My children don't eat well. They refuse to eat anything but certain foods. I cook three different meals at night. What do we do?'

This is typically a problem only in families with enough money to indulge their offspring with the food they feel like eating. You don't get this issue with families who are struggling to put food on the table, where siblings might squabble over food because they're worried they won't get enough. I'm not suggesting poverty as the solution, but I expect your situation is probably exacerbated by abundance.

In my experience this issue is made worse by parents' fears that their child won't eat anything. It becomes a stand-off between the child, the parent and the particular vegetable or meal on the child's plate. Unfortunately, a parent's fear their child will starve leads them to give in and make them a ham sandwich, or get out the sugary cereal. You will always worsen a picky eating tendency when you give in and offer their preferred option.

It is preferable to give them a few opportunities to taste a new food to get them used to it. Don't make a big deal out of presenting a new food to them, or put a lot of pressure on them to eat it. The bigger deal you make of it, the bigger deal they will make of refusing it. Don't try withholding dessert on condition they eat their vegetables: you are not teaching them to choose the healthy option, you are teaching them how to get the dessert. Just because a contestant on a game show swims with sharks to win a million dollars, doesn't mean they will voluntarily swim with sharks the next day for no reward.

Often picky eating simply indicates a child is trying to be in control of the family's mealtime, so don't make a fuss and reward their power play. Involve them in planning and preparing the meal to get them excited about the menu options. Try to be a little nonchalant about what they are eating. Offer healthy options and one meal only, and let them either eat it or not. When they get hungry enough, they will eat their meal; not eating for a short time won't leave them starving. If there is one food they cannot stand, they won't eat it; however, this system will ensure they are not too fussy.

'My child is a worrier. What can I do?'

Fear is an important and potentially helpful emotion as it alerts us to danger. Many fears are somewhat typical. Worries in young children often include fear of the dark and becoming separated from their parents. Older children tend to fear negative social evaluation from peers or others.

When fear becomes excessive to the situation and begins to rule people's lives, we call it anxiety. It's the most common mental health issue in children.

Anxious people often can't tolerate uncertainty (not being able to definitively answer what is going to happen and plan accordingly) so they try certain actions to feel better about what might be coming (for example, they attempt to manage the situation through a routine such as keeping their 'blankie' with them; or they refuse to go along with another person's plan so they feel they are in control and can cope). They also predict things (good and bad) and then either worry in advance about the bad outcomes, or become upset when the good outcomes don't happen.

Be careful your well-meant parenting actions aren't inadvertently encouraging your child's anxiety.

Parenting an anxious child is difficult for a range of reasons; the main one is that often the actions you think will be helpful to the child inadvertently amplify their fears. When you step in and do things for them or excessively reassure them, you don't challenge their tendency to worry: you actually keep them fearful because your actions suggest they are unable to do the activity without your help.

When dealing with sensitive, fearful or anxious children, avoid sending them signals about upcoming events that might make them worry. If you have long conversations about events to come, or constantly reassure them that everything will be okay, you suggest they have every right to be concerned. Avoid modelling worry or bonding with your child over your own anxiety – 'I was scared of school too and it was awful, so I understand' – because you will inadvertently encourage them to be anxious. Try not to overprotect them or pay lots of attention to their fear. Don't help them too much or let them avoid things.

The only treatment for worry or anxiety that works is to challenge or alter the thoughts that make them unreasonably scared, get them nonchalant about these thoughts, and gently start to expose them to the worrisome situation. This will enable them to realise it is not so terrible and they can cope with the outcome, good or bad. Try my recommendations above and your child may worry less. If this is not sufficient, I recommend you see a clinical psychologist for specific advice on helping your anxious child. I also recommend an excellent book by Ron Rapee and others called *Helping your Anxious Child*, which includes a step-by-step guide to what you can do.

'I've got an attention-seeking child. Can I do something about that?'

Attention-seeking children are becoming much more the norm in these days of bonsai parenting. You will often see children hold court on buses, at restaurants and in large groups of adults. Occasionally providing lots of attention to your child is good for them, but continually making them the focus of all gatherings is not.

I understand many parents believe good self-esteem comes from making their child feel special and important. However, when a bonsai child needs this attention all of the time in order to feel good, they remain dependent on others' responses and aren't able to cope well without constant attention and appreciation. If they can't manage when they are not in the spotlight, they won't be able to face working independently later in life.

It's also important to remember that when someone is the centre of attention, they feel in control of the situation and are less likely to take direction. I often find when parents complain about their child's attention seeking, they also complain about their poor compliance.

Think of attention as acting like a drug to your child: giving it to them all of the time keeps them addicted.

You will have to deliberately wean them off being the sole focus of the conversation. Start by not responding in an animated fashion to everything they say and do. Try not to give too much attention to your child all of the time; and sometimes let them play independently, away from your rapt gaze. Focus on other members of the family as well, particularly the adults, and ensure your child is able to cope when you are talking on the phone in their presence. Re-read chapter 11 so you can help them cope with being one of many, not reliant on your constant attention.

'I've done everything for my child and they are always asking for more. What should I do to make them grateful?'

Simple. Stop giving them so much.

Basically, your actions teach others what to expect from you. If you have always granted their every wish, of course they expect their every wish to be granted. There will come a time when you can't do this, particularly when the stakes are higher and it's not just buying them the ice-cream they demand, it's buying them the car they demand. If they have a history of getting exactly what they desire, you can't blame them when they get angry with you and upset when life doesn't go according to their plan.

If you are angry because your child is not grateful, it suggests you are doing too much for them and you are expecting some reward for your sacrifice. I have worked with many parents who always tell their children how appreciative they should be of the school they send them to, or the things they do for them. It suggests the parent indulges their child in order to be rewarded with the child's appreciation and love. This is not good for the child or the parent.

There are steps you can take. Challenge their sense of entitlement and expectation by reducing the number of things you buy for them. Take back their salary and put them on commission so they learn they need to earn things rather than simply expect them. Finally, when they complain about what they don't have, either don't respond or respond in a neutral way without showing you feel the slightest bit of guilt.

'What do I do about tantrums?'

Tantrums occur when a child is frustrated with the way things are going. This is typically when the child doesn't get their way because their parent's agenda is different to theirs – for example, the parent wants to leave the park but the child does not.

People only do things that work for them in some way or another, and tantrums work for the child in many ways.

Parents are often so upset by their child's distress that they cave in to their desires, or apologise profusely and offer them another good thing. Sometimes parents get particularly angry with the child, which gives the child a lot of negative attention. The child also gets to let their emotion go in a dramatic attention-seeking display that can be almost cathartic for a short time.

If a child regularly gets away with throwing tantrums, they are not learning essential skills of self-regulation. They also begin to believe they can have everything they want, which is clearly not possible.

The best way to manage tantrums is not to give any attention or pay-off for this behaviour. Don't raise your voice, go into lengthy justifications of your actions, comfort them, or change your plans; simply ignore the tantrum and their verbal and non-verbal behaviours. If they start to harm themselves, others or property, you can step in and give a consequence such as the ones discussed in chapter 13, which will keep them and those around them safe.

It is important to identify patterns in tantrums, including when and where they occur and over which decisions. Ask yourself whether your child may have had the impression they were going to decide the outcome of the event that prompted a tantrum. Your actions may have inadvertently given them this impression. For example, you might have said, 'Right, we are going to have five more minutes here and then we are going home, okay?' In your mind, this may be a means of ensuring they are ready to leave, but according to them you are asking if they agree with that plan, particularly because of 'okay?' at the end of your statement. Consequently, in five minutes they may firmly let you know that, no, they don't think it's a good idea.

I expect tantrums to decrease after you adopt the strategies in this book. If they continue to be an issue, get some professional help.

And talking about professional help, let's discuss that in more detail in the next chapter.

CHAPTER 16

When to get professional help

Sometimes, even when parents do all the right things, children and parents need professional assistance to teach them how to cope with their particular challenges. Here is my guide for when to seek professional help and how to find the best assistance.

This book has been written to alert parents to problems that can occur in children, teenagers and young adults as a result of some lovingly intended parenting practices. It has also been designed to assist parents with strategies to manage behavioural issues in their child or teen.

If you face these issues with your child, first try the solutions suggested in this book. Read the book from cover to cover, and write a list of the strategies you think you need to adopt. Try these, re-reading relevant chapters every week or two in the process, to check you are on track and haven't forgotten key points or allowed old habits to slip back in.

If you haven't seen any changes in a couple of weeks, or if you find it difficult to implement the strategies, I advise you to get some professional assistance. I strongly recommend you do this sooner rather than later.

As a clinical psychologist who helps people to improve their lives and the lives of their loved ones, it frustrates me when people come to me with long-standing issues. There are some issues that become more difficult to treat if left too late. Long-term issues make the process of change more challenging because one-off behaviours have become established habits.

Signs to seek professional support

If any of the following scenarios apply to you or your child, professional support will help.

Your child's behavioural or emotional issue was diagnosed by you

As a society we are much more aware today of psychological issues in children. While this may be the result of better education and a more caring approach, it has some downsides. With greater psychological knowledge, parents feel they can diagnose and then treat the issues they believe are causing their child difficulty. Frequently they do this by increasing their assistance to their child to help them feel better. This may make the child's life easier, but it's not proper treatment and the parent may inadvertently make the problem worse.

Simply recognising a problem in children goes no way toward treating it. Children need to be taught better ways to cope with challenging emotions and difficult situations. Issues such as anxiety are not fixed by removing your child from challenging circumstances; you treat the issue by getting them to face anxiety-producing situations and learning how to cope, both cognitively and behaviourally. This is a difficult process to get right and one for which you need to engage a qualified professional.

It is preferable to seek and receive this help sooner rather than later – particularly for issues such as anxiety or depressed mood. The teen years and their rush of hormones and life changes often challenge even the most robust adolescents. If your child has difficulty coping in primary school and you suspect anxiety, depression, or any other psychological issue is holding them back, get them early assistance so they are in the best position to face the teen and young adult years.

Your child gets through because of your efforts

Today some parents orchestrate their bonsai child's school and social life. As I often point out in this book, involvement in your child's life is a good thing, but there is a point where you can become too involved.

Ask yourself, 'Is it primarily my effort that is getting my child through, academically or socially? Is it my motivation and not my child's that is producing their scholastic or social success? Do I have many conversations with my child about their academic, social or behavioural difficulties, without actually seeing any improvement over time in these areas?'

If you still answer yes to any of these after reading the book and implementing the strategies, you would be wise to engage a professional to teach your child or teen better ways to develop their confidence and abilities, or to teach you better ways to manage their behaviour and coach them to develop skills they need. A professional may also help by assessing children's strengths and weaknesses, and helping parents and children determine what can be changed and what needs to be accepted.

Your child will not do what you want them to do

Can you honestly say you can get your child to do what you want them to do with a minimum of fuss? Do you wake up confident that your child will mostly comply with your wishes for the day to come or do they always want to be in charge? Can you say your child is usually respectful to you and, if they are not, you have a system in place to give them meaningful consequences that will ensure they improve their attitude? (As you now know, yelling at them or being angry with them for a period of time are not meaningful consequences.)

If any of these situations remain problematic for you after reading the book, I encourage you to get some qualified parenting assistance. Nearly everything is treatable or able to be improved, but again, I recommend getting help sooner rather than later. Noncompliance in children is much easier to treat than noncompliance in teens, and teen disrespect is easier to treat in younger teens than older teens.

Your worry about your parenting is affecting your wellbeing

We are often so worried about our child's self-confidence that we underestimate its effect on our own confidence in how we go about the very important job of raising children. Being a parent is difficult enough without lack of confidence in your parenting choices making your tough job even more challenging. If you constantly doubt your skill as a parent, seek one-on-one sessions with a parenting professional. Tailored parenting advice often confirms to a parent that their actions are indeed in the best interests of their child. Professional one-on-one parenting sessions can also fine-tune strategies parents already use to improve the family dynamic and harmony. Many parents receive an enormous confidence boost when a professional confirms their parenting choices are appropriate; get this support if you think you would benefit from it.

How to find good treatment

How do I find a professional?

The easiest way to find a good psychologist is to speak to your family doctor. Most have a group of trusted professionals they recommend. Another way is to go to the 'find a psychologist' page of your country's psychological association website, for example the Australian Psychological Society, the American Psychological Association, or the British Psychological Society. This will assist you to find a range of appropriately experienced professionals located close to you.

How do I tell if they are suitably qualified?

There has been an alarming trend recently of people claiming to be experts as a result of having a few children themselves, reading a couple of books on parenting, or just wanting to be helpful. Their good intentions almost always outweigh their qualifications and experience. A lot of advice found on the internet and in blogs can be filed under this category.

The process of becoming a registered psychologist takes six to eight years for good reason. Psychologists, particularly clinical psychologists, have an extensive education in mental health and are well trained in treating psychological issues. There is a lot to learn before they can qualify and call themselves a professional. More importantly, they are regularly required to update their knowledge and training in the latest research and treatments in order to remain members of professional associations.

People without genuine skill can cause harm if they delve into people's psyches without having the expertise to treat them. How can you judge whether a counsellor is appropriately qualified? You can always ask them about their educational qualifications, whether they are a member of a professional association, and their experience in treating your particular issue. You can also check whether private health insurers pay for some of the cost of psychological treatment provided by them. Health funds generally do not pay for unproven treatments, which may be a waste of money for the insurer and the client; insurance companies have standards for professional services they consider legitimate.

How do I know if the treatment will work?

The only treatments I use have empirical evidence of success. As a clinical psychologist, I am not professionally allowed to do something in treatment because it seems like a good idea. I am genuinely shocked that many people think good intentions are sufficient qualifications. I have heard of many charlatans who provide potentially dangerous procedures when they manipulate people's emotions, bring up their past issues, and practise some nonsense affirmations and pseudo-psychology, while genuinely believing they are helping people.

To help you discern professional from non-professional treatments, you can ask questions. You have every right to ask a therapist why they have chosen the particular treatment they propose and how long it will take to show results. A true professional will give you or your child actual strategies to cope with your issue and indicate how long it will take for the treatment to be effective. They should be able to justify their treatment choice with empirical evidence published in professional journals. Showing you testimonials is not true evidence; that is their marketing material.

Effective therapy teaches you better ways to cope. A good therapist actively guides you to become capable of coping with things yourself, without the need for regular therapy. 'Talk therapy' (or what psychologists call 'supportive counselling'), where you just unload your day or your past, has little evidence of success. In some cases it can exacerbate issues by dwelling on difficulty without resolution.

Simply downloading your week by regurgitating your issues to someone who says 'how awful' or 'I understand' is not therapy. This will only make you feel bad while you tell the tale and then reassured when the counsellor confirms your experience was difficult. It won't bring about lasting change unless you are taught specific ways to overcome your feelings by learning how to accept a situation you cannot change or using psychological strategies to change your current difficulty.

When working with a psychologist, you should see an improvement in the way you or your child is coping within weeks or months of commencing treatment. It concerns me how many people see counsellors for years. Unless you have a particularly traumatic past, treatment should not take more than a few months. In my private practice, most of my clients see me for four to ten sessions. In general, most parents who come to me for parenting advice have only a couple of sessions with me; generally, I'd say most parenting programs should take no longer than ten sessions, unless you also have personal mental health issues to overcome.

Remember a psychologist is primarily there to teach you strategies and better ways to cope with tricky things in your life, and help you to accept the things that are out of your control.

When you look for a therapist, be wary of people who promote a particular program as the only solution they offer. If they only have one answer to every issue – their $1000 'Study Success' or 'Be Happy' course – they aren't properly diagnosing issues and tailoring genuine solutions. They are just herding cattle into their yards.

Who should be involved in the treatment?

My rule of thumb is that the people experiencing a problem and actively looking for a solution are the ones who should be involved in treatment. So, if a child is behaving badly and it is causing a problem for their parents, it is the parents who should be seeking assistance and ways to manage their child's behaviour. Indeed, I would only recommend the child attend these sessions if they genuinely want to change and wish to be part of the team that improves their behaviour. I don't see any benefit in sitting two eager parents and one eye-rolling, crossed-arm antagonistic child in a therapy room together; it just isn't going to work.

There are a few reasons for this. The first is that parents are more affected by a child's lack of compliance than children. Sure, children become upset by their parent's anger and consequences, but it is likely that the parent is losing more sleep about it than the child, particularly if they continually give in to the child or adjust their own expectations to suit the child's mood and behaviour.

The second reason is that I prefer to empower the parents to work with their child. I would only be with the child for one hour a week at most, while parents are with their child every day. If I teach parents better ways to manage the child's behaviour or their tendency to be depressed or anxious, then the changes will be more effective than if I just work with the child. Parents love their children and want to do what is best for them; this makes them more likely to carry out the strategies suggested in therapy, no matter how difficult. Parents' cognitive capacity means they are also better able to understand the strategies and coach their child; therapy with adults usually takes half the time of therapy with children or teens and is often more effective.

The final reason is that the strategies discussed in therapy are often far too tricky for a child or teen to remember and act upon, particularly in the heat of the moment. The parent is usually better able to keep a cool head and implement the strategies.

Should parents always be involved in the treatment?

Therapy can sometimes inadvertently disempower parents. When a child sees a psychologist for an issue, parents can become cautious and unsure of themselves. They might walk on eggshells around their child and may not keep up the daily routines beneficial to children.

Even when the child or teen is working with a psychologist on their issues or problems, I still think their parents should be involved in some way. These days I rarely work with any child or teen without involving (ideally both) parents in treatment. Unless the child has a problem with an emotionally or physically abusive or unloving parent, I involve parents in treatment.

Without a doubt, parent-child relationships go on for much longer than therapy, and everyone needs to be part of the game plan.

Ideally, psychologists inform parents of the techniques they discuss with children or teens, and teach the family better ways to communicate, or coach the parents on strategies to ensure the family is not overly affected by the child's issues. If I am teaching the child to change their behaviour, then I need to inform the parents of the best ways to support them or the situation won't improve; old habits die hard.

As a parent, make sure you check in with your child's psychologist and confirm the best approach you should take to support your child as they learn to overcome their issues.

How long will it take?

In my experience, if you haven't seen things start to significantly turn around after your child or teen has had three or four sessions with a psychologist, you might be wasting your money if they continue. It may not be because the psychologist is not capable; it may be that your teen has neither the skills nor sufficient motivation to change their behaviour. Be sure to discuss this with the psychologist; sometimes teens present a rosy version of reality and it will be helpful for the psychologist to know of any ongoing issues.

If you don't see much change after your own parenting sessions, discuss this with the psychologist as well. You may not be undertaking the strategies in the right way or there might be other issues contributing to the problem. Either way, therapy has to be effective to be worthwhile and if you are not seeing sufficient change, be open with your professional.

There is no shame in receiving parenting advice or employing a professional to assist you with parenting. Today for some reason it can be more acceptable to go to puppy school than it is to learn how to parent. I applaud the veterinarians and dog trainers who have made this an essential part of owning a dog, but I fail to see how bringing up a dog could be anywhere near as difficult as bringing up a child. So why isn't parenting advice sought more often and unashamedly?

There are so many professionals with extensive training and expertise who can help you. Psychological research has provided us with a wide range of evidence-based programs and therapies to enable adults and children to live their lives unconstrained by major or minor mental health issues. Don't wait too long to avail yourself of this support if you or your loved ones need it.

CHAPTER 17

The most effective parenting manoeuvre of all time

Step right up ladies and gentlemen and witness the greatest parenting manoeuvre of all time. Of all time, I tell you!

When I was training to be a teacher, I learnt many techniques to make lessons interesting, appeal to students' different learning styles, and to inspire children and make them eager to know more. One of the most useful was something called *doorknob lesson planning*. The lecturer asked us to imagine the following scenario. We were busy marking assignments, or working on the school musical or sports carnival, or we had a late night with friends, . . . as a result, we have not prepared the next lesson scheduled to start in five minutes. We realise this only when we are walking down the hallway toward the classroom. He then gave us a fail-safe technique for quick lesson planning, which only takes as long as turning the doorknob to walk inside the classroom.

I understand you may feel you have been bombarded with techniques and strategies in this book. As a reward for ploughing through all of the information I have provided, I want to give you the gift of a similar technique to the doorknob one. This strategy will help in those moments when all of the other strategies escape you.

This is a physical technique so let me give you step-by-step instructions.

1. Sit up straight in your chair
2. Lift your shoulders up, hold for half a second and then drop them
3. Now lift your shoulders up, but tilt your head slightly toward one shoulder before you drop your shoulders back down
4. Now lift your shoulders up, tilt your head as before and screw your face up a little while slightly nodding your head, then drop your shoulders down.

That, dear reader, is a *shrug* and it is the most useful parenting manoeuvre of all time.

Let me clarify when the shrug is useful. When your child explains they are having some very minor difficulty at school, you shrug. When your child says the milk in their cereal is not cold, you shrug. When your child states that their classmates' parents let them watch TV before school, you shrug. When your teen says they don't want to go to Grandma's for lunch, you shrug. When your child says they don't feel like going to school, you shrug. When your teen says their friend's parents bought their 16-year-old a car, you shrug. When your child says they wish they went to a different school . . . well . . . I'm sure you get the picture.

Here's the beauty of the shrug – it sends a very clear message. Your facial expression and nod say you empathise with them a little; the shrug of your shoulders says it's no big deal. The shrug clearly says, 'Yep, I hear you. Ain't life tough, but I'm sure you will cope.'

What are your options other than the shrug? Well, you could talk about it with them for a long time . . . but that would encourage them to ruminate on a minor problem and increase its importance by sending the message that this slightly tricky thing they are facing is a terrible thing that needs to be processed; the processing will make them exaggerate their problems and increase their poor mood. And remember, it is not a terrible thing they face; it is a minor inconvenience or something slightly unfair in their world.

You could also step in and make things better for them, but that will make them dependent on your support, and suggest to them that they can't cope with minor annoyances. When you fix their minor issue, you might also imply that they should never have to cope with inconvenience or slight discomfort. That sort of thinking is not going to prepare them for the real world; it might even keep them trapped in their little bonsai pot. You could justify why you haven't done something, but your explanation will suggest to your child that you feel slightly guilty about not giving them what they want.

The message of the shrug is not that you don't care. That you have even listened to their tale of woe is evidence that you love them. In fact, you care enough about them to teach them how to process their minor issues in a manner that lets them get over small things quickly and independently.

Without a doubt, the shrug is the most popular technique with my parenting session audiences. It's one that parents can put into practice immediately. Here's what one parent wrote to me the day after attending an evening session:

> Thank you for giving us some refreshing and clever ways of looking at how we are approaching parenting. It just made sense and I feel empowered to start using these techniques with my kids to develop resilience and confidence in them and to better prepare them for their future. Have already shrugged four times this morning and it felt great!

Why is the shrug so popular? I believe by simply shrugging you are saying, 'It's a shame you're facing this, but I believe you can cope.'

And that message of confidence in your child is one of the most valuable gifts you can give them.

So – what are you waiting for?

Further reading

As this is a book for parents, not academics, I didn't want it to be bogged down by academic references throughout the text. However, some of you will want to read further, so here are some of the references and some suggestions for further reading.

Part A

2. Parenting today

Australian Institute of Criminology 2012, *Australian crime: facts & figures 2011*, Australian Institute of Criminology, Canberra, viewed 18 October 2014, <http://www.aic.gov.au/media_library/publications/facts/2011/facts11.pdf>.

Baumrind, D 1965, 'Parental control and parental love', *Children*, vol. 12, pp. 230–4.

Brummelman, E, Thomaes, S, Nelemans, SA, Orobio de Castro, B, Overbeek, G & Bushman, BJ 2015, 'Origins of narcissism in children', *PNAS*, vol. 112, no. 12. pp. 3659–62.

Dornbusch, SM, Ritter, PL, Leiderman, PH, Roberts, DF & Fraleigh, M J 1987,

'The relation of parenting style to adolescent school performance', *Child Development*, vol. 58, pp. 1244–57.

Flanders, JL, Leo, V, Paquette, D, Pihl, RO & Séguin, JR 2009, 'Rough-and-tumble play and the regulation of aggression: an observational study of father-child play dyads', *Aggressive Behavior*, vol. 35, no. 4, pp. 285–95.

Lamborn, SD, Mounts, N S, Steinberg, L & Dornbusch, S M 1991, 'Patterns of competence and adjustment among adolescents from authoritative, authoritarian, indulgent, and neglectful families', *Child Development*, vol. 62, pp. 1049–65.

Lester, D 1983, 'Maslow's hierarchy of needs and psychological health', *Journal of General Psychology*, vol. 109, no. 1, pp. 83–5.

Maccoby, EE & Martin, JA 1983, 'Socialization in the context of the family: parent–child interaction', in PH Mussen & EM Hetherington (eds), *Handbook of child psychology*, 4th edn, vol. 4, *Socialization, personality, and social development*, Wiley, New York, pp. 1–101.

Michiels, D, Grietens, H, Onghena, P & Kuppens, S 2010, 'Perceptions of maternal and paternal attachment security in middle childhood: links with positive parental affection and psychosocial adjustment', *Early Child Development and Care*, vol. 180, no. 1–2, pp. 211–25.

Seligman, MEP 1995, *The optimistic child: a revolutionary approach to raising resilient children*, Random House, Sydney.

Steinberg, L, Elmen, JD & Mounts, NS 1989, 'Authoritative parenting, psychosocial maturity, and academic success among adolescents', *Child Development*, vol. 60, no. 6, pp. 1424–36.

3. Overparenting – too much of the good stuff

Baumrind, D 1965, 'Parental control and parental love', *Children*, vol. 12, pp. 230–4.

Locke, JY, Campbell, MA & Kavanagh, D 2012, 'Can a parent do too much for their child? an examination by parenting professionals of the concept of overparenting', *Australian Journal of Guidance and Counselling*, vol. 22, no. 2, pp. 249–65. Download this paper at http://eprints.qut.edu.au/55005/

4. The bonsai child

Thanks to Bonsai Boy of New York for information on the art of bonsai, viewed 4 November 2014, <http://www.bonsaiboy.com>.

6. Bonsai parenting – what I see in the clinic

Bernstein, G & Triger, Z 2011, 'Over-parenting', *UC Davis Law Review*, vol. 44, pp. 1221–79, viewed 5 November 2014, <http://papers.ssrn.com/sol3/papers.cfm?abstract_id=1588246>.

Part B

10. Help your child develop confidence

Bowlby, J 2005, *A secure base: clinical applications of attachment theory*, Routledge, London.

Gottman, J & DeClaire, J 2001, *The relationship cure: a 5 step guide to strengthening your marriage, family and friendships*, Three Rivers, New York.

Henderlong, J & Lepper, MR 2002, 'The effects of praise on children's intrinsic motivation: a review and synthesis', *Psychological Bulletin*, vol. 128, pp. 774–95.

Lepper, MR, Greene, D & Nisbett, RE 1973, 'Undermining children's intrinsic motivation with extrinsic reward: a test of the "overjustification" hypothesis', *Journal of Personality and Social Psychology*, vol. 28, pp.129–37.

Mueller, CM & Dweck, CS 1998, 'Praise for intelligence can undermine children's motivation and performance', *Journal of Personality and Social Psychology*, no. 75, pp. 33–52.

12. Help your child develop resilience

'Adolescence; a lesson for parents: arguing in front of your teens has lasting impact, researchers find' 2009, *Life Science Weekly*, 24 March, p. 181, viewed 15 November 2014, <http://www.prnewswire.com/news-releases/a-lesson-for-parents-arguing-in-front-of-your-teens-has-lasting-impact-researchers-find-61778012.html>.

Peris, TS, Goeke-Morey, MC, Cummings, EM & Emery, RE 2008, 'Marital conflict and support seeking by parents in adolescence: empirical support for the parentification construct', *Journal of Family Psychology*, vol. 22, pp. 633–42.

13. Help your child learn self-regulation

Fitzsimons, GM & Finkel, EJ 2011, 'Outsourcing self-regulation', *Psychological Science*, vol. 22, no.3, pp. 369–75.

Mischel, W 2012, 'Self-control theory', in PAM Van Lange, AW Kruglanski & ET Higgins (eds), *Handbook of theories of social psychology*, vol. 2, Sage Publications, Thousand Oaks, CA, pp. 1–22.

14. Step back - so they step up

Aagard, S, Chen, D & Yang, X 2012, 'The empty nest syndrome: ways to enhance quality of life', *Educational Gerontology*, vol. 38, no. 8, p. 520–9.

Berman, L 2009, *The sex ed handbook: a comprehensive guide for parents*, viewed 25 November 2014, <http://media.oprah.com/lberman/talking-to-kids-about-sex-handbook.pdf>.

Dillon, P 2009, *Teenagers, alcohol and drugs: what your kids really want and need to know about alcohol and drugs*, Allen and Unwin, Sydney.

Gilbert, D 2007, *Stumbling on happiness*, Vintage, New York.

Livingston, M & Pennay, A 2015, 'Don't believe the hype, teens are drinking less than they used to', *The Conversation*, 22 May, viewed 23 May 2015, <http://theconversation.com/ dont-believe-the-hype-teens-are-drinking-less-than-they-used-to-41884>.

15. Frequently asked questions

Campbell, M 2014 'The difference between "bullying" and "everyday life"', *The Conversation*, 8 August, viewed 16 December 2014, <http://theconversation.com/the-difference-between-bullying-and-everyday-life-27861>.

Mössle, T, Kleimann, M, Rehbein, F & Pfeiffer, C 2010, 'Media use and school achievement – boys at risk?', *British Journal of Developmental Psychology,* vol. 28, no. 3, pp. 699–725.

Rapee, RM, Wignall, A, Spence, S, Lyneham, H & Cobham, V 2000, *Helping your anxious child: a step-by-step guide for parents,* New Harbinger Publications, Oakland, Calif.

Rappaport, SR 2013, 'Deconstructing the impact of divorce on children', *Family Law Quarterly*, vol. 47, no 3, pp. 353–77.

Rekart, JL 2011, 'Taking on multitasking', *Phi Delta Kappan*, vol. 93, no. 4, pp.60–63.

16. When to get professional help

For assistance finding a qualified psychologist in your area:
Australia: <http://www.psychology.org.au/FindaPsychologist/>.
Canada: <http://www.cpa.ca/public/whatisapsychologist/PTassociations/>.
China: <http://www.cpsbeijing.org/en/index.php>.
Europe: <http://www.efpa.be>.
Hong Kong: <http://www.hkps.org.hk>.
India: <http://www.naopindia.org>.
Ireland: <http://www.psychologicalsociety.ie/find-a-psychologist/>.
Japan: <http://www.psych.or.jp/english/>.
Malaysia: <http://www.psima.org.my>.
New Zealand: <http://www.psychology.org.nz/community-resources/find-a-psychologist/>.
The Philippines: <http://pap.org.ph>.
Singapore: <http://www.singaporepsychologicalsociety.com/sps-membership/singapore- register-of-psychologist/>.
South Africa: <http://www.psyssa.com/search.asp>.
United Kingdom: <http://www.bps.org.uk/psychology-public/find-psychologist/find-psychologist>.
United States: <http://locator.apa.org>.

Acknowledgements

My interest in this topic came from a range of people, careers and experiences. I would like to thank all of those who contributed in many ways: the students, teachers and leadership teams I worked with in my teaching career; the companies and staff I worked with in my workplace training career; the lecturers, supervisors, managers, and peers in my student and practising days as a clinical psychologist; and my former colleagues at Triple P International. I particularly want to thank the many clients in my private practice, and in my training organisation, Confident and Capable – your experiences indicated to me that there was a somewhat unexplored parenting issue that needed to be examined.

I would like to thank my former supervisors and current research colleagues, Professor Marilyn Campbell and Professor David Kavanagh from QUT, who have both helped me develop as a researcher and academic.

My gratitude and thanks to Sue Webster, my editor, who has been diligent, resourceful and supportive (and to Ami for finding her). Thanks to Nic Lehman for the design of the book and Justin Nicholas for the photography. Many thanks to Kate and Max for their patience and talent when being photographed for the cover.

I cannot help but acknowledge the influence of Professor Martin Seligman, my academic leading light, whose main research areas have helped me find the way in my own. I also recognize that I stand in the shadows of the parenting giants – Professor Gerald Patterson, Professor Rex Forehand, Professor Robert J McMahon, Professor Carolyn Webster-Stratton, Professor Matt Sanders, and Professor Mark Dadds. I thank Linda Chamberlain, Dr John Moulds, Dr Karen Salmon, and Dr Katie O'Neill who guided me so well in my early years as a clinical psychologist. I appreciate the support of Arna Bennett, Dana Wedge, David Ogilvie, and Karon Graham in furthering my research and parenting programs, and also to Dr Rod Kefford for his early support of my career as a psychologist. Big thanks to Machelle Flowers-Smith for her excellent advice and support.

And finally, but most importantly, many, many thanks to my family and friends; your support, assistance and love has been much appreciated.

Coming in 2016 . . .

Judith Locke's next book

The Bonsai Student

In *The Bonsai Student*, Dr Judith Locke takes her experience as a clinical psychologist working with students, schools and parents, and combines it with her knowledge as a former teacher, to give parents crucial strategies to ensure their child gets the best out of their schooling years.

In this essential companion book to *The Bonsai Child,* Judith describes the true purpose of your child's school education, how to choose the right school for your child, who should take responsibility for different aspects of their schooling, and how to help them start successfully at a new school. Most importantly, she gives you practical strategies to assist your child to develop the motivation and confidence to make the most of their education.

Sign up now at bonsaichild.com to be notified when *The Bonsai Student* is released.

Index

This index doesn't cite pages – it cites chapters. There's a reason for that.

I designed this book to be read from cover to cover: this approach will help you get the most out of it. If you choose to read bits of strategies in isolation, you will find implementing them less straightforward than if you read from start to finish. For those of you who are re-reading certain sections, I list the following topics and the chapters where they are mentioned to assist you to find the information. I recommend you re-read the whole chapter to gain assistance for the issue.